THE BIG WELFARE MESS

Publication No. 888

AMERICAN LECTURE SERIES

A Publication in
The BANNERSTONE DIVISION OF AMERICAN LECTURES
IN SOCIAL AND REHABILITATION PSYCHOLOGY

Consulting Editors

RICHARD E. HARDY, Ed.D.
Chairman, Department of Rehabilitation Counseling
Virginia Commonwealth University
Richmond, Virginia

and

JOHN G. CULL, Ph.D.
Director, Regional Counselor Training Program
Department of Rehabilitation Counseling
Virginia Commonwealth University
Fishersville, Virginia

The American Lecture Series in Social and Rehabilitation Psychology offers books which are concerned with man's role in his milieu. Empahsis is placed on how this role can be made more effective in a time of social conflict and a deteriorating physical environment. The books are oriented toward descriptions of what future roles should be and are not concerned exclusively with the delineation and definition of contemporary behavior. Contributors are concerned to a considerable extent with prediction through the use of a functional view of man as opposed to a descriptive, anatomical point of view.

Books in this series are written mainly for the professional practitioner; however, academicians will find them of considerable value in both undergraduate and graduate courses in the helping services.

THE BIG WELFARE MESS

PUBLIC ASSISTANCE AND REHABILITATION APPROACHES

JOHN G. CULL
RICHARD E. HARDY

CHARLES C THOMAS • PUBLISHER
Springfield • Illinois • U.S.A.

Published and Distributed Throughout the World by
CHARLES C THOMAS • PUBLISHER
BANNERSTONE HOUSE
301-327 East Lawrence Avenue, Springfield, Illinois, U.S.A.

©*1973, by* CHARLES C THOMAS • PUBLISHER
ISBN 0-398-02796-X
Library of Congress Catalog Card Number: 73-222

With THOMAS BOOKS *careful attention is given to all details of
manufacturing and design. It is the Publisher's desire to present books
that are satisfactory as to their physical qualities and artistic possibilities
and appropriate for their particular use.* THOMAS BOOKS *will be true
to those laws of quality that assure a good name and good will.*

Printed in the United States of America
A-2

CONTRIBUTORS

C. D. AUVENSHINE, Ph.D.: Director of Rehabilitation Counseling and Associate Professor in the College of Education at the University of Kentucky. He holds degrees of Bachelor of Arts, Master of Education, and Doctor of Philosophy from the University of Missouri at Columbia. His studies were in psychology, education, counseling, rehabilitation, and guidance. He has worked as elementary teacher, rehabilitation counselor and psychologist. He has taught graduate courses in counseling and rehabilitation at the University of Missouri, the Pennsylvania State University and the University of Kentucky. He is the author of several articles in professional journals pertaining to counseling, the rehabilitation process and psychosocial aspects of disabling conditions. He serves as consultant to educational institutions and various government and private agencies.

MONROE BERKOWITZ: Professor of Economics, Rutgers College, Rutgers—The State University, New Brunswick, New Jersey. Member—Panel of Arbitrators; Federal Mediation and Conciliation Service; American Arbitration Association; New York Office of Collective Bargaining. Consultant: New Jersey Department of Labor and Industry, Vocational Rehabilitation Commission, National Commission on State Workmen's Compensation Law, and Social Security Administration. Member: Board of Trustees—National Institutes of Rehabilitation and Health Services, Kessler Institute of Rehabilitation. Associations: American Economic Association, Industrial Relations Research Association, National Academy of Arbitrators, American Association of University Professors. Publications: Monroe Berkowitz and William G. Johnson, towards an Economics of Disability: The Magnitude and Structure of Transfer and Medical Costs, *Journal of Human Resources,* Summer 1970, John F. Burton, Jr., and Monroe Berkowitz, Objectives Other Than Income Maintenance for Workmen's Compensation, *The Journal of Risk and Insurance,* September 1971, Monroe Berkowitz and John F. Burton, Jr., The Income-Maintenance Objective in Workmen's Compensation, *Industrial and Labor Relations Review,* October 1970.

JOHN J. CODY, Ph.D.: Chairman, Department of Guidance and Educational Psychology; Professor, College of Education, Southern Illinois University, Carbondale, Illinois; Test Consultant; Evaluator of Counseling and Testing Programs, Southern Illinois; Co-authored *Books in*

Educational Psychology A Behavioral Science and "Appraisal of Disadvantaged Youth," *Counseling the Disadvantaged Youth.* Dr. Cody has contributed numerous articles to the literature in counseling, measurement and education.

WILLIAM A. CRUNK: Deputy Commissioner for Rehabilitation and Self-Support Services, Social and Rehabilitation Services, Department of Health, Education and Welfare (Region III). Formerly, Field Representative, Office of Field Coordination, Office of the Secretary, Department of Health, Education and Welfare; Administrator, Central Alabama Rehabilitation Center and Crippled Childrens Clinic; Rehabilitation Supervisor and Counselor, Alabama Division of Vocational Rehabilitation. Special Assignments: Manpower Program Coordination Team, President's Committee on Manpower; Staff Member, Secretary's Task Force on Handicapped Children and Child Development.

JOHN G. CULL, Ph.D.: Director, Regional Counselor Training Program and Professor, Department of Rehabilitation, School of Community Services, Virginia Commonwealth University, Fishersville, Virginia; Adjunct Professor in Psychology and Education, School of General Studies, University of Virginia; Technical Consultant, Rehabilitation Services Administration, U. S. Department of Health, Education and Welfare; Vocation Consultant, Bureau of Hearings and Appeals, Social Security Administration; Lecturer, Medical Department Affiliate Program, Woodrow Wilson Rehabilitation Center; Consulting Editor, *American Lecture Series in Social and Rehabilitation Psychology*, Charles C Thomas, Publisher. Formerly Rehabilitation Counselor, Texas Commission For The Blind and Texas Rehabilitation Commission; Director, Division of Research and Program Development, Virginia Department of Vocational Rehabilitation. The following are some of the books Dr. Cull has co-authored and co-edited: *Vocational Rehabilitation: Profession and Process, Contemporary Field Work Practices in Rehabilitation, Social and Rehabilitation Services for the Blind, Fundamentals of Criminal Behavior and Correctional Systems* and *Drug Dependence and Rehabilitation Approaches.* Dr. Cull also has contributed more than 50 publications to the professional literature in psychology and rehabilitation.

LARRY R. DICKERSON, Ph.D.: Assistant Professor of Education at the University of Arkansas and a Senior Research Scientist with the Arkansas Rehabilitation Research and Training Center. His background includes direct rehabilitation experience in serving the emotionally disturbed, mentally retarded, physically handicapped, blind and culturally disadvantaged. Besides teaching in the rehabilitation field, he has been a Work Adjustment Counselor in a private rehabilitation center in Milwaukee, Wisconsin, a Rehabilitation Counselor for the Blind in Harlem and the Bronx, New York, a college counseling center counselor at Coe College,

Cedar Rapids, Iowa, plus serving as a consultant to private and state rehabilitation centers. He is currently the principal investigator of two projects directed toward offering effective rehabilitation services to the rural public assistance recipient. Dr. Dickerson has recently been nominated to the National Advisory Council for Vocational Rehabilitation.

CARL E. HANSEN, Ed.D.: Associate Director of the Rehabilitation Counselor Education Program, and Graduate Advisor for the Department of Special Education, The University of Texas, at Austin. Formerly employed with the California Department of Rehabilitation as a counselor. Consultant, Technical Assistance Consultation to Sheltered Workshops, Department of Health, Education and Welfare, Social and Rehabilitation Service. President of the National Rehabilitation Counseling Association; Secretary American Rehabilitation Counseling Association. Dr. Hansen has presented numerous papers at state and national professional meetings as well as having published widely within rehabilitation, employment, and special education journals.

RICHARD E. HARDY, Ed.D.: Chairman, Department of Rehabilitation, School of Community Services, Virginia Commonwealth University, Richmond, Virginia; Technical Consultant, Rehabilitation Services Administration, U. S. Department of Health, Education and Welfare; Consulting Editor, *American Lecture Series in Social and Rehabilitation Psychology*, Charles C Thomas, Publisher; and Associate Editor, *Journal of Voluntary Action Research*. Formerly Rehabilitation Counselor in Virginia; Chief Psychologist and Supervisor of Training, South Carolina Department of Vocational Rehabilitation and member South Carolina State Board of Examiners in Psychology; Rehabilitation Advisor, Rehabilitation Services Administration, U. S. Department of Health, Education and Welfare. The following are some of the books Dr. Hardy has co-authored and co-edited: *Social and Rehabilitation Services for the Blind, Vocational Rehabilitation: Profession and Process, The Unfit Majority, Fundamentals of Criminal Behavior in Correctional Systems* and *Drug Dependence and Rehabilitation Approaches*. Dr. Hardy has contributed more than 50 publications to the professional literature in psychology and rehabilitation.

ROBERT A. LASSITER, Ph.D.: Associate Professor and Coordinator, Work-Study Program, Rehabilitation Counseling Department, School of Community Services, Virginia Commonwealth University, Richmond, Virginia. Formerly Director, Rehabilitation Education and Research Unit, Chairman, Rehabilitation Counseling Program, University of North Carolina at Chapel Hill; Technical Consultant to the Rehabilitation Services Administration, Social and Rehabilitation Service Department of Health, Education, and Welfare. Consultant in Continuing Education for the Training and Research Departments, North Carolina; State Director, North Carolina Division of Vocational Rehabilitation;

Executive Director, North Carolina Society for Crippled Children and Adults; Rehabilitation Counselor, Florida Division of Vocational Rehabilitation. Publications include: VOCATIONAL REHABILITATION IN NORTH CAROLINA, School of Education, University of North Carolina, 1970; "Vocational Rehabilitation in Public Schools," HIGH SCHOOL JOURNAL, 1969; "Help for the Mentally Retarded Person," NORTH CAROLINA EDUCATION JOURNAL, 1967.

RICHARD E. LAWRENCE, Ph.D.: Associate Professor and Director, Rehabilitation Counselor Education, University of Maryland, College Park, Maryland. Ex-officio member of the advisory council for Regional Rehabilitation Research Institute and Regional Rehabilitation Facilities Training program; Member, American Psychological Association; Research consultant, Association of Rehabilitation Centers; Consultant, D. C. Division of Vocational Rehabilitation; Coordinator, Maryland Partners in the Alliance Project in Rehabilitation. Formerly, Prison Counselor, State Prison of Southern Michigan at Jackson; Disability examiner and Rehabilitation Counselor, Michigan Department of Public Instruction. Journal publications include: "The Relationship Among the Factors of Counselor-Client Social Class Similarity, Emphatic Understanding, and Felt Similarity;" "Practicality of Existentialism for the Employment Counselor." Projects include "Characteristics of Disabled Population at the University of Maryland;" "Description Study of the Needs of Handicapped Students on Campus." Dr. Lawrence has contributed his services and other articles to the profession of rehabilitation and psychology.

W. ALFRED McCAULEY, M.A.: Executive Director, National Rehabilitation Counseling Association, Washington, D. C.; Visiting Lecturer, Virginia Commonwealth University and Pennsylvania State University, Rehabilitation Education. Formerly, Associate Regional Representative, Rehabilitation Services Administration, Department of Health, Education, and Welfare, Region III, and Coordinator of Rehabilitation Counselor Training West Virginia University. Mr. McCauley is the author of *The Blind Person as a College Teacher,* American Foundation for the Blind, a writer of various conference proceedings and contributor to various rehabilitation publications, including "The Professional Status of the Rehabilitation Counselor," *Vocational Rehabilitation, Profession and Process,* Charles C Thomas, Publisher, Springfield, Illinois, 1972.

Wm. HEYWARD McELVEEN, M.S.W.: Coordinator, Welfare-Vocational Rehabilitation Services, Virginia Department of Welfare and Institutions. Formerly the Chairman of the Richmond Area Community Coordinated Child Care Program (4-C) and Social Worker in the Richmond Social Service Bureau Serving In Protective Service, Special Foster Care, Foster Home Funding, and Supervisor of Day Care.

RUSSELL A. NIXON, Ph.D.: Professor of Social Policy, Columbia University School of Social Work; Consultant on Manpower and related areas to various governmental and other agencies including Office of Economic Opportunity, U. S. Department of Health, Education, and Welfare, Vocational Rehabilitation Program, Community Services Committee (New York City), A.F.L.-C.I.O. Central Labor Council, American Rehabilitation Foundation (Minneapolis, Minn.), New Careers Manpower Project, National Rehabilitation Association, Research and Training Center in Vocational Rehabilitation (PT-14), School of Education at University of Pittsburgh, Milburn Health Center (Syracuse, N.Y.), Council on Social Work Education, National Committee on Employment of Youth, Division of Manpower and Training Programs, National Institute of Mental Health, Mobilization for Youth (New York City), Juvenile Delinquency Program at Fordham University. Member of various Advisory Committees and Task Forces of projects relating to manpower. Co-Chairman of National Conference of Public Service Employment, and Chairman of Committee on Public Service Employment, New York Urban Coalition. Has taught at New School for Social Research, Rutgers University, Radcliffe College, Massachusetts Institute of Technology, and Harvard University. Has lectured widely and contributed numerous articles to professional literature on manpower economics, New Careers use of non-professionals, social policy, and social legislation.

RALPH R. ROBERTS, Jr., Ph.D.: Associate Professor of Rehabilitation Counseling, the University of Iowa. Formerly Assistant Director of the Rehabilitation Institute and Coordinator of the Rehabilitation Counselor Training Program at Southern Illinois University; prior Assistant Professor, Rehabilitation Counselor Training Program, University of Pittsburgh. Has served on the Joint Liaison Committee, APGA Senate, and Editorial Board of the Rehabilitation Counseling Bulletin. Currently is serving as Director of Region VII CRCE and member of the Executive Committee. Has co-authored an RSA supported long-term study on Continuing Education for Rehabilitation Counselors and contributed various articles to the professional literature of Psychology and Rehabilitation. Has been active in professional organizations such as APGA, ARCA, NRA, NRCA, and CRCE.

CHARLES R. ROUSELLE, M.S.W., holds degrees from Morgan State College and Howard University. He is Chief of the Offender Rehabilitation Division Public Defender Service for the District of Columbia. Formerly he was Director of the Offender Rehabilitation Project for the District of Columbia; Associate Superintendent of Community Services for Youth Services Division, D.C. Dept. of Corrections, and Chief Psychiatric Social Worker for the District of Columbia Department of Vocational Rehabilitation. He was listed in *Who's Who in the South and Southwest* in 1971.

BROCKMAN SCHUMACHER, Ph.D.: Coordinator, Rehabilitation Counselor Training Program, and Associate Professor, Rehabilitation Institute, Southern Illinois University, Carbondale, Illinois; Member, National Study Committee Social and Rehabilitation Services Department of Health, Education and Welfare; Chairman, Committee on Rehabilitation Education for Standards and Accreditation; Formerly Director of Comprehensive Manpower Programs, Human Development Corporation, St. Louis, Missouri; Director of Rehabilitation Services, St. Louis State Hospital, St. Louis, Missouri. Edited *Problems Unique to the Rehabilitation of Psychiatric Patients*. Dr. Schumacher has also contributed articles to the professional literature in rehabilitation.

STANLEY J. SMITS, Ph.D.: Director, Rehabilitation Counselor Education Program, and Professor, Department of Counseling and Psychological Services, Georgia State University, Atlanta, Georgia; has been engaged in rehabilitation counselor education, research and practice for ten years; Authored and edited monographs and research reports include: The Interdependence of Rehabilitation Facilities, Workshops and State Agencies and Leadership Behavior of Supervisors in State Rehabilitation Agencies; Dr. Smits has written numerous articles dealing with the psycho-social impact of disability, and with the utilization of manpower in rehabilitation service delivery system.

JERRY S. TUREM, Ph.D.: Currently Project Director on Social Services Research with the Urban Institute, Washington, D. C. His prior positions included two years as Executive Assistant to the Commissioner of the Rehabilitation Services Administration, Social and Rehabilitation Service, The Department of Health, Education and Welfare. Dr. Turem performed analytical studies of Welfare and Social Services for the President's Commission on Income Maintenance Programs and for the Office of Management and Budget, Executive Office of the President.

JOHN B. WADE, M.S.: Director, Vocational Rehabilitation—Welfare Programs, Virginia Department of Vocational Rehabilitation; Lecturer, Regional Counselor Training Program, Virginia Commonwealth University, Fishersville, Virginia; Formerly Vocational Rehabilitation Supervisor and Counselor, Virginia Department of Vocational Rehabilitation.

KEITH C. WRIGHT, M.A.: Professor, Department of Rehabilitation Counseling, School of Community Services, Virginia Commonwealth University. Formerly, Research Analyst, West Virginia Division of Vocational Rehabilitation; Counselor and Research Analyst, United States Public Health Service, Past President Virginia Rehabilitation Association; Past President Virginia Association of Workers for the Blind; Coordinator Short-Term In-Service Training Institutes in Rehabilitation. Mr Wright is the contributor of numerous articles to the professional literature.

This Book is Dedicated to

DR. DILL D. BECKMAN
for his outstanding service
and leadership
in rehabilitation

PREFACE

THIS BOOK IS AN OUTGROWTH OF our interest and those of our colleagues in attempting to offer practical information in order to move agencies and personnel of agencies toward more basic understanding of the problems of the recipients of their services and the difficulties in working together to achieve common goals. The scope of this book is broad out of necessity. The problems associated with rehabilitation of the welfare recipient are as varied and complex as any of those facing rehabilitation and other social service workers. Problems include a gamut of concerns from the loss of purpose in life to the development of appropriate vocational interests and capabilities.

In the development of this book we have meticulously selected those individuals who could most ably contribute. These individuals are those who are most involved in improving the system and helping it work more cooperatively and effectively. As could be expected these persons are practitioners of high order. We have gained much from our work with them and are pleased to offer the results of combined efforts in this book which shows that cooperation among various disciplines can be most effective and beneficial.

The book will be of real value to rehabilitation counseling personnel, psychologists, social workers, psychiatrists, sociologists, and others in that all professions and personnel in these areas are concerned with the problems presented here.

There seems to be general agreement in our society that people on welfare really are not encouraged to work. The welfare system contains widespread inequalities in payments and standards; it delivers too little for what it costs and benefits are generally too low to provide for basic necessities of life.

The welfare system should provide incentives for working instead of penalties. The benefits should be uniform nation-wide and people should be trained for jobs that exist.

This book describes public service programs, how they function and how they should function. It offers information on how these programs are viewed and how the recipients of the services are viewed. It covers special problems of persons who are disadvantaged and disabled and offers a coverage of special techniques and approaches to their rehabilitation. The book offers extensive information on what research has shown and what a complex society requires. It also outlines some innovations which could improve our current state.

JOHN G. CULL
RICHARD E. HARDY

CONTENTS

PART IV

PART V

THE BIG WELFARE MESS

PART I

Overview of the State-Federal Vocational Rehabilitation Program

Cooperative Efforts in the Rehabilitation of the Welfare Recipient

The Impact of Welfare Reform on Rehabilitation

Cooperative Alternatives to Duplication in Social and Rehabilitation
Services

CHAPTER I

OVERVIEW OF THE STATE-FEDERAL VOCATIONAL REHABILITATION PROGRAM

ROBERT A. LASSITER

Background

Legal Precedents

Chronology

References

BACKGROUND

THE STATE-FEDERAL PARTNERSHIP in Vocational Rehabilitation in America began on June 2, 1920, when President Woodrow Wilson signed the first congressional act to provide vocational rehabilitation services to handicapped civilians (Public Law 236). The following quotations from this act indicate the emphasis and direction considered important by Congress in this new program: ". . . to provide the promotion of vocational rehabilitation of persons disabled in industry or in any legitimate occupation . . . the term 'person disabled' shall be construed to mean any person who, by reason of a physical defect or infirmity, whether congenital or acquired by accident, injury, or disease, is, or may be expected to be, totally or partially incapacitated for remunerative occupation."[1]

A two-fold program of vocational guidance and vocational education for physically handicapped people, as contained in this act, was evidence of the federal government's increasing concern for the welfare of individuals. It was also the result of a greater awareness in this country of the need to conserve human resources for economic benefit to society as a whole. For an understanding of this new legislation, it must be viewed in the light of certain social movements of the late nineteenth and early twentieth centuries.

The origins of the vocational rehabilitation movement can be found in an examination of some of these social movements at the turn of the century, and a better perspective of the problems can be gained by analyzing some of these movements which were developing prior to and parallel with the program of vocational rehabilitation. Esco Obermann, in his history of vocational rehabilitation, stated: "The history of vocational rehabilitation is the history of a long struggle to establish dignity and opportunity as a right of disabled persons, just as history in general is the story of the long struggle to establish dignity and opportunity as a right of every human being."[2]

In a thirty-year span (1890-1920), many forces were at work in America which would provide the background necessary for the beginning of a vocational rehabilitation state-federal program. Some antecedents of this new program were: (1) the tremendous progress made in the medical science and medical practice field; (2) the development of governmental programs concerned with society's health such as Public Health and Workmen's Compensation; (3) the developing profession of psychology and its impact on the mental health movement; (5) the work of early pioneers in social work, for example, Jane Addams' Hull House in Chicago; (6) the free public education system advancing to compulsory education laws to all states by 1920; (7) the establishment of vocational guidance programs by social workers and school officials.

Of greatest impact on the developing vocational rehabilitation movement would be vocational guidance, a relatively new discipline. Only twelve years before the act was passed by Congress, Frank Parsons, a social worker, organized and established the Vocational Bureau in Boston, the first organized vocational guidance program in America. "It was his concern that the strengths and weaknesses of individuals be understood and brought into harmony with vocational opportunities." In his book, *Choosing a Vocation*, Parsons stated three broad factors in outlining a theory for vocational guidance: "1. a clear understanding of yourself, 2. a knowledge of the requirements and conditions for success . . . in different lines of work, and 3. true reasoning of the relation of these two groups of facts." Parsons' intelligent spirit of social reform and his far-seeing vision are reflected in this passage from his book:

> Not til society wakes up to its responsibility and its privileges . . . shall we be able to harvest more than a fraction of our human resources, or develop and utilize the genius and ability that are latent in each new generation. When that time does come, education will become the leading industry, and a vocation bureau in effect will be a part of the public school system in every community, — a bureau provided with every facility that science can devise for the testing of the senses and capabilities, and the whole physical, intellectual, and emotional make-up of the child, and with experts trained as carefully for the work as men are trained today for medicine and law.[3]

The first World War (1914-1918), provided an opportunity for increased emphasis on the need "to choose the right man for the right job" which Parsons stressed in his vocational guidance theory. Selective tests were devised to determine aptitude as well as intelligence. The first group of intelligence tests, the Army Alpha and the Army Beta, were used for literate and illiterate recruits, respectively. Tests were constructed also to measure skills in the various trades. After the war, these techniques and methods would be extended to all areas of vocational guidance, including the new program in vocational rehabilitation.

LEGAL PRECEDENTS

Legislation passed by Congress during World War I led directly to the enactment of Public Law 236 which established the state-federal partnership in vocational rehabilitation. The National Defense Act of 1916 indicated the importance Congress attached to the area of vocational training: "In addition to military training, soldiers while in active service shall hereafter be given the opportunity to study and receive instruction upon educational lines of such character as to increase their military efficiency and enable them to return to civil life better equipped for industrial, commercial, and general business occupations. Civilian teachers may be employed to aid the Army officers in giving such instruction, and part of this instruction may consist of vocational education either in agriculture or the mechanic arts."[4] In addition, the Smith-Hughes Act of 1917 set a precedent for federal funding of educational programs of all types, and also established a pattern of vocational education in the United States. This act created the Federal Board for Vocational Education which would lead to the establishment of state boards in vocational education in all states. These boards, at the state and federal level, would later administer the early state-federal program in vocational rehabilitation. Also, this same Federal Board for Vocational Education was authorized by Congress in 1918 to operate a program of vocational rehabilitation for veterans (The Soldier Rehabilitation Act). This act which became known as the Smith-Sears Veterans' Rehabilitation Act of 1918 provided the first definition for governmental vocational rehabilitation services: "an act to provide for the vocational rehabilitation and return to employment of disabled persons discharged from the military or naval forces of the United States and for other purposes."[5] Eligibility for services was outlined and a disabled veteran was defined as one who "is unable to carry on a gainful occupation, to resume his former occupation or to enter upon some other occupation, or having resumed and entered upon such occupation is unable to continue the same successfully, shall be furnished by the said board, where vocational rehabilitation is feasible, such course of vocational rehabilitation as the board shall prescribe and provide."[6] Many of the same legislative, professional, and lay leaders who were active in the work of this legislation for veterans were also committed to a program of vocational rehabilitation for civilians, and the new law providing for vocational rehabilitation for civilians which was passed in 1920, came as a result of their efforts. Some of the key leaders included: Senator Hoke Smith of Georgia, Representative William Bankhead of Alabama, Dr. R. M. Little, of the United States Employment Compensation Commission, (workmen's compensation), W. F. Faulkes, a supervisor of vocational education in Wisconsin, who represented the growing interest in vocational rehabilitation by some state departments of education.[7]

Following the passage of the Vocational Rehabilitation Act of

1920, thirty-four states within an eighteen-month period, had passed acceptance or enabling legislation and had taken steps to organize a program of services to accommodate federal funds which were made available through the Federal Board of Vocational Education and state boards of education or vocational education.

Prior to the federal legislative action in June, 1920, several states had enacted vocational rehabilitation laws to accept provisions of the anticipated federal act.

The first legislative action occurred in Massachusetts in 1918 with the passage of an act to provide for training and instruction of persons whose capacities to earn a living had been destroyed or impaired through industrial accident. Other states followed, and by June, 1920, twelve had enacted vocational rehabilitation laws. Most states' legislation consisted of a few brief statements amending a public law dealing with vocational education. This procedure represented only an acceptance act; no attempt was made to define the scope of the work or to advise the State Board of Vocational Education on procedures to follow; and all regulations and policies were left entirely with the federal legislation. Funds were appropriated to match the federal monies made available in the act on a fifty-fifty federal-state matching ratio.[8]

The Federal Board for Vocational Education issued a statement of policies for use by states in the administration of the vocational rehabilitation act in September, 1920. This publication made it clear that the federal government was reluctant to establish a new federal program:

> Under this act the Federal Government does not propose to undertake the organization and immediate direction of vocational rehabilitation in the states, but does agree to make substantial financial contributions to its support.[9]

Congress, by passing only temporary legislation, probably held the opinion that the funds would stimulate the development of programs carried on entirely by state governments at some future time. This first policy statement reflects the philosophy of responsible officials in the federal vocational education agency who viewed vocational rehabilitation as being synonymous with vocational education, except that this new area would be concerned only with handicapped people. The authors of the bulletin state:

The industrial rehabilitation law provides practically the same administrative procedures as is required in the administration of the vocational education act. In so far as possible, the same methods of administration and relationships with state boards will be maintained.[10]

Requirements for a state's participation, which were based on the federal act, were provided in the bulletin:

1. The expenditure of funds in the state must be equal to the amount expended in federal funds (a fifty-fifty matching formula established with all states);
2. The development of a state plan for approval by the federal agency (guides were provided but emphasis was placed on each state developing an individual plan which would meet its unique needs);
3. Submission of an annual report to the federal board;
4. Administration of the state program placed under the state vocational education board and a cooperative agreement established with the state's workmen's compensation commission or bureau;
5. A prohibition of expenditure of funds for buildings or equipment (setting the early policy of a "purchase of service plan").[11]

Information was also provided on the forms to use in statistical and financial reporting. A question and answer section was included in this early bulletin to provide an interpretation of the law by the various state departments of vocational education:

The Board interprets the term "vocational rehabilitation" as used in this act not to include the work of physical rehabilitation, although such work may be necessary preliminary to or accompaniment of vocational rehabilitation.[12]

The question of purchasing artificial appliances was presented since the experience of workmen's compensation programs showed the majority of serious industrial accidents resulted in amputations. This question was answered in a somewhat ambiguous way which may have helped to set a pattern for the future establishment of a comprehensive physical restoration and treatment program: "In such a case it would be clear that this would be outside the purview of vocational rehabilitation, since like medical care and occupational therapy, it is physical restoration . . ."[13]

But, in response to the question of providing "specialized" vocational prostheses, the authors of the bulletin replied: "If in these instances they are real supplies of an instructional nature necessary for the individual in training, it is possible . . ."[14] The question regarding the provision of job placement *only* was answered in the negative, and this, for many years, resulted in the reluctance of rehabilitation workers to assist a handicapped person who needed only counseling and job placement services:

> A rehabilitation agency which contemplates placement only is not in harmony with the spirit of the Federal Act. The emphasis is laid by the act upon courses of studies, supervision, etc. and it is made clear that the chief thing in mind was the vocational re-training of the disabled.[15]

In answer to the question of a minimum age, the Federal Board provided an answer that was accepted as a policy in all states: "The Federal Act does not specify a minimum age. It is evident, however, that the minimum age in any state would be the minimum age of legal employability in that state."[16] Rigid adherence to this interpretation (and not to the law) over the years hampered efforts to provide counseling and other services of a prevocational nature to people under age sixteen. The answer given to the following question was answered affirmatively, "What about homemaking as an occupation? Persons engaged in homemaking, whether working for a wage or not, will be considered as engaged in a legitimate occupation." This interpretation, however, was based on the vocational education act which had included home economics as a major educational program and the implications for the future development of vocational rehabilitation services for housewives and other unpaid family workers were not foreseen.

It is clear that an action and service-oriented program was envisioned from the beginning. In answer to a question about the use of funds for preliminary surveys (research) prior to establishing a program, the federal official stated:

> The general principles on which the work should be constructed are fairly well recognized and are easily ascertainable. Further progress depends upon the contacts with individual cases, and actual work in vocational rehabilitation. A preliminary survey should include contacts looking toward an early beginning of training since the Federal Act has clearly in mind a definite undertaking of the work of vocational rehabilitation. Such a survey would be only incidental to the actual starting of the work.[17]

This last statement may have been needed in order to encourage a pioneering-type activity which was necessary in the development of a new program; however, it may have been somewhat shortsighted in the exclusion of an early emphasis on research and study which could have accompanied the developing service program—to provide the data needed for improvement of services and sound planning for the extension of services in future development and growth.

The Federal Board for Vocational Education issued its second bulletin on vocational rehabilitation in March, 1921. Additional interpretive data for the states to follow in setting up new programs were provided in this second bulletin. The first clear statement on the techniques and methods to be used by rehabilitation agents (later called rehabilitation counselors) was included. This was a case method approach adopted from the social work field.[18] The employment of federal supervisors to work specifically in vocational rehabilitation and the experiences of a few states in attempting to rehabilitate people helped to establish this method.

Even before the state agencies began to function, th methods for providing services moved from those of instruction, supervision and courses of studies to the case method technique. Vocational guidance and vocational testing are not mentioned in this second bulletin; however, early vocational guidance principles were implied by stating that the purpose of the person contacting handicapped people was:

> to inspire the disabled man with a feeling of receptivity and . . . of confidence. This may be accomplished by tact in giving encouragement, and proffering assistance, and by acquainting the injured man with the achievements and accomplishments of others who have suffered from similar or other disabilities. There should be induced, so far as possible, a mental state of hopefulness which will tend to counteract the almost inevitably discouraging effects of accidents or illnesses.[19]

A discussion of specific case procedures to be followed in the management of services was provided: (1) Determination of eligibility is made by the agent in three distinct areas—age, physical disability and feasibility (2) Determination of the job objective, "the whole interview should be conducted so that the disabled person rather than the agent is led to make a decision as to the selection of a job objective," and yet stress was placed on what the agent does for the handicapped person: "In order to determine what particular occupation or employment is best in the case of any disabled person, it is necessary that an intensive study be made of the case (again, no mention is made of an objective appraisal by tests). (3) Formulation of a tentative plan of rehabilitation, "when a specific employment objective has been determined upon, the agent of the State Board will be face to face with the issue of making at least a tentative plan of vocational rehabilitation for the disabled person." (4) Follow-up during training and the determination of employability: "This follow-up on the job must continue until, beyond a question of a doubt, the disabled person is independent, confident, and happy, and all reports show that he is producing at his maximum efficiency."[20]

In these early bulletins, no information was provided on the qualifications of rehabilitation agents nor was any concern shown for their training other than the distribution of various policy statements. Perhaps the federal supervisors followed the tradition established in the federal board's work with states on the Smith-Hughes legislation, which, for the most part, left selection and training of vocational education personnel to the state boards and departments of education. In 1927, a report of the subcommittee on vocational guidance of the Commission on Reorganization of Secondary Education described the process as applied to Rehabilitation: "Vocational guidance should be a continuous process designed to help the individual to choose, to plan his preparation for, to enter upon, and to make progress in an occupation."[21] This statement indicates the direction rehabilitation work was taking—moving from an educational emphasis to a social work approach, then to the field of vocational guidance and psychology, and retaining parts of all three areas in attempting to meet the needs of a unique and somewhat neglected group in America, the physically handicapped.

Obermann's review of this period reflects this development: "The years from 1921 to 1926 were filled with the spirit of development and growth for the State-Federal vocational rehabilitation program. The national conferences in St. Louis, Washington, and Cleveland reflected this in their programs and proceedings. The philosophical base for the new movement was being formulated, the administrative machinery was being established, definitions were being agreed upon, the limitations of operations under the federal act were being explored, and the techniques of rehabilitation practice were discusssed."[22]

The first sectional meetings for the professional staff in vocational rehabilitation were held at the National Society for Vocational Education Annual Conference at Buffalo, New York, in 1923. At one of these sectional meetings, leaders from the state-federal vocational rehabilitation agencies established the National Civilian Rehabilitation Conference; and, in 1925, this organization began operating as a separate organization as it held its first annual meeting in Cleveland, Ohio. In Memphis, Tennessee, at its annual conference in 1927, the name of the organization was changed to the National Rehabilitation Association.

The objectives of this new organization were listed as follows:

(a) to provide through its meetings a forum in which all phases of vocational rehabilitation of disabled civilians and problems incidental thereto may be discussed (b) to conduct a campaign of education to bring the general public to an adequate understanding of the importance of the civilian rehabilitation movement, (c) to further so far as possible and desirable agreement upon the principles and practices in the field of civilian rehabilitation and to promote comity between the various agencies, (d) to set up a medium through which expression may be given to the views of the membership upon pending legislation and public policies affecting the civilian rehabilitation movement.[23]

The other national forum for state supervisors and directors of vocational rehabilitation was provided by the Federal Board for Vocational Education as it sponsored national conferences on vocational rehabilitation. At the second national conference in Washington, D.C., in 1924, one state director related his philosophy in the selection of rehabilitation agents: "There is no place in vocational rehabilitation for a routine worker or one who is contented with his present knowledge and methods of rehabilitation." His speech continued with the outlining of the duties of a rehabilitation professional worker:

1. interviewing applicants
2. setting up feasible plans of rehabilitation
3. supervision of training
4. job placement

5. soliciting funds for areas not covered
6. securing cooperation of individuals and agencies.

He then described the kinds of personal qualities needed to carry out these duties as

> Tact, careful observation, patience and sympathy tempered by good judgment . . . a complete knowledge of the rehabilitation laws, policies and best practices, thoughtfulness, alertness, resourcefulness, ingenuity, and common sense, . . . one must have a liberal education in order that he may meet all classes favorably and deal with them on their own level. One must be socially agreeable, that is, be able to get on well with people. This requires courtesy, tact, poise, cheerfulness, and a good sense of humor. He should be a graduate of a standard college and should have some experience in rehabilitation, social services or other work that has given him experience . . .[24]

Later, in this speech, he commented on his "necessary qualifications" list:

> Someone may say that we cannot afford the type of men described, I want to say that you cannot afford any other type of men. The success of the work depends upon the kind of men who are administering it, and, rightly so, that of administration (salary). The poorest economy that can be practiced in rehabilitation work is the employment of cheap and incompetent officers. The effectiveness of the work in any state will depend upon the ability of the staff that is in charge of the program.[25]

This speech by Homer L. Stanton of North Carolina, recorded at the national conference in 1924, is the earliest known statement on qualifications of professional staff made by any state or federal vocational rehabilitation leader.

Despite the growing body of knowledge that contributed to professionalization of the work of the rehabilitation agent during this period, little growth, in terms of the number of people served, took place in the early 1930's. These early depression years created conditions that restricted growth and, on some occasions, threatened the very existence of this small federal-state program which was not well known by the general public, nor by many of the politicians. This more static and inactive period did provide an opportunity for consolidation of gains made in the development of a new concept. The framework for future growth was built as rehabilitation leaders were called on to participate in some of the federal government's attempts to improve the plight of America's middle class as well as its poor who were suffering from a major economic depression.

Later, in 1933, vocational rehabilitation became involved with the administration's total governmental effort to combat the depression, President Franklin D. Roosevelt's New Deal. A monthly national allotment of $70,000 was made available through the Federal Emergency Relief Administration to the state vocational rehabilitation programs for the purpose of extending rehabilitation services to the unemployed handicapped people who were on relief.

People on relief who received vocational rehabilitation services were also provided living expenses while they were in training. This inclusion of maintenance for a limited group led to legislation and regulations which came later when the total rehabilitation program was made more comprehensive.[26]

When the functions of the Federal Board for Vocational Education were transferred by an executive order by President Roosevelt to the Department of the Interior in 1933, the Secretary of the Interior assigned the vocational rehabilitation division to the Office of Education.

Terry Foster was the author of the first rehabilitation bulletin published by the Office of Education in the Department of the Interior. This bulletin, written in 1934, presented "a manual of instructions, policies and practices for the guidance of case workers in the field of vocational rehabilitation." Sample forms for record keeping and reporting were based on those developed by Foster and the director of the vocational rehabilitation program in Pennsylvania. For example, Foster wrote guidelines for counselors to use in making decisions about "re-opening" cases, stating that a case could be re-opened, but "careful investigation should be made however before re-opening such cases." Emphasis was placed on the indigent "crippled" person, even though some services were available to people in all economic groups, e. g. counseling and guidance and tuition for training; and, limited services also were available to people with disabilities who were not crippled or orthopedically handicapped. It is clear that this program in 1935 was a limited one and a priority of service was necessary; therefore, the needs of the indigent person with an obvious disability that could be corrected or minimized received the highest priority.[27]

The Social Security Act of 1935 provided the first permanent base for the federal vocational rehabilitation program. The Social Security Act thus accomplished three objectives of rehabilitation officials, namely a permanent authorization, increased grants, and in 1936;[28] a new publication from the federal office provided additional information in the development of a vocational rehabilitation philosophy: John Kratz, Chief of the Federal Division, wrote *Vocational Rehabilitation of the Physically Handicapped,* and in one section stated:

"Of fundamental importance is the principle that from the inception of a rehabilitation case to its conclusion only one agent should deal with the disabled person. Functional handling of cases was tried in the soldier (sic) rehabilitation work, and it proved a failure."

Kratz expressed his ideas on the importance of counseling.

> One of the most important services given by a rehabilitation agent is that of counsel and advisement. It is a continuous service designed to assist the disabled person in choosing, preparing for, entering upon, and making progress in an occupation . . . Such devices as psychological, individual, group, trade and intelligence tests have been used only to a limited extent, but it is not likely that they can ever be used in all cases as a general procedure in rehabilitation. A practical common sense trial and error process has been the procedure followed in most cases . . .[29]

Kratz also provided a statement that reflected the growing recognition of the need to look at a client as a person of worth and dignity, and, who still needed some manipulation and direction:

> It is a far better procedure to have the person assume a measure of initiative and responsibility for the development of his own rehabilitation . . . the rehabilitation supervisor must be skillful in assisting the applicant to appraise his own abilities, capacities and deficiencies.

And, yet he goes on to say,

> If the agent is skillful, he leads the disabled person to follow his guidance and to enter into the rehabilitation plan which the agent suggests, as freely and as enthusiastically as if he himself had suggested and originated it.[30]

In this same bulletin, Kratz commented on the problems of ad-

ministration, and outlined the types of administration, observed in
the states without making a recommendation for the use of any
particular kind. There were two basic types of organization: a central office which handled all services in the smaller states, and a
central office with district offices established throughout a larger
state. In addition, Kratz mentioned two basic approaches used in
administration—a centralized program with all or most decision
making taking place in the central office and a decentralized program which provided for some autonomy in the district offices.

The Federal Security Agency was established in July, 1939, and
all education, welfare and health organizations were transferred to
this new department. The Office of Education moved from the Interior Department of the new agency, and vocational rehabilitation
was set up as a separate division within the Office of Education.
"Thus, administrative reorganization, rather than legislative change
. . . ended the subordination of vocational rehabilitation to vocational education . . . It remained within the Office of Education,
however, an agency concerned with different problems."[31]

World War II affected the vocational rehabilitation agency in
many ways as it influenced all activities in the nation and the world.
The consequences of this war, for rehabilitation, however, were
different from the effects that the war had on other peacetime programs supported by the government: federal legislation passed by
Congress at the height of World War II resulted in the greatest
period of expansion in the twenty-year history of vocational
rehabilitation.

Certain events in the early years of the war, led to the development of a new federal act for vocational rehabilitation in 1943.
Known as Public Law 113, this law was to have the greatest
impact on the growth of the program since the original act was
passed by Congress in 1920.

Obermann, in his history, states that

> It was a time when rehabilitation workers and their disabled clients
> were being given the opportunity to demonstrate to a broad and re-
> ceptive audience that disability need not be an employment and pro-
> ductive handicap . . . The tragedy of the war, and the new approaches
> to personal practices required by it (the need to seek out all work-
> ers who could be productive, e.g., "Rosie the Riveter") was ad-
> vancing the cause of vocational rehabilitation far faster than would

have been possible under conditions of peace and labor surpluses.[32]

During the war, the agency's services were in demand by industry and business because of the serious manpower shortage. Governmental agencies began to increase referrals to vocational rehabilitation by substantial numbers. The Selective Service agency referred people who were rejected for the armed services because of disability and the Employment Security Commission and the War Manpower office referred people who were needed as productive workers despite their disabilities.

The major changes in the Barden-Lafollette Act of 1943 were:

1. All administration and guidance and placement costs, including salaries for professional and clerical staff, were paid by the federal government. This led to a rapid expansion of staff in the state program. (Services to clients remained on a fifty-fifty matching ratio)
2. The use of federal funds for physical restoration services including hospitalization, surgery, and therapeutic treatment.
3. Maintenance for living expenses and occupational tools and equipment was authorized.
4. The mentally handicapped were included so that mentally retarded and mentally ill people for the first time were eligible for vocational rehabilitation services.[33]

The objectives of this new legislation were clear: "During the year (1943-1944) the two primary objectives defined by the Federal Security Agency on establishing the Office of Vocational Rehabilitation have been foremost: first, to channel disabled manpower into war production and essential business as rapidly as possible and second, to provide a comprehensive service to enable the disabled to prepare for and secure employment in peacetime pursuits."[34] For the first time, the state vocational rehabilitation programs were given the opportunity to develop a comprehensive service program for disabled civilians.

In the federal program of vocational rehabilitation in the early fifties, events were taking place which would lead to the enactment of the most significant legislation since the amendments of 1943. Miss Mary E. Switzer, a long-time government administrator in related programs, was named Director of the Office of Vocational Rehabilitation in the Federal Security Agency in 1951. In 1953, President Eisenhower appointed Mrs. Oveta Culp Hobby as Secretary of the newly organized Department of Health, Education and

Welfare and Nelson Rockefeller as Under-Secretary. Eisenhower's philosophy of "dynamic conservatism"[35] fitted in well with the vocational rehabilitation concept of helping handicapped or dependent people help themselves to a productive life, thus bringing about economic benefits to the nation. Mary Switzer presented to Mrs. Hobby and Mr. Rockefeller a greatly enlarged program in vocational rehabilitation which had the potential of performing a humanitarian service for the welfare of handicapped citizens, and at the same time, providing an opportunity for the government to "do something about what was considered by the administration as an increasing dependence of citizens on the welfare state." Mrs. Hobby was impressed with the possibilities presented by Miss Switzer; and Nelson Rockefeller was able to recommend this program to Mrs. Hobby as he had worked with Miss Switzer on committees previously and was a strong supporter of the vocational rehabilitation goals and objectives. When the Health, Education and Welfare proposals were presented to the President and the Cabinet in 1953, they were approved and plans were made to ask Congress for the greatest expansion of rehabilitation goals and objectives.[36]

Public Law 565, cited as the "Vocational Rehabilitation Amendments of 1954," became law on August 3, 1954. The purpose of this new act was stated in the Department of Health, Education and Welfare Annual Report of 1955:

> The law's avowed aim is to assist "the states in rehabilitating physically (and mentally) handicapped individuals so that they may prepare for and engage in remunerative employment . . . thereby increasing not only their social and economic well-being but also the productive capacity of the nation . . .[37]

Public Law 565 authorized thirty million dollars for federal grants-in-aid for 1955; the use of federal funds for the training of doctors, nurses, rehabilitation counselors, physical therapists, occupational therapists, social workers and other specialists to meet the personnel needs of the expanded rehabilitation program; extension and improvement grants and special project grants for research and demonstration.[38]

A stronger financial structure allowed for federal funding for case services and administration to be determined by a formula which gave consideration to the state's per capita income and population. This new formula eliminated the previous funding in full by the federal government for salaries and administrative costs; however, the new formula for allotment of federal funds to states helped the poorer states, particularly those in the Southeast. No major changes were made in the policies regarding eligibility, nor were any new definitions provided for terms such as "disability" and "handicapping condition" which might have extended services to new groups. The state agency was allowed, for the first time, to use its funds in expanding or remodeling buildings to make them suitable for the rehabilitation of severely disabled persons, e.g. rehabilitation centers and sheltered workshops.[39]

From 1964 to 1968, there was an unprecedented period of growth in vocational rehabilitation on state levels, due to special legislation for the mentally retarded, joint program agreements for the mentally ill, and other jointly administered units, e.g. public school special education programs, private and public rehabilitation facilities, etc. Also, significant events at the federal level contributed to this growth. Three key events which occurred in three of these years, 1965, 1967 and 1968, influenced the direction and the magnitude of this extraordinary era of expansion.

First, the Vocational Rehabilitation Amendments of 1965 were passed unanimously by Congress. Obermann states that these new expansive amendments "could almost have been written by an enthusiastic professional in the state-federal vocational rehabilitation program."[40] The new amendments provided for a substantial increase in federal spending and also provided a broader base for extending services to additional handicapped people. The definition of disability was revised to include people with "socially handicapping conditions" as determined by a psychologist or psychiatrist, e.g. juvenile delinquents and adult public offenders were eligible without regard to a specific physical or mental diagnosis. An extended plan for evaluation was authorized in the new act, which, in effect, permitted the agency to waive the third item of eligibility: a reasonable expectation that vocational rehabilitation services may render the individual fit to engage in a gainful occupation (extended evaluation). This 1965 act also provided special grants for construction and operation of sheltered workshops and other rehabilitation facilities to the state agencies or to private agencies which held joint program agreements with the official agency for vocational rehabilitation.[41]

The second of these events occurred in 1967 when the Department of Health, Education and Welfare was reorganized and the Social and Rehabilitation Service was established to provide a rehabilitation emphasis to many of the welfare and health programs in the department. John W. Gardner, who was Secretary of Health, Education and Welfare, asked the late Mary Switzer, Commissioner of Vocational Rehabilitation to head up this new administrative unit. "To better coordinate the programs, Health, Education and Welfare Secretary John Gardner has gathered five major welfare agencies under one office, named the Social and Rehabilitation Service (SRS). To Washington's surprise, Gardner went over the heads of HEW's brightest young men and selected as the first boss of SRS a 67-year old spinster . . . Mary Elizabeth Switzer has spent forty-six years in government, the last seventeen as the highly successful head of the Vocational Rehabilitation Administration, which aids the handicapped."[42] In addition to the vocational rehabilitation agency which the Social and Rehabilitation Services administers, the Children's Bureau, Administration on Aging, Medical Services Administration (Medicaid) and the Public Welfare Assistance Payments Administration were consolidated in the new Social and Rehabilitation Service.[43] The reorganization, which appeared to favor vocational rehabilitation, provided greater visibility and a national recognition for the total state-federal program, and occurred just two years after the landmark 1965 federal legislation. It strengthened the federal base for future growth at the state level.

The third major event of this period occurred when Congress passed the 1968 Vocational Rehabilitation Amendments. Among the important changes and additions contained in this act were:

1. Substantial increases in appropriations with the basic programs moving from a 75-25 matching ratio to a new formula for all states (80% federal-20% state),
2. Approval for Vocational rehabilitation to expend funds in new construction of rehabilitation facilities,
3. The definition of rehabilitation services was completely rewritten to include follow-up services in maintaining an individual in employment, services to families of the handicapped individual when

services can contribute substantially to the rehabilitation of a group of individuals,

4. The state was permitted to amend its state plan to enable it to share funding and administration responsibility with another state agency to carry out a joint project (a policy already established in most states).[44]

Thus, vocational rehabilitation was reorganized as a program which could provide substantial assistance to the administration's "war on poverty."

In concluding the study of this period, a chronological accounting of events and developments in the vocational rehabilitation program for 1965-1972 is presented:

CHRONOLOGY

- Adoption of statewide medical consultation programs with a state administrator and physicians employed on a part-time basis at district and facility offices.
- Sheltered workshops organized by local non-profit groups in cooperation with the Division of Vocational Rehabilitation or established and maintained by rehabilitation agencies. Special counselors employed to work only with mentally handicapped clients.
- Rehabilitation homes (half-way houses) established with departments of mental health, or other agencies.
- Following the passage of the Civil Rights Act of 1964, the state rehabilitation agencies adopted formal policies and procedures to meet the provisions for compliance with the act—"that no person shall, on the grounds of race, color, or national origin, be excluded from participation in, be denied benefits of, or be otherwise subjected to discrimination in the provision of any care or service."
- In-service training programs were initiated or strengthened for orientation of new staff and tuition payments for non-credit and credit graduate work, resulting in greater utilization of university programs in rehabilitation counseling.
- Joint sponsorship of amputee clinics and audiological centers in various rehabilitation centers and university facilities in the states.
- Counselor Advisory Committees were formed to improve communication between the State Office and the field, in several states.
- Graduate training programs in rehabilitation counseling developed rapidly to include over seventy universities in the nation.
- The initiation of a joint program with Social Security, utilizing funds received from the social security trust fund for the rehabili-

tation of severely handicapped people who received disability payments.

• The first statewide planning efforts were started in the establishment of the governors' study committees in Vocational Rehabilitation.

• The first undergraduate courses in rehabilitation were provided through federal grants at several colleges and universities.

• Correctional rehabilitation programs were established to provide rehabilitation services at the training schools and prisons.

Program development became an important area of administration, resulting in the establishment of numerous joint programs with other agencies and in the development of rehabilitation facilities statewide. Equally important was the emphasis placed on the improvement of services through medical and psychological consultation, staff training, and staff participation in evaluation and planning activities.

Vocational Rehabilitation's major challenge now is the adaptation to change that is required to provide new and additional services for new clients who can benefit from them. The growth of the vocational rehabilitation program from 1921 until 1963 was an orderly process (except for those beginning years) with the first major expansion occurring twenty-two years after it started in 1943, prompted by war needs; and, then, in 1954, eleven years later, in answer to the government's search for an answer to the mounting welfare and dependency problems. There was time for consolidation of gains made and sufficient experience to make a case for new needs. In the more recent period (1965-1972) the situation has been much different. As one prominent, contemporary leader in rehabilitation said, "There is a sense of urgency not only in our own field (rehabilitation counseling) but throughout the American Society."[45]

As we look toward a more effective integration of social and rehabilitation efforts for the benefit of public welfare recipients in the seventies, it is imperative that state-federal programs in vocational rehabilitation and social services take aggressive steps to establish joint programs at the local community level. Former President Lyndon Johnson, in reference to the problems of welfare in this country, stated: "The Welfare System today pleases no one. It is criticized by liberals and conservatives, by the poor and the wealthy, by social workers and politicians, by Whites and Blacks in every area of the nation." It appears that a stronger alliance between social workers in public welfare agencies and rehabilitation counselors in the state-federal rehabilitation service program may offer the greatest hope to the people of this country who want an opportunity to participate in the "American Dream."

The following quote is taken from the National Citizens Advisory Committee report on Vocational Rehabilitation published in 1968:

> We are a humane nation and we are a nation of businesses. Yet we violate the principles of humanity and business when we continue to permit large numbers of Americans to languish in the shadow of a serious handicap which could be mastered. Both the conscience and the purse suffer when men and women who could be self-reliant and productive are consigned to futility and dependency.

REFERENCES

1. *United States Statutes at Large,* Vol. 41, Sixty-sixth Congress, 1920, p. 735.
2. C. Esco Obermann: *A History of Vocational Rehabilitation in America.* Minneapolis, T. S. Denison Co. 1965, p. 47.
3. Frank Parsons: *Choosing a Vocation.* Cambridge, Houghton-Mifflin Co., 1909, p. 165.
4. *United States Statutes at Large,* Vol. 39, Sixty-fourth Congress, 1916, p. 186.
5. *Ibid.* Vol. 40, Sixty-fifth Congress, 1918, p. 617.
6. *Ibid.*
7. Obermann, *op. cit.,* pp. 216-226.
8. C. H. Patterson (Ed.): *Readings in Rehabilitation Counseling.* Champaign, Illinois, Stipes Publishing Company, 1960, pp. 25-26.
9. Federal Board for Vocational Education: *Industrial Rehabilitation—A Statement of Policies to be Observed in the Administration of the Industrial Rehabilitation Act,* Bulletin No. 57, Industrial Rehabilitation Series No. 1. Washington, Government Printing Office, September, 1920, p. 7.
10. *Ibid.,* p. 9.
11. *Ibid.,* p. 13.
12. *Ibid.,* p. 31.
13. *Ibid.*
14. *Ibid.*
15. *Ibid.,* p. 33.
16. *Ibid.,* p. 37.

17. Ibid., p. 33.
18. Federal Board for Vocational Education: *Industrial Rehabilitation - General Administration and Case Procedures,* Bulletin No. 64, Industrial Rehabilitation Series No. 2. Washington, Government Printing Office, March, 1921, p. 31.
19. *Ibid.*
20. *Ibid.,* pp. 33-36.
21. Homer L. Stanton: The Rehabilitation of Disabled Civilians in North Carolina, Master's thesis, North Carolina State College of Agriculture and Engineering, Raleigh, North Carolina, 1927, p. 7.
22. Obermann, *op. cit.,* p. 246.
23. Obermann, *op. cit.,* pp. 354-358.
24. Federal Board for Vocational Education: *Proceedings of the National Conference on Vocational Rehabilitation of Disabled Persons,* Bulletin No. 136, Vocational Rehabilitation Series, No. 18. Washington, Government Printing Office, 1928, p. 30.
25. Federal Board for Vocational Education: *Proceedings of the National Conference on Vocational Rehabilitation of Civilian Disabled Persons,* Bulletin No. 8. Washington, Government Printing Office, 1924, p. 123.
26. Lloyd E. Blauch: *Vocational Rehabilitation of the Physically Disabled,* Staff Study No. 9. The Advisory Committee on Education. Washington, Government Printing Office, 1938, p. 8.
27. United States Department of Interior, Office of Education: *Manual for Caseworkers,* Bulletin No. 175, Rehabilitation Series No. 23. Washington, Government Printing Office, 1934, p. 47.
28. Mary E. McDonald: *Federal Grants for Vocational Rehabilitation.* Chicago, University of Chicago Press, 1944, p. 80.
29. United States Department of Interior, Office of Education, *Vocational Rehabilitation of the Physically Handicapped,* Bulletin No. 190, Vocational Rehabilitation Series No. 25, Washington, Government Printing Office, 1936, p. 44.
30. *Ibid.,* pp. 49-50.
31. McDonald, *op.cit.,* p. 100.
32. Obermann, *op.cit.,* p. 289.
33. Harry A. Pattison (Ed.): *The Handicapped and Their Rehabilitation.* Springfield, Illinois, Charles C Thomas, Publisher, 1957, p. 849.
34. The Federal Security Agency: *Annual Report for the Fiscal Year, 1944-45.* Washington, Government Printing Office, 1945, p. 151.
35. Samuel Eliot Morison: *The Oxford History of the American People.* New York, Oxford University Press, 1965, p. 1082.
36. Obermann, *op.cit.,* pp. 311-312.
37. United States Department of Health, Education and Welfare: *Annual Report,* 1954-55, "Office of Vocational Rehabilitation." Washington, Government Printing Office, 1955, p. 182.

38. *Ibid.*
39. Obermann, *op. cit.*, p. 316.
40. *Ibid.*, p. 323.
41. *Newsletter,* National Rehabilitation Association, Vol. 23, No. 4, August, 1968, p. 2.
42. "The Administration," *Time,* Vol. 10, No. 9, September 1, 1967, p. 14.
43. John W. Gardner: To extend the concept of rehabilitation. *J Rehabil, 34,* N. 1, January-February, 1968, p. 12.
44. *Newsletter,* National Rehabilitation Association, Vol. 23, N. 4, August, 1968.
45. Kenneth W. Hamilton: Perspectives and prospects in rehabilitation. *J Rehabil, XXXIV,* No. 1, January-February, 1968, p. 19.

CHAPTER II

COOPERATIVE EFFORTS IN THE REHABILITATION OF THE WELFARE RECIPIENT

WILLIAM A. CRUNK

⊕⊕

Attitudinal Consideration
Definition and Discussion
Cooperation With Private Agencies
Cooperation Programs Using Third-Party Funds
Conditions Governing the Use of Third-Party Funds in Cooperative
    Programs
A Guide to Planning
Development of Programs Plans
Historic Perspective

⊕⊕

I T REMAINS A MATTER of deep concern for all citizens that in this land of super abundance there remains a significant segment of our people who do not share in this bounty. This is a matter of special significance for those who are involved in planning and directing the Nation's attack on deprivation, dependence and disadvantage—the prime elements characterizing the unemployed and underemployed in our society.

A most acute aspect of this problem is represented by the millions of persons made dependent by disability. Significantly, for a large segment of these disabled, the problem confronting them is one of unemployability rather than unemployment. This is frequently characterized by both the lack of capability to work and the motivation to work. The incapacity is not based solely upon physical or mental disability but is frequently aggravated by a strong overlay of cultural, educational and economic deprivation as well.

Thus, the design of contemporary rehabilitation programs must recognize the need for new approaches and services which can deal with the special characteristics of the disabled such as:

Social and economic immobility

Inadequate education

Marginal health

Loss of hope and expectation

Meager (or no) job experience background

Frequent rejection and hostility toward the helping services

While the foregoing is a generalization, it represents factors that illustrate the complexities inherent in comprehensive rehabilitation planning with a disabled individual.

Any serious student of the contemporary scene in America cannot be other than perplexed with the lack of decisiveness inherent in the manner that society has dealt with its poor and impoverished. This indecisiveness permeates all interest groups, the young and old, ultraliberals, middle roaders and staunch conservatives. It ranges from those advocating abdication of all responsibilities as a requisite to sharing the bounty of this nation to those who believe that such returns should be in absolute equation to assumption of such responsibility. Responsibility as used here means responsible citizenship in relation to social, civic and employment concerns and endeavors.

While this great American debate goes on, a significant segment of our citizens are drawn deeper into the morass of dependency— their lives slipping away and never to be recovered—because we continue to procrastinate, in reality, over the value of the life of an individual.

ATTITUDINAL CONSIDERATION

It has been said that we are now in a period of social revolution that promises a full measure of social and human rights to all individuals in our democratic society. Yet, for the poverty stricken, there is a growing sense of rejection and hostility toward all segments of our society, the private as well as the public sector. For example,

- Congress has been inept in trying to develop legislation that would intervene in the cyclic dependency syndrome.
- Middle income families have developed misconceptions relative to the poverty population and are comfortable with such concepts.
- Youth, though many are well motivated, have been unable to impact upon causative factors of poverty.

Moral Cretinism

Obviously, this writer, because of the potential readers of this chapter, is not co-opting for student adherents to his thesis. He already believes that sufficient moral cretinism (Ellsbery usage) exists among college students as well as professionals in the field, and the general public, to show the promise for any substantive action that will benefit the poor. Rather, he believes that the thoughtful student will consider the issues, debate the facts and reach a commitment for career goals that will be conscionable.

Youth today are seriously interested in ecology with its attendant factors which threaten the survival of this nation and the world. Yet, they must join their elders in sharing in the "Pollution" that is contributing to dependency. For example,

— Venereal Disease has reached epidemic proportion in this country and in Canada. Involved are those fourteen to twenty-five in predominant numbers. In this case, the sins of fathers and mothers will be passed on to generations to come in disability and misery.

— Youth are "copping out" in ever-increasing numbers through the use of drugs in a frantic effort to escape reality. Tragically, few know the meaning of the word until their habit catches up with them.

— Automobile accidents cause more deaths and injuries per year than all of the American casualties from the Vietnam war. Youth to age 25 are the largest causative group for such tragedy.

While such examples do not characterize the majority of youth, they lend credence to the fact that the student mood of today reflects a deep underlying skepticism about the society in which we live, and many doubts about its ability to cope with inequalities, injustices and social problems, the interspection of the "new naturalism" and its rejection of power. Such attitudes seem to hold little promise for reversing the trends or correcting causative factors of poverty during this decade. In 1970, nearly one out of five American families had to live on $5,000 or less. In 1980, one out of five families will have an income of $7,000 or less with over half of these coming under $5,000. With the depreciation in the dollar, the very poor *will be worse off in 1980 than they are now.* This is simply unacceptable.

The decade of the seventies will see a population heavily weighted with young marrieds and new careerists—37 million of them aged 25 to 34 (unprecedented in the nation's experience). In addition, although elementary and secondary enrollment will be down, college enrollment will be up 55 percent by 1980 to a total of 13,300,000.

Thus, no longer will society accept the moral platitudes and cretinism that characterized the more vocal of student leadership during the sixties. More credence will be given to the dedicated youth who will work to change the "system" as was exemplified in the 1972 presidential campaigns. It is in the unrealized potential of such youth that I have the courage to hope for a reversal in the trends and standards for services that perpetuate the dependency of the poor upon society.

Rehabilitation of the Welfare Recipient—Made Difficult

As has already been suggested, this writer believes that the difficulties encountered in working with welfare recipients lies more with the practitioner than with the client. Attitudes, values, language and a whole host of barriers are invoked when we know we are dealing with a welfare client.

Unknowingly, many rehabilitation counselors and other practitioners work quite well with and achieve respectable results from their efforts with such clientele. *It's when we know* that such difficulties crop-up.

In Maryland, for instance, only 37.4 percent of the disabled welfare clients closed in fiscal year 1970 were referred by welfare. The balance came from other sources including self-referral, employment offices, etc. In many of these cases (62.6%) it was not established that they were welfare recipients until they were well along in the rehabilitation process.

Such accountability grew out of a national thrust to identify such persons and the percentage increase over fiscal year 1968 in welfare client rehabilitation was 139.2 percent. Thus, I draw the conclusion that the identification (because of the average length of time a person is in the VR process) of such persons came after their acceptance for rehabilitation services.

Additionally, *welfare recipient* is a misnomer since it generally characterizes only those receiving income assistance. While the "characteristics of welfare recipients" are amply discussed elsewhere in this text, I suggest that there are more persons eligible for welfare in this country *than are receiving welfare*. Thus, the characteristics are similar for those *except* that they do not receive a cash payment. (Check it out.)

Thus, we are dealing with up to 32 million persons in this country who do not share fully in its productivity and resources. To varying degrees they share in the deprivation called poverty.

In reviewing the characteristics of this large population, I would suggest that the common characteristic or common denominator among this group is *poverty*. Further, I would suggest that few readers of this chapter have any valid understanding of the overwhelming and often conclusive impact of poverty upon the individual.

While poverty, to be understood, is a condition to be experienced (as experienced by this writer) there are some truths concerning this condition that can be factually stated. Among these are:

Poverty means marginal health. Except for those who are poverty stricken, youth of today are the best fed, healthiest and best educated in the history of this country. Yet, how many poor children are retarded or even die from lead paint poisoning, rat infestation, untreated chronic disease and malnutrition?

Poverty means loss of hope and expectation. Misery breeds misery. Today, most crimes against Blacks are carried out by Blacks. While this is a negative example, it suggests the cancerous effect of oppression, loss of opportunity and isolation of a people when the world rushes by without empathy and concern. Another example is Appalachia. This is tragic illustration of a people and land raped by the corporate structure leaving in its wake a large measure of frustration and loss of hope.

Add to these meager illustrations, the deficiency in education, work opportunity and experience, social and economic immobility and a whole host of other deprivations and the uninitiated might just begin to sense the magnitude of the problem of being very poor.

Challenge of the Seventies

Since 1935 we have condoned a relief system that has not worked and appears to be unworkable. The next few years presents the opportunity, ours collectively, to turn the system around and attain an equitable opportunity for those dependent upon society.

While I have "shot-gunned in" on a serious social problem, I wish now to change from bird-shot to buck-shot. It is easy to generalize about our shortcomings as professionals and emerging professionals—ringing in a few shots at Congress and the general public at the same time.

However, the talents story found in the New Testament is applicable here. This chapter is directed at those who presumably have made a career choice to enter one of the helping professions. If so, we cannot diffuse our accountability over so wide a field as to excuse or justify our failure to intervene in the causative factors of dependency. In essence, the buck passing stops with us. *Because we chose to engage the issue,* we carry a proportionate larger share of the responsibility for doing something about the problem of poverty and the dependency it breeds.

In the decade of the 60's, it became obvious that vocational rehabilitation was not impacting upon our most vulnerable population—the welfare recipients. As a matter of fact, services to disabled welfare recipients actually decreased between 1961 and 1969 when related to the growth of vocational rehabilitation during the same period. This is reflected in the following table.

	Rehabilitated Persons		
Fiscal Year	*Total No.* *Rehabilitated*	*Public* *Assistance*	*Percent* *of Total*
1961	92,416	13,528	14.6
1969	237,500	24,500	10.3

Source: Rehabilitation Service Adm., SRS, DHEW.

It is quite likely that neither Vocational Rehabilitation Administrators nor practitioners were conscious of this reduction in program effort. This lack of perception and sensitivity, in a period of growing social crisis and upheavals, required the formulation of a national strategy that would coordinate and concert the combined efforts of welfare and rehabilitation agencies in the restoration of welfare recipients to a status of full or partial self-support. This plan is known as the *Vocational Rehabilitation of Public Assistance Applicants and Recipients—A Plan of Action.* It was released by the late Commissioner of Social and Rehabilitation Services, Miss Mary Switzer, to all welfare and vocational rehabilitation administrators in February, 1969.

This *Plan of Action* remains a viable planning document since it envisions that results obtained collectively would be greater than results attained by either agency going their singular ways. Additionally, early results seem promising in view of the fact that in fiscal year 1972, rehabilitation goals for disabled welfare recipients totaled 65,000 or approximately 20 percent of the total expected number of rehabilitations.

A secondary and more subtle need for such a plan was to counter criticisms that had at their roots a challenge to the rehabilitation program and process itself! Unresponsive to emerging needs; middle class programs, creaming of easy cases—clients selected who needed little or no rehabilitation, etc. Such charges were made (and continue to be made) from both within and outside of the rehabilitation movement. Such were made by serious minded and often sincere people whose frustration in seeking resolution to the growing welfare problems was heightened by the relative failure of "new-born" and costly innovative programs of the sixties.

Thus, in this chapter it has become apparent that I view the problem of rehabilitating the welfare recipient as attitudinal rather than one of procedure or process. The rehabilitation process, for instance, is the most individually oriented procedure employed by any agency known by this writer. Yet, as a close observer of the implementation and initial results of the *Plan of Action* referred to previously, I must draw two conclusions:

First, there appears to be relatively modest commitment in either rehabilitation or welfare to mount a cooperative program really responsive to the welfare group. Much of what has been accomplished has been through Federal pressure—closer scrutiny and resource deployment (earmarking of expansion funds). Obstacles range from misconceptions (myths) to "turf protection" and everything in between. There are, of course, notable exceptions and it is from these that the promise noted above is born.

Second, there has been relatively poor use of combined resources. This includes the lack of joint housing, social and rehabilitation plans, single case records including medicals and judicious use of joint funding. Many administrators and practitioners alike seem to be waiting for welfare reform legislation and subsequent appropriations which mandate and prescribe respective roles and responsibilities before taking definitive actions in respect to the disabled welfare population.

These conclusions are quite contrary (by implication) to the early pioneering role of vocational rehabilitation in which leadership and a "damn the torpedo attitude" prevailed. Thus, the real hope of correcting the causative factors of dependency among disabled welfare recipients might well rest upon a "can do" attitude of the *new leadership* in the rehabilitation movement and that which will emerge for tomorrow!

Legislative and Funding Considerations

A "can do" attitude can be completely supported by existing social legislation. In fact, there is so much social legislation and funds available that a monumental problem facing agencies and practitioners is how to put it all together. Additionally, legislation existing now is so broad in its coverage that courts are daily making decisions that create new or expanded services and mandate their delivery. The Region III Social and Rehabilitation Services, with help from the Office of General Counsel, DHEW, has repeatedly taken positions that would broaden the interpretation of Vocational Rehabilitation legislation and has had such positions sustained. Students in rehabilitation counseling might take one provision found in the VR Regulations, "other goods and services necessary to a person's rehabilitation" and list, as an exercise, what might be possible under this one provision. Is the relocation of families and the purchase of day care services possible under this provision.

Social Services' legislation under Title IV-A and the Adult Titles in Social Security Legislation, is so broad that efforts are underway to *specify*, through regulations, what social services are and build into the delivery system a measure of accountability for results to be attained. While rehabilitation funds (Federal) are closed-end, social service funds are open-end funds as of this date. The point is that since the Action Plan of 1969, states have had available legislation that allowed the provision of any and all rehabilitation and social services that might be required by a disabled welfare recipient and, potentially at least, an open bank account to finance such services. This funding potential was *surfaced* and *underlined* by action by SRS in Region III and subsequently extended nationwide through the development of a *program aid* that spelled out the provisions and requirements that would permit *welfare agencies to purchase vocational rehabilitation services* from vocational rehabilitation agencies. This purchase of services arrangement provided linkage of the VR agency to an open-end source of Federal funds to *carry out vocational rehabilitation*.

Such welfare funds could support *administration, counseling and guidance and all rehabilitation services defined in the VR regulations for eligible disabled welfare recipients,* served beyond a maintenance of effort tied to previous expenditures by state vocational rehabilitation agencies of Section 2 VR funds for such purpose. Hence, the disappointment in the growth of disabled welfare recipients served and rehabilitated in the period 1969 to the present.

I cannot cry out too loudly or implore too strongly that the same opportunity exists today. Congress might get around to passing welfare reform legislation; closing social service appropriations; providing new definitions as to what constitutes rehabilitation; or exercise any number of legislative options including Federal Revenue sharing with States. If vocational rehabilitation is competitive, it will be the "razor's edge" in developing responsive programs under any of these options. However, vocational rehabilitation as a movement, along with its supporters can no longer assume a favorable position in Congress or with the Administration—regardless of party.

Somewhere along the way there must be a payoff from our investments. There is no question as to where the national domestic priority lies, our priority must deal with our more costly domestic outlay of funds. I know many fiscal management people and find most warmly human but "hard-nosed" when debating the issues of who should have priority in respect to social services.

Their arguments are persuasive but fade into insignificance when the long range options are faced. Either through our wisdom, ability and efforts, a program of services will be evaluated to meet the needs of welfare recipients—including former and potential— or a program might well be regimented through sheer economic necessity. The latter might well be fraught with requirements that dehumanize and relegate to a commonality that will be little less than forced servitude.

The Client's Perspective

One has only to look at the recent emergence of forces representing the welfare recipient and the poverty-stricken. Granted, much of this grows out of their just belief that they have been denied a proportionate share of the bounty of this nation. Furthermore, I believe, it represents an inherent fear that the oppressed become more oppressed, and on occasions irrational stands have been taken by such groups that grew more out of fear than a a desire for equitable treatment.

Reflect for a moment on the misconceptions listed above, the relative poor performance of service delivery agencies, the less than adequate subsistence provided by an "enlightened" society, complacency of most people to their plight, threatening legislation (in fact or fantasy). Could you be trusting of the establishment if you were among the welfare population of this country? How would you view the social worker or rehabilitation counselor?

Also, reflect upon our communication linkage with the welfare recipient—particularly in the hard core poverty areas such as those in our large cities. The problem exists also in rural poverty areas but is diffused by the relative lack of concentration of recipient groups.

Communications are simply inadequate. We just don't live where they live. Young people today glibly use four-letter words to shock their elders or impress their contemporaries. Yet, I have seen sophisticated, idealistic youngsters, armed with college degrees drop their marbles when confronted with the vernacular of the street— a vernacular that strips away all pretense and game playing.

Many of the people we seek or need to contact are unreachable during the day. They are hustling at night, making out the best way they can and spend much of the day in cheap theaters— sleeping in seasonable comfort at a reasonable cost. I recall an instance while serving on the *President's Committee on Manpower,* of discussing work with seven young unemployed Black men in a pool parlor. (This was in early evening and I would have never been there without the blessing and protection of the local gang leader.) This was where I learned that the language could be used as an endearing term, one of friendship, or one used in hostility— such is the vernacular of the street!

To shorten this first person experience, my purpose was to offer employment opportunities, including training, to any who desired such. Arrangements were made to meet the following morning at 11:00 a.m. (even I knew it would be impossible to get them there earlier). Only one person showed up. Was this individual motivated and the others not? This personal experience could be the basis of a good discussion on motivation. Obviously, the other six were not motivated as I expected them to be in terms of my expectations.

Rehabilitation of the Welfare Recipient Made Possible

I have concluded that we have sufficient legislative authority, resources and procedures to deal adequately with the rehabilitation needs of the disabled welfare recipient (definition in broadest terms).

The problem from my viewpoint lies in the relative lack of administrative commitment and practitioner dedication and ability to deal with the attendant factors rather than the disability of the recipient.

I suggest a moral cretinism that makes us feel comfortable in perpetuating the misconceptions (myths) which malign those in poverty—particularly the welfare recipient.

I predict the development of an isolated society that will eventually react from fear and distrust and *will not* become a subculture

—complacent and docile as some predict.

These conclusions grow out of my perception of 37 years of what I view as a demeaning, degrading, disincentive welfare system which the State and Federal Governments have ineptly used.

However, I can be persuaded that this system *can be turned around* during this decade. We have the tools and the programs necessary to achieve this happening!

Establishing Credibility

We must solicit the aid of consumers of our services before we can even begin to bridge the credibility gap. We must desist in the imposition of middle class values upon this target population. In addition to the differences noted above—or in support of them— we must recognize:

— the need for availability of services at times that don't coincide with our regular 8 to 5 work-day.
— the difference in language.
— the differences in social and moral values—with an acceptance of such differences.
— the need for services that are relevant to the needs—perceived or actual—of the target group.
— the need to respond to basic as opposed to elective services of the clientele group. Basic sanitation, health, recreational, safety and transportation needs.
— the need to recognize the human worth and value of the individual.
— the need for short-circuiting the laborous process of dealing with the individual as a total person.
— the need to care—really care.
— the need to eliminate the bull-shit and get on with basic and prompt decisions regarding eligibility for programs and services (automatic referral and prompt, automatic acceptance).
— the need to decentralize referral and intake centers.

There are no ready answers to the rehabilitation of welfare recipients. I frequently believe we make mountains out of relatively minor problems. We need to think, act, and respond to welfare recipients as people and not as a categorical entity. (Remember the Maryland experience.)

It is interesting, if perplexing, to see state agencies consolidate their efforts in times of natural disaster—the Pennsylvania flood of 1972 as an example—but fail to recognize the human disaster that has existed since the time of recorded history. In such current disasters, there is the coordination and concerting of services— single service centers for another example—that reflects an urgency of the minutes rather than an urgency of the times.

Specific accomplishments in the vocational rehabilitation of the welfare recipients depend, in the judgment of this writer, on the following process and procedures between VR and social services (and other helping professions).

1. Joint housing of staff. This is not considered essential but is desirable to insure less fragmentation of services.
2. Development of a *single social and rehabilitation plan for the individual. This is essential* to insure the commitment, in appropriate sequence, of the required services needed by the individual.
3. Common case service forms. Intake, medical, psychological, etc., requirements to develop a case record should be acceptable by the two primary agencies and *all others* involved in the rehabilitation process.
4. Utilization of paraprofessional staff to insure attention to details of the individual's needs such as transportation required to keep appointments, baby-sitting for similar purposes, etc.
5. Automatic referral (by welfare) and automatic acceptance (by VR) of welfare clients. This would be based upon the joint development of selection and referral criteria.
6. Less specific, but of ultimate significance is the provision of prompt, efficient and high quality vocational rehabilitation and social services for persons accepted into the VR-PW programs.

DEFINITION AND DISCUSSION

A relatively new approach to rehabilitation planning for priority or "target" groups of disabled persons has been cooperative programming. Simply defined, cooperative programming as used here means concerted program planning and action by the public or private agencies in an effort to maximize their effectiveness in restoring disabled individuals (and their families) to economic and social independence.

Early target populations for which cooperative programs were designed included the mentally retarded, the mentally ill and the unemployed disabled. Subsequently, programs have been developed for the public offender, the disabled welfare recipient and, to a lesser degree, for the older adults, the deaf and the blind. The most recent group targeted for cooperative programming is miners disabled by pneumoconiosis and other dust diseases. Thus, agencies most frequently entering into cooperative agreements with the public vocational rehabilitation agency are the public schools, correctional, welfare and mental health agencies; workmen's compensation boards; and nonprofit, private groups such as sponsors of workshops and facilities.

Cooperative program development means more than just the provision of services from the two (or more) agencies to a common clientele group. As conceived by this writer, it involves the formalized commitment (written plan) of the agencies involved to plan, organize, improve and focus in the most effective way their respective services on the needs of the disabled to be served through the joint action program. This means prescribed commitment of resources which might result in new organizational and staffing patterns, new and creative use of staff, development of new programs and facilities and full utilization of community resources. Additionally, the formal commitment must address procedural modification, such as client selection and referrals and changes in administrative policy, institutional or agency rules which might retard program development and operation. Following the development of cooperative program content and procedures, the costs of the program must be determined and budgets established. Financial commitments, it should be noted, are crucial to the success of cooperative program efforts whether or not the mechanism of third-party funding (which will be discussed later) is employed. Finally, joint decisions must be reached and recorded as to responsibility for program evaluation and accountability.

While cooperative program planning and implementation is not an easy task, its effectiveness cannot be disputed. Literally hundreds of cooperative programs are in operation throughout the nation.

Scores of such endeavors are underway within single states. Probably the most numerous outside of workshop and facility programs are public school vocational rehabilitation programs. Among the earliest cooperative programs established were those for the mentally ill. Several states now have cooperative programs at each of their mental hospitals and have extended this approach to community mental health centers as well. Most cooperative programs are developed between the vocational rehabilitation agency and one other agency. In Kentucky, an exciting cooperative effort is underway which envisions statewide correctional rehabilitation services for eligible, youthful and adult public offenders. In this effort, five public agencies developed cooperative program plans to coordinate the delivery of services to eligible persons within this target group. Thus, it is self-evident that through appropriate administrative and staff action, joint action programs can be developed which provide the basis for long-term commitments to an effective interagency operating pattern resulting in the optimal rehabilitation and well-being of the disabled persons served.

The California Department of Rehabilitation, in a report to the state legislature on April 1, 1969, pointed out some general benefits of cooperative programs as follows:

> It has been possible for the Department of Rehabilitation to bring its services to larger groups of mentally and physically handicapped persons. It has been possible to do this while conserving the state general fund, and at the same time, maximizing federal funding participation. It has permitted the cooperating departments to enrich and expand their programs to the benefit of their clients. Lastly, the cooperative programs have provided a guide for the diverse vocational interests represented in the various departments so that maximum gains were achieved for the eligible client population.

While cooperative program planning is frequently difficult by the nature of the task, it can be further complicated by applicable state and federal laws and regulation as well as by the "professional jurisdictions" sometimes "staked out" by one of the partnership agencies. However, there is no mystery surrounding their development as some imagine. Such planning is almost always successful when conducted by persons who have sincere concern for the well-being and betterment of the clientele group to be served, who are creative and not fearful about trying new approaches to rehabilitation and self-support and who are willing to invest in hard work to assure that the cooperative effort will be successful. Since all sections authorizing funding of services under the Vocational Rehabilitation Act, as amended, are on a project basis except for Section 2 (basic support to State Vocational Rehabilitation Programs), cooperative programs as discussed in this chapter relate to programs for which the public vocational rehabilitation agency elects to use the latter source of funding (Section 2) for its share of cost in such activities.

COOPERATION WITH PRIVATE AGENCIES

The fact that the private sector has benefited from cooperative programs is attested to by the hundreds of workshops and rehabilitation centers that have been started or expanded since 1954. Hundreds of such facilities have been assisted and many states have statewide networks of such resources which make possible services to thousands of disabled persons who could not otherwise be served. Assistance to workshops and facilities included remodeling, renovation, expansion of the building, equipment and initial staffing. Until 1965, the total cost of such workshop improvements was borne essentially by the state agency.

In 1965, Congressman Melvin Laird initiated an amendment to the Department of Health, Education, and Welfare's appropriation bill that made possible the earmarking and use of contributed funds by local nonprofit organizations as the state's share for earning the federal share in these projects. The Laird Amendments were continued from around 1965 through 1968. The 1968 amendments to the Vocational Rehabilitation Act incorporated all authorities allowed under the amendments to the Appropriation Act and added provisions to provide new construction of workshops and facilities. The 1968 amendments also provided for new construction of such facilities.

A further note on the Laird Amendments: Cooperation among agencies—public and private—is being extolled today as a necessary approach to the resolution of problems confronting our society. It is a "theme song" at all levels of government and a similar chorus is heard from various segments of the private sector. The Laird Amendments were responsive to an early recognition of such need by the enlightened leadership in vocational rehabilitation at the time—federal and state—and by members of both Houses of the Congress. The uniqueness of using an amendment to the Appropriation Act as a vehicle in achieving this specific purpose and the support of such amendments through the years without dissenting votes in either House reflect the degree of approval this pioneer effort received in Congress.

The success of state and local private agencies and organizement was significant in securing passage of the 1968 Amendments to the Vocational Rehabilitation Act which, as now evolved, probably represents the most liberal and enlightened piece of social legislation in existence. Beneficiaries from such legislative authority in the private sector has included many independent community workshops administered by local boards of directors and organizations providing services to disabled persons such as associations for retarded and crippled children, organizations for the blind, Goodwill Industries and others. Of course, the real beneficiaries have been and continue to be the disabled, many of whom receive concurrent services from the private facility and the public vocational rehabilitation agency.

COOPERATIVE PROGRAMS USING THIRD-PARTY FUNDS

As noted previously, the Laird Amendments and subsequent changes in the Vocational Rehabilitation Act permitted the use of private, nonprofit funds as the state's share in attracting Federal Section 2 funds for use in "establishment" and construction of rehabilitation workshops and facilities. Similar provisions apply to the public sector as well. In other words, state funds available to public agencies other than the public vocational rehabilitation agency can be used to attract Federal Section 2 funds.

The use of the "other" agency's funds, both private and public, is conditioned on a number of requirements. The latter (public) presents a more complex set of conditions due to the various federal and state laws applicable to each agency and the resultant and traditional functions of the agencies involved in cooperative programming.

Such funds, when made available from another public agency, are known as "third-party funds" and are defined as follows: Third-party funds are that part of the state's share in the cost of vocational rehabilitation services and their administration which is borne by a state or local public agency under an agreement (and program plan) and can be made available in two ways: administrative transfer in cash by the cooperating public agency to the state vocational rehabilitation agency and expenditure of funds (for vocational rehabilitation purposes) by the cooperating agency. Third-party funding, whichever method used, is predicated upon the premise that the cooperative program will result in the reaching and serving of more handicapped persons while improving the quality of rehabilitation services over that which could be provided singly by either of the cooperating agencies.

CONDITIONS GOVERNING THE USE OF THIRD-PARTY FUNDS IN COOPERATIVE PROGRAMS

It has already been established that third-party funds may be made available in two ways. Cash transfer to the state vocational rehabilitation agency and/or acceptable expenditures for rehabilitation services (and their administration) by the host agency.

The first method is the easiest way to make funds available. It is a cash transfer and, as such, both the state and federal share of costs for services are expended by the vocational rehabilitation agency. The second method frequently involves host agency staff assignment to the rehabilitation program and other services provided by the host agency such as maintenance, heat and other utilities for cooperative program staff and facilities. In this instance, the cost of staff so assigned and services provided constitutes the host agency's contribution to the program and such costs may be considered the state's share for use in attracting Federal Section 2 funds.

The financial significance of third-party funding to the states is quite clear. Let us assume that a cooperative welfare rehabilitation program is priced out at a total cost of $250,000. Further, we assume that the state rehabilitation agency's state appropriation was insufficient to attract all of its Federal Section 2 allocation and that a balance of $300,000 in unearned funds remained in the federal "account" which would be lost to the state.

In this instance, if the welfare agency makes available the state share at the current state-federal ratio of 20/80, it would transfer in cash or "in kind" a total of $50,000. The social service bureau would have infused into its program a rehabilitation component not previously existing and the state vocational rehabilitation agency, and hence, the state would earn a more equitable share of federal funds available for rehabilitation purposes. In the early days of cooperative programming, as discussed later, guidelines covering program content and funding arrangement were rather meager. Through a vast amount of experiences in mounting such efforts, including the resolution of many audit questions and issues, a sound program and legal base now undergirds this type of program activity.

Where third-party funding is used in financing a cooperative service program, both the third-party share and the federal funds earned must meet certain conditions imposed upon any Section 2 expenditures made by the state vocational rehabilitation agency. These conditions are stipulated in both the vocational rehabilitation regulations governing the vocational rehabilitation program and in Chapter II of the Vocational Rehabilitation Manual. Additionally, cooperative program activity, if adopted by the state agency, must be covered in the approved state plan covering the vocational rehabilitation program in that particular state. These provide essential references for anyone seriously interested in cooperative program planning and operation. However, it might prove useful to discuss briefly some of the principles and criteria governing cooperative programs as discussed in this chapter.

Source of third-party funds. While either of the methods of making funds available is acceptable as noted it is important to observe here that with few exceptions federal funds cannot be used to attach federal funds. The only exception known to this writer are certain Appalachian regional development funds and housing and urban supplemental funds made available to model cities agencies. Otherwise, third-party funds must represent state monies and be subject to verification that they so qualify. Also, the state cannot use the same state monies to attract federal funds from more than one federal source (non-duplicating matching).

Third-party funds must be spent for vocational rehabilitation purposes. This simple statement becomes more complex in its essence when we realize that many agencies provide rehabilitation-type services. Since it is not the purpose or intent in cooperative programs to supplant existing and adequate rehabilitation services or finance existing services of the third-party agency for which a handicapped person would be entitled if he was not an applicant or client of the vocational rehabilitation agency, we reach this important conclusion. Rehabilitation services for which third-party expenditures are claimed must represent new rehabilitation services or new patterns of rehabilitation services which are not available through the cooperating agency, and such expenditures for new or new patterns of services must be under the control of the state vocational rehabilitation agency.

The principles of control derive from legislative requirement that the state vocational rehabilitation agency must be the final authority on the quality, ends, scope and extent of vocational rehabilitation services provided disabled people with the funds, from whatever source, for which it is responsible. Also, the agency is required to determine eligibility, rehabilitation potential and scope of services to be provided a handicapped individual. Control, as used here, is not the harsh requirement as it might seem. We are talking about new services or new patterns of vocational rehabilitation services which are nonexistent without the development of the cooperative program. Also, the cost of these new or changed services is borne principally by the state vocational rehabilitation agency (80% Federal Section 2 funds) which becomes involved in the provision of services after careful joint planning and agreement as to program content, priority for services in respect to the clientele group and similar program content has been completed. After these discussions, and only then, does the state vocational rehabilitation agency exercise its responsibilities under state and federal laws requiring such control over the vocational rehabilitation part of the program. The cooperating agency would likewise be expected to administer, according to applicable laws, its part of the program.

Additionally, control of expenditures for either new services or new patterns of services may be achieved through direct expenditures by the state vocational rehabilitation agency or the disbursement by the cooperating agency when made in accordance with the cooperative program plan, budget and agreement and by such method that satisfies the vocational rehabilitation agency as to fiscal accountability.

New rehabilitation services are those services which are not and have not recently been a part of the cooperating agency's program. They may be services for which the cooperating agency is authorized to provide but for some reason has not elected to do so. However, they may not be services for which the cooperating agency is legally obligated to provide. The key words here are authorized and obligated. It goes without saying that it would be unlikely that a cooperating agency could make funds available to the vocational rehabilitation agency if it did not have the authority to provide the services envisioned. However, state enabling legislation is frequently more specific on obligatory services which a state agency must provide. Rehabilitation agencies could establish services which a state agency must provide. Rehabilitation agencies could establish services in the former or authorized area if they were nonexistent but not in the latter category. State attorney generals can help make such distinctions in applicable state laws, policies and regulations.

New patterns of rehabilitation services might include previously existing services of the authorized category provided by the cooperating agency. The cost of such services, to constitute a third-party expenditure, would have to be modified or otherwise changed and reoriented to vocational rehabilitation. If existing staff (employed by the cooperating agency) is assigned, control in terms of program assignment and supervision would become the responsibility of the state vocational rehabilitation agency. Thus, the new pattern must provide discernible contrast favoring vocational rehabilitation activity. Occupational therapy, although previously existent might be either medically or recreationally oriented in a setting such as a psychiatric hospital. This modality might be redirected to provide personal adjustment or vocational evaluation services within the cooperative psychiatric rehabilitation program established at the hospital. Under such circumstances, new patterns of services would be established. However, under ordinary circumstances, the psychiatric care and treatment, room and board, medications and similar services for which the hospital is obligated, under law, to provide could not be so modified to constitute acceptable third-party expenditures.

A GUIDE TO PLANNING

In an effort to simplify the approach to cooperative program planning, the writer developed an outline, with brief comments under each heading, that might be useful to persons interested in this kind of program development. It is a composite outline drawn from several joint action plans now in operation. It is not intended as a prototype plan guide but as a stimulator since each cooperative program opportunity has its own uniqueness for expression in plan development.

A. Introduction.

This can be a statement that presents traditional or historical developments or other content which supports, in a general way, the need for and timeliness of the effort to be made. Planners should keep in mind that the implementors might cover a range of professional, paraprofessional and volunteer staff. For educational purposes alone, an introduction or background statement is frequently desirable.

B. Statement of the Problem.

This is simply an assessment of the problem as it now exists in respect to the client group to be served, availability of existing services (or lack thereof) and other information that establishes the nature of the problem and establishes the need for a coordinated, concerted joint program effort.

C. Action Plan Development.

1. Goals and objectives.

Certain program objectives might be specified here and then the establishment of more specific goals in terms of numbers of persons to be served and rehabilitated.

2. Priorities for services.

This is a critical plan provision which is required since joint agency resources are rarely adequate to serve a total population group. In correctional rehabilitation planning, for instance, will the program be directed toward youthful or adult offenders, long-termers or those on probation and parole? It is also important, since it establishes, quite

specifically, the target group for participating agencies.
3. Selection criteria.

To assure controlled and effective referrals to the program and to assure referrals of those who can profit most from a concerted program effort, it is usually accepted practice to establish such criteria. They can be modified as the program matures to expand coverage. Another reason for selection criteria should be to establish an automatic referral and acceptance procedure. If selection criteria is jointly determined then it follows that the host agency—mental hospital, school or welfare agency—would automatically refer those meeting the selection criteria and vocational rehabilitation would automatically accept them for evaluation to determine eligibility for services.

It is, of course, hardly necessary to mention that the criteria for extended evaluation under the vocational rehabilitation service program would constitute two of the selection criteria.
4. Services to be provided by vocational rehabilitation.
5. Services to be provided by other cooperating agency (ies).

Under each of these headings a concise description of services to be provided is presented.
6. Case planning and management.

Describe how the counseling and planning required to develop and activate a rehabilitation program for the individual is to be carried out. In the mental hospitals, for instance, the cooperative program unit is usually located in space made available on campus by the hospital administrators. The client served through the unit is also a patient in the hospital. This poses questions as to the role of the hospital's social workers who obtain intake data, social histories and the like. Frequently hospital social workers are assigned to the unit staff. How does her role change? Is the counselor's role modified following such assignment? Considerations should be given to all aspects of case planning and management including plan development, progress reports, case reviews, case closures and so forth.
7. Plans for housing.

In institutionally-based programs the plan should provide for adequate housing of professional and support staff assigned to the cooperative program and for adequate evaluation, adjustment and training areas. Such space is made available by the host institution and is frequently renovated or remodeled by vocational rehabilitation. In cooperative programs with public welfare and similar community-based programs, joint housing of social workers and counselors may be desired.

8. Commitment of resources.

   Each agency should indicate the extent of financial and staff commitment. Program utilizing third-party funds will develop operational budgets and, after the first year, prepare expenditure reports as well.

9. Target coverage area.

   Cooperative programs, except those directed toward residents in the big city ghettos and in specified rural areas, such as Appalachia, should ultimately be planned for statewide coverage. Orderly program implementation, tight money conditions or other reasons might require phasing in of the new program in selected geographic areas or selected institutions.

10. Staff development.

    Should be jointly planned, funded and carried out.

11. Interagency reporting system.

    Should be adequate for purposes of each cooperating agency.

12. Public information system.

    Usually describes the method used for making known to potential clients and others the services available under the program plan.

13. Supportive services from other agencies.

    Usually indicated here are services from other agencies that will be utilized in the cooperative program such as
    • Services under Medicaid
    • Crippled Children's Service
    • Day-Care Facilities and Services
    • Manpower Programs

14. Program evaluation.
    Describe here the method and procedures jointly developed
    for use in measuring the strength and weaknesses of the
    program operation including results obtained.

DEVELOPMENT OF PROGRAM PLANS

In view of the possibilities for joint cooperation, state administrators should review their existing relationships and methods of
operation to determine most effective means for achieving a major
expansion of services for target groups. They should jointly set in
motion steps that will result in a program plan which would be
expressed in a formal cooperative plan of operation.

Specific actions in planning and initiating the cooperative program which might be taken by program administrators include
the following:

A. The appointment of an interagency task force to be charged
   with
   1. The development of the program plan, including the iden-
      tification of agency resources each agency plans to commit
      and use in achieving program goals.
   2. Assignment of responsibility for its implementation follow-
      ing administrative acceptance.
B. The establishment of target dates for program implementation,
   including sequential target dates for statewide coverage (if
   not initially planned).
C. The preparation of operational manuals and guide material
   for use in implementing and operating the program.
D. The development of material for use with the information
   media to interpret and explan the program to the general
   public.

HISTORIC PERSPECTIVE

Strong advocates for the use of third-party funding to carry out
vocational rehabilitation service programs emerged at both the
state and federal levels in the early fifties. In fact, some of the
more aggressive state directors were experiencing audit problems
prior to the 1954 Amendments to the Vocational Rehabilitation
Act. These amendments vindicated such cooperative program prac-

tices including funding arrangements by legitimizing such practice in federal laws and "grandfathering in" or covering many of the prior activities of state agencies for which audit exceptions were pending.

The strength of character of those state directors and those at the federal level who supported their cause in forcing changes in vocational rehabilitation legislation and practice in the recognition that a disabled individual was a total being, with sundry and complex problems requiring an array of social, medical, psychological and vocational services beyond the capacity of any one agency to provide is to be admired.

Such persons were ahead of their times as can be recognized with today's hue and cry for coordinated services. Yet, while their intuitive wisdoms of the emerging needs of many of our citizens, disabled and disadvantaged, was denied by policy makers at the time, they and many who followed gave those of us in the rehabilitation movement today ample legislative authority and program experience to provide aggressive leadership in developing new and innovative cooperative programs for the disabled (and if required, the disadvantaged) during the decade of the seventies and beyond.

CHAPTER III

THE IMPACT OF WELFARE REFORM
ON REHABILITATION

JERRY S. TUREM*

೫೫

History of Welfare Reform
The V. R. Role in Welfare Reform
Size of the Task
Policy Impact of Welfare Reform on V.R.
Unresolved Policy Issues
Rehabilitation of Children
References

೫೫

VOCATIONAL REHABILITATION has always had an important, though not central, role in working with handicapped persons dependent on public assistance. For any number of reasons—good and bad, ideological and practical—the prime focus of V.R. until recent years has not been on this population. The impetus for welfare reform has brought about something of a revolution in the concern and services to be focused on this group of handicapped persons. The implications of this focus reverberate throughout the rehabilitation movement. Seldom has there been an example of a

*The author is grateful to his colleagues at the Urban Institute, Robert Harris and Alan Fechter who reviewed early drafts, and to Edward Newman, Commissioner of the Rehabilitation Services Administration, SRS, DHEW, who read and commented on the paper. His able staff contributed many thoughtful comments, Kay Arneson, Jack Bailey, Bill Bean, Joe Abrams, Larry Mars, Dick Melia, Fred Sachs, and Sylvia Vela. The work reported in this paper was supported in part by Grant No. 18-P-56665/3-01 from the Social and Rehabilitation Services, Department of Health, Education, and Welfare, Washington, D.C.

major policy shift in one area having such profound, and anticipated, implications for another. Interestingly enough, it is viewed in many circles not as welfare coming to rehabilitation, but the infusion of rehabilitation concepts into the welfare field.

HISTORY OF WELFARE REFORM

Welfare reform has been long needed and long in coming. The 1962 and 1967 Amendments to the Public Assistance Titles of the Social Security Act recognized both a need for services for public assistance recipients, and that many could participate in the labor market. However, the legislation tended to focus upon welfare department caseworkers and traditional Department of Labor manpower services rather than upon the rehabilitation system. The handicapped assistance recipients as a group were ignored as far as employment was concerned.

Lyndon B. Johnson appointed a President's Commission on Income Maintenance Programs in 1968 to examine the full range of welfare and related programs. Alternatives were to be proposed. The Commission report, made after President Nixon was inaugurated, recommended a major overhaul of public assistance programs and in many ways underpinned the President's Welfare Reform Program: federalize payments and administration, remove categorical constraints, provide adequate guarantees and lower the rate by which benefits are reduced by earnings to encourage people to work.[1]

President Nixon introduced welfare reform with his message of August 11, 1969,[2] and his proposed welfare reform bill, dated October 3, 1969, was introduced to the House as H.R. 14173. In the Nixon proposal, for the family program, persons were required to register for employment unless excluded by a specific set of conditions, one of which included incapacity. His proposal for the disabled and blind did not include any work requirement. For persons in the family program who claimed exclusions for incapacity, however, referral to V.R. was required. The major features of his pro-

---

[1]*Poverty Amid Plenty.* Report of the President's Commission on Income Maintenance Programs, U.S. Government Printing Office, November, 1969. Also *Background Papers* and *Technical Studies.* U. S. Government Printing Office, 1970.

[2]Reprinted in T. R. Marmor (Ed.): *Poverty Policy.* Aldine-Atherton, 1970. This volume also contains Secretary of HEW Finch's message in support of the Administration's bill.

posal were: a national minimal guarantee in a federally-administered program. The rate at which benefits were to be reduced by other income was less severe than existing law, and working poor families with a male head were included. The income break-even points for coverage were generally higher than current law.

The House Committee on Ways and Means considered the President's Welfare proposals and made modifications. When the Ways and Means Committee voted out their Welfare Reform bill, H.R. 16311, there were references to a mandatory referral of incapacitated family members for evaluation of their need for and use of vocational rehabilitation services. And, as in the President's bill, the House bill did not require V.R. or manpower services for the aged, blind and disabled.

H.R. 16311 passed the House in April, 1970, and was sent to the Senate Finance Committee chaired by Senator Russell Long of Louisiana. Senator Long and most of the Finance Committee, especially the Republican members, were opposed to most of the welfare reform principles embodied in the bill.

The Administration, meanwhile, was preparing its proposed amendments to H.R. 16311 and, from that point on, the rehabilitation interests were directly involved in welfare reform. Representatives of the Rehabilitation Services Administration became involved in the welfare reform process on a continuing basis to shape those aspects of the program relating to handicapped people and the V.R. role. Time after time questions of equity between able-bodied and handicapped arose and in most cases were resolved in favor of adding provisions for the handicapped paralleling those for the able-bodied. One example was the provision for incentive allowances for those in V.R. comparable to allowances given to able-bodied participating in manpower programs. Additional examples were coverage of certain cost to the handicapped and similar funding requirements for reimbursements to states for programs to both the able-bodied and handicapped at 90 percent federal. While the bargaining process both within the Administration and between the Executive Branch and Congress was slow, progress was made. For example, an RSA proposal to have the V.R. agencies in the states perform the determinations of disability under the welfare Title XVI Aid to Disabled program was accepted, since V.R. was doing most of the determinations under the Social Security Disability Trust Fund Program and would be doing those for the incapacitated under revised Title IV.

For the first time in the history of a major domestic policy change, the implications of different alternatives, and the impacts on various populations, were projected through a model which could simulate program elements and population variables.[1] Almost immediately it became required that V.R. estimates be included on this new basis. This challenge was accepted by the Rehabilitation Services Administration and work began on forecasting-simulation models so that cost, caseload and other impacts could be better estimated and planned. If nothing else, federal planning for rehabilitation took a major step forward.

H.R. 16311 died when the 91st Congress adjourned without taking action. It was reintroduced in the 92nd Congress by Ways and Means Committee Chairman Mills as H.R. 1, a recognition of its high priority and importance. Once again his Committee began work on the bill and voted out what became the House passed version of welfare reform. The bill was again hung up in the Senate Finance Committee.

From a V. R. perspective, H.R. 1 contains many improvements over its predecessor. For one thing, the proposed funding for V.R. services to assistance recipients became 100 percent federal, rather than 90 percent as in the prior version. There would be requirements for the blind and disabled as well as for the incapacitated in families. Handicapped children receiving benefits in the Disabled Program could be V.R. clients. V.R. would have claims on incentive money for disabled clients, child care funds and, if agreements are worked out with the Department of Labor, for work-evaluation-work-adjustment services for the non-disabled disadvantaged. H.R. 1 would have Federal (Social Security Administration) administration of the assistance program for the blind and disabled as well as

---

[1] Gail R. Wilensky: "An Income Transfer Computational Model," *Technical Studies.* The President's Commission on Income Maintenance Programs, USGPO, 1969. Nelson McClung, John Moeller, and Eduardo Siguel, "Transfer Income Program Evaluation," Urban Institute Working Paper 950-3, Washington, D.C., March, 1971. Jerry Turem, "Impact on Current Public Assistance Programs of Adopting a Universal Income Supplement," *Technical Studies,* op. cit.
A version of this simulation is being run by the Social Security Administration which provides the cost and caseload estimates being used in discussions with the Congress.

the aged, with rules similar to those in the Title II (Disability Insurance Trust Fund) program. This would mean that in most states, V.R. agencies would be performing determinations of disability for both the Trust Fund and Welfare Programs under nationally uniform definitions. This would be a broad step in providing equity for the disabled compared to the existing practice of allowing each state to adopt its own definition of disability in the welfare program.

Some defects remained in the bill, from the V.R. viewpoint. Some handicapped persons in families who would have another exemption from the work requirement not only would be referred for V.R. services but could even volunteer through H.R. 1. Thus a female head of household, both handicapped and with a child under six, could not get V.R. through H.R. 1. Thus she could not get the incentive allowances or other benefits her able-bodied counterpart could get, nor indeed those her handicapped counterpart without a child under six could get. Administration proposals were made to correct this inequity. If this policy were corrected, and if H.R. 1 passed with these V.R. provisions intact, it would mean that every public assistance recipient who was blind, disabled or an incapacitated member of a family would be referred for assessment of rehabilitation potential, and, if served, would have his services reimbursed to the State Agency at 100 percent federal rate.

The thrust to include V.R. in Welfare Reform was, of course, viewed by some as less than a blessing. Animosities on the part of some segments of the rehabilitation movement, public and private, to welfare as a system, welfare agencies as competitors for state funds, and toward welfare recipients themselves emerged. At first some in the rehabilitation movement were reluctant to even consider inclusion into welfare reform as being significant. Initially there was a great deal of concern with separate financing for these recipients, so that service to incapacitated and disabled recipients of public assistance would not displace funds needed to serve the "handicapped." The traditional clients were seen as being the staple of V.R.: They were perceived as deserving while the welfare caseload were perceived of as dependent, unmotivated, hostile and unskilled.

Then came the questions more closely rooted to real problems:

How dependent are they? What do we know about motivating them? Can V.R. deliver? The answers to these questions started appearing even though welfare reform had not passed.

While welfare reform was wending its way through Congress, the federal agencies began placing greater emphasis on assistance recipients as priority clients for service. In the Social and Rehabilitation Services Administration, rehabilitation was at the center of this movement. The Office of Management and Budget even went so far as to support increased appropriations to cover increased services to welfare recipients served under V.R. The percentage of the caseload and clients rehabilitated who had been on public assistance at some time during V.R. began a steady rise. In fiscal 1969 28,200 persons receiving public assistance at any time were rehabilitated (11.7% of the total number rehabilitated). By fiscal 1971 the number of welfare recipients at any time during the rehabilitation process who were rehabilitated was 40,300 (or 13.8% of the total). And in fiscal 1972, it is expected that 203,-000 welfare clients will be served by V.R. and 58,000 will be rehabilitated (19% of the total).

Efforts were made to search out answers to questions of service provision to the handicapped assistance recipients. Some practitioners pointed out glibly that these clients were not different from many other clients served by V.R. Others pointed out the problems of those suffering from years of dependency made this group far more difficult. Old research was reviewed. New projects and studies were initiated. V.R. became involved in part of a simulation of the operations of welfare reform in Vermont. Increasing emphasis and funds were provided to collect data on the recipients being served. Large sums were authorized for expansion grants. A National Task Force on V.R. and Welfare Reform was organized. The V.R. movement was gearing up to take on a job.

THE V.R. ROLE IN WELFARE REFORM

H.R. 1, as it passed the House, contained two new titles to the Social Security Act concerning welfare income maintenance payments. Title XX is a federalized program for the aged, blind and disabled. Title XXI is a family program for all families with children who come within the income tests, including intact families with a male head who is working. Title XXI is divided into two parts, Part A allocates to the Secretary of Labor those families with a member available for employment, training or already working. Part B allocates to the Secretary of Health, Education and Welfare those families without a member available for employment as specified in the bill: persons are exempted from work registration if they are aged, ill, incapacitated, if a spouse is already registered, if one is a caretaker of a child under age six, if one is sixteen to twenty and in school, if one is needed to care for another who is incapacitated, or a child under sixteen.

Title XX has two provisions of special interest in defining V.R. roles. It puts the program administered by the Social Security Administration on essentially the same basis and definitions of disability used in the Title II program. It also eliminates a minimum age for disabled children. The bill requires that all blind and disabled beneficiaries, after a determination of disability is made and payments begin, be referred to the State V.R. agency for review of rehabilitation potential and the provision of rehabilitation services with penalties for refusal without good cause. These provisions all parallel the requirements of the Trust Fund Program with the possible exception that children may be referred in Title XX. Thus three distinct aspects of the V.R. role in Title XX emerge: (1) determinations and redeterminations of disability and blindness similar to the process now done for Title II beneficiaries. These contracts for disability determinations units are with V.R. agencies in all but seven states; (2) evaluation of rehabilitation potential; (3) provision of services. All of these would be reimbursed to the state with 100 percent Federal funds.

Title XXI, Part A (Opportunities for Families Program) under the jurisdiction of the Secretary of Labor, contained two distinct kinds of provisions. There are those mandating referral of the incapacitated similar to those for the blind and disabled. But the Secretary of Labor also would have had an authorization of $100 million to purchase supportive services, including Vocational Rehabilitation Services, necessary to assure certain persons had their needs met in order to participate in employment or training. Among the things included might have been minor medical services and work evaluation services for the able-bodied.

Title XXI requires that the Secretary of H.E.W. make a determination of those persons who would be excluded from the work registration requirement of Part A. Thus a determination of incapacity, a term undefined in the bill, and redeterminations are required. The bill is silent on who should do these determinations, but the clear presumption among welfare reform planners was that V.R. would do them.

Both Parts A and B of Title XXI contain like provisions requiring referral to V.R. of recipients who are exempt from the work registration requirement solely by virtue of incapacity for an evaluation of rehabilitation potential and for services where appropriate.

In Title XXI, then, the V.R. role would include determinations and redeterminations of incapacity, evaluation of rehabilitation potential and provision of V.R. services to the incapacitated, and the provision of supportive services to the Department of Labor recipients as may be jointly agreed.

SIZE OF THE TASK

Just what does this set of potential roles mean for rehabilitation? How many people would be involved and what would the costs look like? The effort to make creditable estimates of the V.R. roles in welfare reform led to what was probably the most extensive and intensive use of a variety of data sources and development of simulation models that has ever been done for a rehabilitation effort. Special analyses of the Survey of Economic Opportunity and the Current Population Surveys were made to pull out of them those persons who would be eligible under a simulation of the provisions of the welfare reform rules and who were handicapped. Analyses were made of the Social Security Survey of the Disabled, and of special studies of the blind, disabled and aid to family with dependent children populations. Interagency working groups of representatives of labor, Social Security, welfare reform planning and rehabilitation staff met to agree on definitions, data sources and estimates. And the terrible weakness and absence of data for such planning became so evident, that one wondered how rational planning ever went on in the past. As a result of the Welfare Reform experience a new recognition of the need for adequate information on which to plan has begun to set the analytic agenda for the next few years.

The welfare reform planners made different assumptions about the implementation dates of different aspects of the bill. Estimates for Title XX determinations for part of fiscal year 1973 and all of fiscal year 1974 were about $110 million for about 1.1 million determinations. About 187,000 individuals would have been referred for V.R. with about 93,000 accepted with a service cost estimated at about $83 million. Thus Title XX would have brought almost $200 million of new funds into the rehabilitation system.

The program for the families with children was assumed to be in effect only for half a year of fiscal 1974. The determinations of incapacity would have been about 423,000 costing about $30.5 million. About 105,000 would have been referred from both Part A and B with about 53,000 being accepted above the number already being served who were carried as public assistance recipients prior to the effective date of the bill. The new costs would have been about $44 million for the last six months of fiscal year 1974. Therefore, Title XX would have brought about $75 million into rehabilitation. The policy of converting the existing caseload of persons who would be eligible for benefits under the welfare reform provisions, and thus for 100 percent federal reimbursement, had not been settled.

Clearly then, the welfare reform program would bring about a significant expansion of V.R. programs. Close to $275 million of new federal funds would be added to a system which would otherwise be spending about $750 million. This 37 percent increase would happen within a period of under two years. These financial impacts would be large. In addition, the Federal role in determining the nature of state V.R. programs would be expanded.

One important effect would be to expand V.R. services to the non-poor. If one were to expect a reasonably stable pattern of appropriations for V.R., then the services to welfare recipients paid for from H.R. 1 would leave funds now used for welfare recipients for service to other handicapped groups. With the emphasis on severely disabled persons, both in the proposed amendments to the V.R. Act and the H.R. 1 emphasis, these handicapped persons may represent important beneficiaries of the welfare reform effort whether they are poor or not.

POLICY IMPACT OF WELFARE REFORM ON V.R.

Clearly the implications of welfare reform for rehabilitation are far greater than the dollars and numbers involved, even if the money is 100 percent federal and the numbers of rehabilitation cases reflect a growing stream of public assistance recipients. The implications of the impacts range from the place of vocational rehabilitation in the federal establishment to the technology used by counselors. An example of a precursor change in 1965 permits some insight into what may happen. When the Social Security Trust Fund Beneficiary Rehabilitation Program began, the overall number of severely disabled served by vocational rehabilitation was very small. Since then the number has grown significantly, not only in terms of trust fund cases rehabilitated, but also in terms of the numbers of severely disabled served out of the regular program funds. One can easily expect far more profound changes with the onset of welfare reform.

One example of the impact this process is having on rehabilitation is the fact that review of long standing policies and definitions is underway. Indeed, one of the most profound may be the question what constitutes a "rehabilitation." In the regular V.R. program an individual is "rehabilitated" by completing a service plan and being placed in a job for thirty days, or more. In welfare reform it is entirely possible that a handicapped individual can complete services, be placed on a job, earn to his maximum potential and still be eligible for assistance payments. Is this person then "rehabilitated"? Does his case transfer from V.R. and H.E.W. responsibility (which would be for unemployables) to the Department of Labor? Should there be new definitions of rehabilitation? These could include: Rehab-one, people who get off welfare assistance after rehabilitation; Rehab-two, those who earn at their maximum capacity but who still receive supplementary assistance payments; and Rehab-three, people whose ability to benefit from rehabilitation services is great, but not reflected in terms of their participation in the labor force. In all but the first, a "rehab" case may never be closed.

Much has to be done in terms of turning around the attitudes of many counselors in the field. Elizabeth Kramm reviewed a number of projects on rehabilitation of public assistance recipients.[1] Although she refers to project findings, there is much that seems to reflect beyond them. Many problems in these projects, and this refers only to the V.R. part, were partly associated with the "numbers" game of producing successful closures. V.R. counselors seem to have somewhat more stringent middle-class values with respect to the work ethic than the welfare caseworkers and, by and large, were under pressure to produce. As a result, the multiple complications, emergencies, and difficulties faced by many welfare clients resulted in their being seen as bad V.R. risks. Indeed, the world of the welfare client is far removed from the concerns of many V.R. counselors.

V.R. counselors often see little potential for successful case service due to emotional problems as well as handicapping conditions among the P.A. recipients. Many V.R. counselors claim that welfare workers are oriented to dependency and, as such, use the payment process to keep clients dependent. Caseworkers thought that many clients should not be responsible for self-support, and therefore many implicitly and explicitly discouraged work efforts. Many welfare clients believe that they must remain unemployed, unemployable or disabled and passive to remain eligible for assistance. Certainly when one is poor, this is hardly an irrational stance unless the counselors and caseworkers make the facts very clear. Then too, the nature of the welfare system with the many disincentives due to the steep rate of reduction in benefits as other income increases lead many clients to wonder why they should bother working at all unless they can make significantly higher incomes than the welfare grants. Of course, this is not possible in many states. In New York, for instance, an AFDC mother with three children would have to earn well above the minimum wage per year to make the same as she can on welfare without work. If she worked, she would be better off only by a small amount.[2] Many welfare recipients, as a recent study points out, do not understand the workings of the earnings disregard instituted in the 1967 welfare amendments where they can keep part of their earnings before their grants are reduced.[3] Many states, even with programs for an unemployed male, measure his hours worked and not his income. For those men with larger families, the individual can go to work and, even earning a respectable hourly rate, if his hours worked exceed the definition, he is no longer considered unemployed. His family could be worse off in terms of total income. This is especially true when one considers that they not only lose their cash payment but could lose Medicaid and food stamp eligibility as well.[4]

It is clear that many counselors do not view welfare recipients as being good rehabilitation risks. Yet in most projects, and since the onset of the public assistance-rehabilitation cooperative working agreements, most counselors agree that there is a great deal more potential then they originally believed. On the whole this may be very good because the impetus in welfare reform is toward rehabilitation of the client. It seems unlikely a casual discounting of clients would be allowed when the Federal government is paying full cost. Certainly rehabilitation acceptance procedures would have to be quite different. A relatively casual decision on the part of a counselor that a client does not have rehabilitation potential may not be adequate under welfare reform. This, in turn, seems to indicate that substantial work-evaluation-work-adjustment activities would be included in the way the recipients would be processed. The finding of "no rehabilitation potential" would have to be an affirmative finding, and not just a way for a counselor to decide not to work with a difficult client.

Of course, this, in turn, suggests that the way counselors are required to produce rehabilitations will have to change, which in turn, may change the entire incentive system. (Under the impetus of welfare reform, R.S.A. had given grants for studies on weighted case closures.) Related to these kinds of changes is the fact that welfare recipients may turn out to be more labor intensive for counselors than are other handicapped clients. This suggests that greater emphasis on this client group means that substantial new numbers of rehabilitation positions will have to be created, with somewhat smaller case loads and perhaps correspondingly smaller case service budgets. Rehabilitation in this group may be more a function of counseling skills than of purchased service. This suggests more experienced, highly qualified counselors on one hand, and greater numbers of para-professionals experienced in working in poor communities on the other. With greater work evaluation demands, greater use of rehabilitation facilities would be required.

One would expect that if a state rehabilitation agency could get significant amounts of federal funds, it may have an incentive to try to work with more difficult clients over a longer period of time before a case is rejected or closed as "not rehabilitated." On the other hand, since it is not expected that skilled manpower will significantly increase at first, the technology of disability and incapacity determinations and better referral criteria may have to be improved so that less than the usual skill level will be required. The criteria used in the Disability Trust Fund Program (in which only 14 percent of all approved beneficiaries end up being referred to and accepted by rehabilitation) probably provides an inadequate basis for servicing welfare recipients. A whole new advance in disability definitions and the determination processes will likely be developed. These disabilities would be related to "employability" in a somewhat more scientific fashion than at present.

Among the other fairly profound changes welfare reform means for rehabilitation is a reduction in state autonomy in definitions and procedures. There are now essentially 54 general rehabilitation programs with great variation between states in client selection, types of services provided, and types of occupations for which individuals are rehabilitated. It is clear that different states have different preferences. Handicapped persons in one state may be at a disadvantage compared to their counterparts in another state. It is clear that, in a national, federally-administered program, with national policy settings, national standards in rehabilitation will follow. It seems unlikely, if such standards were imposed, that they would remain in effect only for welfare recipients. It is more likely that greater standardization of the rehabilitation program throughout the nation would result.

The major rationalization for the current policy is usually stated as the fact that not enough funds are available to serve all of the handicapped who need V.R. services. But if welfare reform brings to rehabilitation open-ended, federal money to serve public assistance recipients, such arguments become trivial. One can fully expect that the inherent biases and rationalization among various rehabilitation professionals will be uncovered as the resource argument, behind which they have long hidden, is stripped away.

UNRESOLVED POLICY ISSUES

In November of 1971, the Nixon Administration organized an interagency task force on welfare reform. One subcommittee of that task force developed a set of papers on the major rehabilitation issues embodied in welfare reform. Because this was planning for implementation at the federal level, assuming the House-passed bill, the issues tended to be somewhat preoccupied with federal administrative and related questions. Nonetheless, the issues concerning disability and incapacity determinations, V.R. services, and questions of administrative organization at the federal and state level, all serve to illustrate the nature of the policy questions. A very brief review of those questions and issues follows.

A number of issues revolve around one set of background facts: those relating to the needs for organizing and delivering several related aspects of disability and incapacity determination and rehabilitation services. Issues include the question of the federal agency (or agencies) responsible for developing guidelines, monitoring and management of the determinations process in Titles XX and XXI. It has already been pointed out that Title XX requires that a determination of blindness and disability be made by the Secretary of H.E.W. in order for benefits to begin. A beneficiary is then referred to the state V.R. agency for V.R. services which are mandatory if the individual is suitable. Title XXI requires that the Secretary of H.E.W. make a determination of capacity (among other exclusions) to determine if the case belongs to the Department of Labor, or the H.E.W. program. Again, each Secretary will refer persons exempt from work registration solely by virtue of incapacity to V.R. agency for services.

Related to this issue is the fact that Title II, the basic Social Security Program which includes the Disability Trust Fund Program, also requires disability determinations, mandated referrals to vocational rehabilitation, and full federal reimbursement under certain conditions. Thus, it is possible that each income maintenance agency designated to administer the different programs (Social Security Administration, the Family Benefits Administration of Health, Education and Welfare, and the Department of Labor) could develop independent sets of standards, contracts with the states, and systems for determinations of disability and incapacity. Along with the normal relationships that state V.R. agencies have with the Rehabilitation Services Administration, the prospect for administrative complexity is very great. Thus, a series of issues is raised which focus on the need to consolidate functions of one or another lead federal agency.

If one separates the determination process from the provision of rehabilitation services, one could ask whether there should be one federal agency responsible for determinations of both disability and incapacity. How should the determinations for welfare clients relate to the Trust Fund clients? The Social Security Administration already has substantial relationships with every state establishing disability determination units (DDU's) to operate the program under Title II. One option clearly would be to have assigned to the Social Security Administration responsibility for setting the rules and regulations and operations for all determinations. The ongoing organizational arrangements for such determinations under Title II would be expanded. In all but seven states the DDU's are in V.R. agencies. Yet in Title XXI there is no reference to SSA doing this job.

Another alternative would be for the Social Security Administration to do the job for Titles II and XX, since these are related and the definitions of disability are the same. Although the determination process for disability and incapacity would be essentially the same, there may be substantial differences in the types of certification utilized for incapacitated persons in the family program. If there were substantially different definitions (as there seem to be between incapacity and disability) it may make sense to have some other agency (such as RSA or the Family Benefits Administration) handle the incapacity question for Title XXI, leaving Social Security to do the others.

Of course, another alternative would be to have, say, the Rehabilitation Services Administration be responsible for all contacts with the state agencies for determination for Titles XX and XXI, and have Social Security retain its responsibilities to Title II. One rationale for this is that the intent of welfare reform is to move people to their maximum of self-support. The determinations process should be closely tied to rehabilitation with provision of minor medical and health screening services from the onset. Determinations would not merely be a procedure for establishing disability status for benefits but of rehabilitation potential as well. Under this option, Social Security would continue to do Title II since, by and large, those determinations are primarily for benefit eligibility.

The final option would have a single federal agency to deal with all state V.R. agencies on all matters affecting them so that the Rehabilitation Services Administration would be the only federal agency dealing with the state V.R. agencies, RSA would contract with the other federal agencies on behalf of this process.

A parallel issue is whether there should be more than one point of responsibility for determinations in each state. Should there be, for example, more than one unit doing determinations of disability and incapacity. Most people agree that one point is most desirable. At such a place a determination of any one individual could be made to see if he would be eligible for benefits under the Trust Fund Program as well as under the welfare disabled or blind program, or if he was incapacitated for the family program. The inherent logic and efficiency of this approach suggests that the states should have one point of responsibility for dealing with the disability and incapacity determination process. The problems with this approach are of "turf" and politics. These are partly related to decisions with respect to the federal counterparts. Part of it will have to do with whether or not incapacity is defined differently than disability with different processes, procedures and implications.

Most people agree that the rehabilitation aspects should be centralized in the Rehabilitation Services Administration with contracts or other agreements between the affected federal agencies and RSA. However, there is much less agreement that the Rehabilitation Services Administration should have centralized budgeting responsibilities.

The question of definitions becomes crucial. Title XX defines disability in the same way as does the Trust Fund Program. This is a vast improvement over the 54 different definitions used by the different jurisdictions in welfare. These jurisdictions also have the right to define incapacity for the incapacitated father in the AFDC program. Somehow, the Congress did see fit to define incapacity and illness in relationship to the Title XXI program. Title XXI states that the Secretary of Health, Education and Welfare shall consider an individual available for employment unless the in-

dividual is determined to "be unable to engage in work or training by reason of illness, incapacity, advanced age," and, further,
"one whose presence in the home on a substantially continuous
basis is required because of the illness or incapacity of another member of the household." Neither illness incapacity nor
advanced age are defined in the bill or in the committee report.

The options for a definition of incapacity range from a self-
definition by clients to a list of conditions which might qualify.
Self-definition may operate as a statement on a form. An individual
is asked to check if he believes that he has had a condition which,
for example, substantially limits the kind or amount of work he
can do and which has lasted over some period of time. If the individual would check such a statement he would then be referred
for a determination. Of course, the other alternative would be to
have a long catalogue of conditions which, if the individual indicates he has one, would result in referral. Illness could be anything
which is less severe than an incapacity. Alternatively, one could
argue that if Congress went to such pains to use different terms
such as illness and incapacity in Title XXI, and disability in Title
XX, it meant different things by the terms. Since disability is defined in terms of something which, (1) would result in death or
which has lasted or is likely to last for one year, and (2) prohibits
substantial gainful activity, one could argue that a poor person
who met this definition should be eligible for the Aid to Disabled
Program. Indeed, the bill seems to indicate that people are expected
to apply for Aid for the Disabled who are also eligible for the
Family Program. A logical argument could then be made that the
disability definition would hold for a severe condition, illness would
be something relatively trivial, and incapacity would be something
in between. Thus a definition of incapacity may be defined something like: a work limiting condition which has lasted or is likely
to last more than a short period, say, but less than twelve months.

The problem with the middling definition of incapacity is not so
much in what it does with respect to removing someone from the
Department of Labor's registration requirement, but what it does
for persons who then have to be referred for V.R. services. Title
XXI requires that recipients whose incapacity is their sole reason
for exemption from work registration be mandated rehabilitation

services if they are accepted. But the rehabilitation definition of eligibility means that the incapacity must also constitute a substantial handicap to employment. There may be a great tension between those who are defined as incapacitated, but found not handicapped enough for rehabilitation services. Unless H.R.1 revises the rules for services to certain recipients beyond those usually used by V.R., in some states some welfare recipients fall between the cracks.

In the pretest of welfare reform carried on in Vermont, many clients were referred from the health screen to the manpower program with notation that the individual is employable, but with work limitations due to handicapping conditions. In these instances, by definition, the individual may be considered incapacitated but not seriously enough to be included in the usual V.R. definition of eligibility. Surely that would be an untenable situation for the rehabilitation program. We would either have to have separate rules for assistance recipients, or change the basic definition of a substantial handicap to employment, or reject many persons defined in welfare reform as incapacitated.

Another portion of the bill allows exemption from work registration for a person caring for another family member who is incapacitated. The question rises as to who determines whether an incapacitated person requires the services of a second family member. This could be a social service responsibility, that of the income maintenance office, or that of whoever does the determination of the original person's incapacity. It seems most logical (although logic doesn't always carry the day) that the agency doing the determination should also gather enough information to see if services to the second family member are required. But this also gets the rehabilitation agencies into the question of services to and on behalf of family members of the handicapped client. While V.R. now has the authority to perform this type of service, counselors have, by and large, done very little.

There is a related question of who has jurisdiction over an assistance recipient under welfare reform. Once a handicapped client is referred to rehabilitation program and is accepted for rehabilitation services, his case management is clearly that of the rehabilitation agency.

But a question remains with respect to setting overall priorities. If all assistance clients cannot be served, for whatever reason, priority should be established. How shall priority be set for the disabled, the blind, and the incapacitated clients; in addition, what shall determine the trade-offs between these groups, groups of non-assistance clients and recipients of the Disability Trust Fund?

What standards need to be developed in order to have a national program emphasizing consistency and equity in acceptance and rejection and closure of V.R. cases? Most of the current planning assumes the state agencies will accept and reject cases on almost the same basis as the present. However, as stated above, a national program funded by 100 percent federal money might require a somewhat more active effort to determine rehabilitation potential than is now the case. This, in turn, has serious implications for the use of facilities and for work evaluation and work adjustment activities. Reasons for rejection or closure such as "lack of motivation" will require close examination under welfare reform. Of course, a comparable question would be what the federal agencies will reimburse. For example, under the provisions of Title II an individual virtually has to be determined as rehabilitable enough so his earnings would be enough to get him off the trust fund. Reimbursement is only for those clients. Too many assistance recipients might not get reimbursement under HR1 if the the rules are this tight. In such a case states might even cut back on their efforts rather than expanding them with respect to this population.

In Title II, the objective of the beneficiary rehabilitation program is to make funds available from the trust fund to finance rehabilitation for selected beneficiaries. The objective is to make it possible for them to get enough income such that the savings from the amount of benefits that would otherwise have to be paid, and the increased contribution to the trust funds, will be at least equal to or greater than the money paid from the funds for rehabilitation costs.

In Titles XX and XXI, however, according to the Committee Report, the program will provide work and training opportunities for those able to work or to be rehabilitated that will enable them to escape from their dependence. Individuals receiving assistance benefits will get rehabilitation services which would be reimbursed at full cost. Thus, the question becomes whether reimbursement will be paid if only the state agency assures that the individual can earn enough to no longer be a beneficiary. For a family of four, an individual would have to earn up to $4,720.00 per year to get no assistance benefits. Some aged and disabled individuals may have relatively higher cut-off points. Clearly, many assistance recipients may not have such an earnings potential, much less the handicapped recipients.

The stringency of Title II seems unwarranted in the assistance titles. The assistance titles had a goal of minimizing federal outlays and maximizing self-support rather than protecting the general revenue, or maintaining certain cost-effective returns. The taxing of earned income at less than 100 percent is specifically designed to encourage partial self-support. This is especially clear in the inclusion of the working poor, who work full-time, but whose earnings are very low, in the welfare reform program. It is inconsistent to allow reimbursement only if a client can earn enough to get completely off the program. The Department of Labor gets funds for serving able-bodied individuals even though they may not earn enough to be completely off welfare. Provisions should be the same for the handicapped.

There are several categories of rehabilitation which have less clear claim for reimbursement eligibility. For example, sheltered workshops, unpaid family workers, and homemakers. In these, the rehabilitated client is not in competitive employment and may not even earn income. Of course, the rationale for these categories is that in the absence of this "work," either the individual would not flourish or alternative funds would have to be spent for such services as for homemakers and the like.

REHABILITATION OF CHILDREN

One of the major, perhaps, and unintended, changes H.R.1 would bring about would be in provision of V.R. services to handicapped children. Under present law children under 18 are prohibited from applying for or receiving benefits under the Aid to Disabled Program. Under H.R.1 the Ways and Means Committee seems to have concluded that the cost of handicapped children to people, especially poor people receiving public assistance, should be offset by allowing these children to receive benefits on their own behalf. Thus the Committee removed the minimum age requirement of the disabled portion of Title XX. The net effect of this would be to increase the family's net income by getting a relatively more generous benefit and certain additional services for a handicapped child.

But whether the Committee intended to or not it did not change its mandatory referral requirements. Since this requirement refers to all persons receiving benefits under the disability provisions as being referred to the V.R. agency, children would be referred also. The Committee report refers to a child in a low income family who would require special assistance in order to help him become a self-supporting member of our society. Making it possible for disabled children to get the benefits under this program rather than under the programs for families with children would be appropriate because their needs are often greater than those of non-disabled children in this group. The question remains as to how V.R. will deliver services to this population.

It is possible that V.R. would simply not serve any but the older children who will be in the age group for which vocational outcomes are appropriate. Since there are no special rules in the bill dealing with children, V.R. may develop any of a set of rules for services to these children and including infants. Among the alternatives available would be for the V.R. agency to take an advocate role, which means it would make sure that children get services from the community. The V.R. agency could do what it has always done in the broker role as the case manager and by using the flow of federal H.R.1 service funds, if that is the policy, to assure necessary and continuous services to the children, even to the point to tracking them through their entire childhood. Of course, it could always take the role as no service provider but a referral agent only with respect to these children. This is a serious and controversial issue since V.R. has not provided services for children and there are many traditional child-serving groups who object to its doing so.

There is another aspect of services to children that Rehabilitation could get into. There are the provisions for child care for children of incapacitated family members. Title XXI would have provided for child care services if these are needed by an individual to accept or continue to participate in vocational rehabilitation services under parts A and B. In part A the Secretary of Labor arranges for child care and in part B the Secretary of Health, Education and Welfare makes such arrangements. Presumably the child care is free to the rehabilitation agency and to the individuals served. Of the 300,000 or so incapacitated family members accepted in rehabilitation programs a large number of children will require some kind of care. Since rehabilitation agencies now by-and-large provide no child care, this will be an entirely new area for them. The director of one state program which is very heavily serving and rehabilitating public assistance recipients, has indicated that as one gets deeply into the assistance population, child care becomes an increasingly crucial element necessary to free the parent for both services and employment. Without wishing for V.R. to get into the child care business itself, it is clear that the rehabilitation program must gather expertise in child care. V.R. should contribute to developing child care not only for the able-bodied children of incapacitated parents, but in developing appropriate child care for handicapped children.

It is clear that in the area of children's services, whether the traditional child-serving groups want rehabilitation to get into the activity or not, should welfare reform pass in its present form rehabilitation will be into the business of serving children.

REFERENCES

1. *Welfare in Review,* March-April, 1970.
2. James R. Storey: *Public Income Transfer Programs,* Studies in Public Welfare, paper no. 1, Subcommittee on Fiscal policy, Joint Economic Committee, U.S. Congress, 1972, p. 12.
3. Storey, *op. cit.,* passim. Also see *Welfare in Illinois,* Illinois Institute for Social Policy, 1972.
4. National Analysts, First Year Report of a Study of Earnings Disregards, DHEW, 1972.

CHAPTER IV

COOPERATIVE ALTERNATIVES TO DUPLICATION IN SOCIAL AND REHABILITATION SERVICES[1]

RICHARD E. HARDY AND KEITH C. WRIGHT

WELFARE PAYMENTS TO INDIVIDUALS and families from federal, state and local funds totaled 16.3 billion in the fiscal year 1971. The average monthly recipient caseload reached 15,513,265 individuals and yet few if any satisfied welfare recipients can be found. Approximately 30 million people are living in poverty even after such an expenditure of welfare funds (HEW, 1971).

It is interesting to note that with all the federal, state, and local programs and professionals attempting to work for the benefit of those individuals who are in need there is not enough coordination of efforts to solve some very basic problems. Illustrative of this situation are the facts that ten percent of clients involved in Work Incentive Programs (WIN) stopped the program because of transportation difficulties; fifteen percent gave up because of child care problems; six percent stopped because of

---

[1]Parts of this chapter appeared in "An Alternative to Duplication," K.C. Wright and R.E. Hardy, *Journal of Rehabilitation, 36,* No. 8, December, 1970.

job orientation difficulties; and twenty-one percent quit due to health reasons of which seven percent were due to pregnancy. Poor interagency working relationships caused an average waiting period of 44 days before the WIN client could begin his program (Smith 1971).

Most professionals in the helping occupations and most agencies serving handicapped people strongly endorse the teamwork concept. Unfortunately, teamwork is more often preached than practiced, and services to the client suffer in the confusion. It seems that we have forgotten the client's problems in our search for specific lines of professional responsibility.

The teamwork concept is discussed in all university programs, across disciplines, and is bandied about in agency in-service training programs. Yet the fact remains that those professionals who must work together following graduation do not study together while in school. We learn or adjust to interdisciplinary relationships and interagency relationships quite often through a trial-and-error process while on the job.

It has long been recognized that no individual, profession, or agency is capable of solving all of life's problems. Failure to provide continuity of services has been a major problem in serving people effectively. Public agency personnel are stymied in their services to clients due to limitations of responsibilities which have been assigned to the agency or the agency has assigned to itself.

It would be grossly untrue to say that delivery systems today are well thought out, well organized, with lines of responsibilities and authority, and with congruent goals agreed upon by all concerned including the client. Indecision, mistrust, and differences in teamwork approach to rehabilitation abound. We have only to observe this in cooperative programs and reorganization activities at governmental levels and on university campuses to verify the confusion.

Some confusion and lack of coordination are caused by variances in training in both college and in-service training programs for service in the various branches of rehabilitation. Some of it is caused by vested interest problems of the agencies. Some of our problems result from the mere fact that we have a proliferation of professional disciplines, volunteer personnel, and agencies serving handicapped people; and some of them are undoubtedly caused by inadequate administrative standards. These are chief among many other valid reasons why our delivery system is under pressure and challenged today as never before.

A brief, historical review of rehabilitation counselor assignments over the years reveals that the old-time counselor was a field counselor with a large caseload. His responsibilities usually included hundreds of clients with all types of disabilities and handicapping conditions; he had a large territorial assignment, and therefore could cover few community rehabilitation facilities. There was less confusion then.

SHARING IS ESSENTIAL

In the early years, the rehabilitation counselor tried to be all things to all people (a one-man operator and a jack-of-all trades). How he worked and functioned, how he selected his clients and his services, and the criteria he used in all aspects of his job were more or less known only by him and his supervisor. In effect, he had his own little bag of tricks which were often not shared with others. The development of such a professional "mystique" is not unique to the rehabilitation counselor.

Yale Law School's distinguished Professor Fred Rodell (Dacey, 1965) has written: "For every age, a group of bright boys, learned in their trade and jealous of their learning, blend technical competence with plain and fancy hocuspocus to make themselves masters of their fellow men . . . a pseudo-intellectual autocracy, guarding the tricks of its trade from the uninitiated, and running after its own pattern, the civilization of its day." He was referring to lawyers, but he could just as easily have been characterizing rehabilitation professionals today.

Present trends in rehabilitation indicate that we have moved into systems of service involving specialization and teamwork. Rehabilitation workers specialize not only by disability or handicap but by work setting. Through cooperative programming and planning, rehabilitation agencies are entering into third-party funding agreements with a variety of interested agencies in order to provide better services to a selected population in which both operating agencies are concerned. This involves a pooling of resources including money, facilities, and staff. Consequently, the rehabilitation counselor, not being able to operate within his former agency-fabricated vacuum, must share his thoughts and actions with other members of the unit team. The mysticism must disappear because methods of operation are exposed for all to see. Sharing is essential in such cooperative settings.

In addition to the emphasis on the team approach, which is often more talked about than practiced, we have been broadening concepts of rehabilitation. During its formative years, rehabilitation was primarily concerned with only those persons disabled in industry. This focus was later expanded, but emphasis was primarily on physical disabilities. It is now evident that rehabilitation concepts applicable to physically handicapped persons are also applicable to those who are mentally ill, mentally retarded, and many other "handicapped" persons. Indeed, rehabilitation concepts are seen as applicable to behavioral disorders, to nondisabled people on welfare, to those under-employed, and to persons with social and cultural handicaps. These concepts apply to families as well as individuals and toward constructive living as well as toward the vocational goal.

OPENING THE COMMUNITY'S RESOURCES TO THE CLIENT

Perhaps because of our historical perspective, vested interests, and political and social organizations, we have in this country developed a highly complex system of helping individuals solve their problems. We have created scores of agencies which, in turn, have developed hundreds of programs aimed at meeting the needs of people. With the wide proliferation of agencies and services existing now in most communities, it is inevitable that there be some duplication and overlapping of services. We must recognize the multiple problems of people, take into account the interrelationships of these problems, and then implement cooperative efforts to solve them.

Rehabilitation, since its inception, has not operated in a vacuum, and its success has been dependent on the condition of public and private resources in the community. Obviously, all of the problems of one individual cannot be dealt with within one system, nor by one agency, nor by one professional discipline.

A man with a leg off is more than an amputee. His problems are usually compounded by what we might have called "the cluster effect." For instance, he would likely have a problem with employment, accompanied by marital difficulties, income maintenance problems, some possible legal trouble and a variety of other medical, social, psychological, and training problems. "Tis neither this nor that, but both and more."

As more difficult cases are dealt with including the welfare recipient, more intensive social contact is needed with professional staff persons, subprofessional staff, etc. It must be remembered that many of these persons have been victims of a highly competitive society which is complicated and whose governmental service programs are filled with complicated regulations and stipulations. Many of them are suspicious not only of governmental agencies but of persons who wish to help them.

The rehabilitation counselor should take it upon himself through his case management procedures to be certain that the client knows that he is coordinating the process through which the client is passing. It is the counselor that the client can always turn to whether he is involved at the time with the physician, psychologist, work evaluator, social worker, etc. The client must strongly feel that continuity of services exists and that the process is coordinated through the counselor.

It is imperative that goal planning be shared and comprehensive for these reasons: all agencies and all professionals evaluate clients prior to delivery of services; most evaluation is concerned with the medical, social, psychological, education, economic, and vocational problem areas; and many rehabilitation clients are known by and served by other agencies and professions. Broad cooperation is necessary to prevent confusion (both to professionals and to clients); to reduce overlapping of services; and to eliminate wasted time, energy, and resources. Teamwork must be practiced as well as preached. We must make interagency and interdisciplinary case planning conferences and staffings a "working reality."

WAYS TO CUT DUPLICATION AND AID THE CLIENT

One suggestion made by Smith (1971) for the elimination of

the present hodgepodge systems is the creation on a nationwide basis of neighborhood centers through which various types of services—medical, economic, social, rehabilitative are brought together under one roof. This model could be seen as a possible replacement for such institutions as the U.S. Department of Labor and the Department of Health, Education and Welfare.

It would certainly seem that the rehabilitation process which has proved to be so successful in work with persons with varied types of problems might be considered for expansion in various areas of service. The process encompasses case finding, referral, diagnostics and evaluation which include various medical, psychological, therapeutic care to enable the individual to become ready for training or employment plus a period of planning for employment, training, placement on-the-job and supervision once the individual has been placed.

Most agencies and organizations require that an intake or initial interview form be completed. Usually this form requires a statement or statements about the applicant's problem(s), in addition to the necessary background data from which they work with the applicant. Actually, the material acquired at intake is similar among all agencies, such as the statement of problem(s), name, age, family composition, resources, etc. A common intake or initial interview form used by several agencies would obviously be very helpful. Such a form would do away with the overlap and duplication plaguing agencies.

And not incidentally, wouldn't a common form help eliminate, to some extent, the irritation and frequent humiliation inherent when the applicant has to repeat many of his failures and problems to several agencies in order to receive their special service? Wouldn't a common intake form have some beneficial effect concerning the acknowledged manpower shortage in most agencies? Indeed, a common intake form might be considered as the first substantial proof of teamwork.

This concept of cooperation can also aid in the economic or financial assessment of the applicant. Many agencies base some of their services on the applicant's ability or inability to provide for himself. Rehabilitation utilizes this evaluation for services based on economic need. Welfare uses the same information for grant award purposes. How many ways are there to identify your assets and liabilities? Why do we continue to expose the client to more embarrassing and frustrating experiences than necessary?

There is little reason why a medical report successfully used by vocational rehabilitation to help in the selection of suitable vocational objectives cannot be used by welfare agencies for grant awards based on disability or for that matter, by Workmen's Compensation or Social Security for the same purpose. Yet we see clients undergoing more than one medical examination, depending on the services they have applied for. With the manpower shortage in the medical profession, this type of duplication becomes confusing and ridiculous. It seems that a single medical form could easily be devised which is applicable to, or can be interpreted by a variety of service programs.

One of the coming developments in all states will be that of the development of what could be called a questionnaire on eligibility for rehabilitation which would be completed by public welfare intake workers and used to identify persons who are applying for welfare and who would possibly also be eligible for rehabilitation. This form should immediately be given to a rehabilitation counselor in order that he may begin his evaluation of the individual for eligibility. One way to cut duplication and aid the client would be that of housing the rehabilitation counselor in the welfare office. Persons who are not eligible for rehabilitation would be referred to some other agencies such as the State Employment Service for possible job development and placement.

If public service agency personnel from vocational rehabilitation, welfare, the employment service, etc., cannot be housed under the same umbrella as suggested earlier, then representatives of these agencies should be in close contact with one another. Whenever possible, rehabilitation counselors should have offices in welfare complexes and do preliminary workups on candidates for rehabilitation from the various welfare categories as individuals are referred to the counselor.

Perhaps we might be able to develop a comprehensive social and rehabilitation plan which would provide an overview of all services needed by the client, the order in which these services will be rendered, by whom, and at what costs. What better way is there to learn the rehabilitation process and to identify your role in it?

The rehabilitation counselor has the responsibility to make certain that social service workers within the public welfare program generally understand the types of individuals who are eligible for rehabilitation in order that they may do some screening of referrals to eliminate the wasted effort, time and money involved when poor referrals are made. Regular conferences should be held between workers of the two agencies in order that a referral process can be established. Welfare and rehabilitation workers should also meet on a regular basis in order to discuss evaluations of each case referred.

Each agency must be willing to examine how the processes of referral and rehabilitation are working for the client. Various re-examinations will be needed before the effective cooperative system can be developed and joint forms used.

Team concepts are designed for the benefit of the client—yet there is considerable disagreement and conflict when we actually attempt to join hands across professions and across state agencies and private organizations to help the client. It sometimes appears that we might be more professionally self-centered or agency-centered than client-centered. Professional immaturity often seems to be what is really keeping us from an effective joint cooperative effort.

Research has shown us again and again that some of the most important variables which contribute to successful client rehabilitation are acceptance, understanding, concern, and support. It would seem that as professional personnel in agencies and organizations mature, they would be able to offer more of these ingredients to our clients, making these variables the nucleus of agreement from which we can all expand our effectiveness in serving the individuals who need their help.

Competence could be defined as the types of behaviors involved in effectively interacting with the environment. This definition and others like it are ones which have been used to evaluate the movement of clients toward their goals. How would we as professionals in rehabilitation rate if we were measured on our effectiveness of inter-action within the varied environment of public and private service organizations?

SERVING THE TOTAL PERSON

If rehabilitation is concerned with the total person, if it is concerned with "rehabilitation of the family as well as of the individual," if delivery of services necessarily involves a variety of agencies, professionals, and others, it then follows that goal planning (the rehabilitation plan) must be entered into with the full cooperation and understanding of all concerned.

This means that the agencies, public and private, and the professional and subprofessional disciplines must get to know each other. It means that any ideas of agency or disciplinary "hierarchy" must be dismissed. It also means that many training programs must include an on-going interdisciplinary approach to teaching. We must not permit isolation on campus between departments or within service agencies. Those of us at colleges and universities must insist that students who will work together on a rehabilitation team following graduation study together often during their training period. Fragmentation of services must be avoided, as well as fragmentation of training.

In this time of job banks and computerization, it would seem that a highly developed reporting system could be used to provide a great deal of useful information to various agencies serving clients. While there are certain dangers, especially those relating to confidentiality, we seem somewhat late in moving forward in attempting to make data readily available which will eliminate duplication and aid the client. While there are some aspects of confidentiality that are most difficult to protect with any kind of data bank unless it contains purely demographic material, the benefits of such a system to the client might be worth the loss of some small degree of confidentiality. Clients must be appraised of any data system process in which information especially of a personal nature is to be housed; however, it is suspected that if services could be expedited and improved such a system of information might be acceptable.

At the present time, rehabilitation should lead the way in cooperative efforts by having its professional staff, within bounds of maintaining confidentiality, share the various types of medical, psychological, and social data which are pertinent with other professional persons in other social service agencies. Again, this can never be done without the consent of the client, but if such a sharing plan could be developed clients would be well known to a number of agencies and would be able to profit from services without having to undergo several social, medical and/or psychological evaluations.

In the development of such a program, committees of not only top level administrators, but middle management, supervisors and professionals should meet on a regular basis. Representatives should come from all social service agencies. These committees should extend also to the training staff and it should become a primary concern of every professional staff person as well as persons in administrative positions. Duplication of efforts which slows down and hinders services to the client must be eliminated wherever possible.

This has been a period of fragmentation, expansion, vested interests, and confusion in social and rehabilitation services. Cooperation at all levels is now a vital necessity. We must put the client and his family first in our priority system and demonstrate the team approach can work for both his and our benefit.

REFERENCES

Dacey, Norman F.: *How To Avoid Probate.* New York, Crown Publications.

Smith, David: *Hodgepodge Delivery Systems Continue Dependency.* The Council of State Governments, Atlantic City, New Jersey, 1971.

PART II

Public Images of Welfare Programs and Recipients of Public Welfare (Myths and Realities)

Legal Problems of the Public Welfare Recipient

Psychological Aspects of Poverty and Disability

Educational and Psychological Appraisal of the Disadvantaged

PART II

CHAPTER V

PUBLIC IMAGES OF WELFARE PROGRAMS AND RECIPIENTS OF PUBLIC WELFARE (MYTHS AND REALITIES)

RICHARD E. LAWRENCE

Public Images of Welfare Programs

Public Images of the Recipients of Public Welfare

Summary and Conclusions

References

"WELFARE EXISTS TO HELP PROVIDE for those who are unable to provide for themselves because of illness, disability, age, abandonment, neglect, and a variety of numerous other reasons."[41] "In today's complex society, almost everyone, at some time and to some extent, needs one or more of the types of services and facilities that are broadly defined as 'welfare'."[51] Recently a high state governmental official indicated that there would be no increase in welfare benefits until "crooks and cheats have been purged from the welfare roles."

These three statements all may be accurate and certainly reflect the impressions of different segments of our society toward welfare programs and welfare recipients. Of course, different persons made each of the three statements, and they were directed to diffrent publics within our country. In addition, the statements apply to different welfare programs and services, and no one statement

89

can accurately reflect the public image of all welfare programs. Herein lies the difficulty in attempting to state one or even a few images that will hold for welfare programs or recipients.

Different publics hold different images toward welfare programs and recipients, and these images are as varied as the publics are numerous. Variables of significance include age, sex, race, level of educational attainment, socioeconomic background, and type of employment to mention only a few. As various combinations of these factors are combined in specific populations, their images of welfare programs and recipients may be expected to differ from persons with other backgrounds.

Welfare programs are too numerous to mention and services rendered by such programs are even more numerous. For children, the services are rendered through juvenile detention facilities, training schools, government sponsored programs such as Neighborhood Youth Corps, receiving homes, and the juvenile court.[42] The standard categories for state programs usually include old age assistance, aid to families with dependent children, aid to families with dependent children—employable, aid to permanently and totally disabled, public assistant to the needy blind, general public assistance, and general public assistance—employable."[32] The United States Department of Health, Education, and Welfare lists welfare programs totalling twenty-three in all. This publication lists programs including the following: grants for health services to school and pre-school children, international maternity and child health programs, internation social welfare, the Cuban refugee program, assistance for repatriated United States Nationals, emergency welfare services, and crippled services programs.[51] In addition, there are general assistance programs in all states as well as the District of Columbia, Guam, Puerto Rico, and the Virgin Islands. Recipients of general assistance aid are generally persons with needs who fall outside of the scope of federal-state programs of welfare assistance.[39]

Another complicating factor is that welfare recipients hold different public images of welfare programs than do nonrecipients. Welfare recipients are children, mothers, aged, blind and disabled, and able-bodied fathers.[50] Ullman conducted a study of welfare recipients and concluded that economic poverty often was secondary to chronic illness and behavioral disorders in recipients. Many were immigrants and an excessive intake of alcohol was yet another characteristic.[37]

The problem of public images is compounded because numerous persons including many prominent persons in government are speaking out in opposition to certain types of welfare programs. Although programs have been established to provide for those who are unable to care for themselves, welfare programs tend to break up families and perpetuate dependency according to the United States Commission on Civil Rights. This report goes on to indicate that escape from the ghetto is becoming increasingly more difficult with the demands of technological society, discrimination, and prejudice as they are. There is a lack of concern for the problems of the slums and an intense frustration built upon unfulfilled expectations and promises and continued deprivation and discrimination.[49]

Although the task of specifying images of welfare programs and recipients is a challenging one, there are many myths and realities that can be specified and focused upon. That will be the task of the remaining pages of this chapter.

PUBLIC IMAGES OF WELFARE PROGRAMS

Several rather popular myths will be mentioned and later discussed. In each instance the myth is one that is either popular and heard frequently or one that is reported in the literature.

Myth—There is no opportunity for participation by recipients or volunteers to be employed in welfare programs since educated professionals have the total responsibility.

Reality—Although this has been true in many welfare programs and continues to be the condition even today in some, the trend does seem to be away from only professionals with higher education functioning within welfare programs. Paraprofessionals and volunteers are finding increased roles and responsibilities, and there is ever increasing participation by recipients in planning welfare programs. The Texas Department of Public Welfare engaged in a program designed to involve recipients directly in welfare programs through actual participation in the formulation of plans for the administration of the program of Aid to Families with Dependent Children. The welfare recipients' views were solicited and his interests were protected through such participation. Participation and involvement were possible because welfare programs were designed to assist rather than regulate welfare recipients. This rather unconventional process was viewed positively and was possible because of the caliber of staff and the openness of the administration of the program.[48]

In 1953, McKinsey reported on new trends in public welfare and included the use of volunteers particularly in governmental welfare agencies. He believed that citizen participation served as a useful means for maintaining a sense of local responsibility for public welfare and assisted with public relations designed to earn support for welfare programs and their goals. He concluded that welfare programs should be challenged to increase the opportunities for participation and to increase their use of volunteers.[22] Because public welfare has a responsibility to educate, recruit, and work with laymen, Martin indicated that citizen involvement must increase. In order to obtain this objective, volunteers should participate in planning and implementation of public and private welfare programs. In Illinois, negative citizen attitudes were altered through active participation with accurate presentation of facts.[20]

As early as 1960, a conference was held in Chicago by the American Public Welfare Association; and the objectives of the conference were summarized in this statement, "only through a true partnership with the people can public welfare meet criticism, dislodge misinformation and fallacious assumptions, and help people to understand the needs of their neighbors and the effects of these needs on the total community." It was suggested that the roles of the public welfare board needed to be expanded and service volunteers could be used to greatly strengthen welfare programs.[26]

There are things that need to be done in order to strengthen volunteer and participant efforts in welfare programs. A study of 200 volunteer cultural, social, and welfare organizations in Philadelphia revealed that social service agencies did not offer steady and vital activities for board members. A recommendation was offered which focused on social welfare reform activity with the suggestion that a partnership between laymen and professionals be provided. This would spur an impetus for needed change in public welfare programs and policies.[18]

Myth—If welfare recipients would only acquire vocational training, they would be able to find satisfying work and could be removed from welfare rolls.

Reality—In recent years there has been some 5 to 6 percent of labor force unemployed according to the Department of Labor Statistics. The Work Incentive Program (WIN) was developed to create a mandatory work situation for the wage earner in families with dependent children. The WIN program was designed to reduce financial burdens and to help develop a sense of dignity which would arise from personal employment. Such a program has many shortcomings including a potential for disturbing important family ties.[47]

Job Corps programs frequently have persons classified as underprivileged who are out of school and out of work. One of the criticisms frequently leveled at such programs focused on the absence of jobs following the completion of training. Review of welfare training programs, including one at Alameda County, California, revealed that non-monetary human values were more impressive than the number of those who became self-supporting through employment. The two most important advantages from training were the trainee's feeling of dignity and independence.[14]

Although work is a desirable outcome from training, it may also be a frustration if no employment is available. Taylor suggests that forcing welfare clients into job training programs with no payoff will produce frustration and anger that may lead to riots. According to Taylor, this could be one of the outcomes of President Nixon's welfare reform which would require able-bodied welfare recipients to enter job training programs or to work if they were to continue to receive welfare benefits. Additional jobs would be necessary in order for this to be a reality.[38]

Rivlin has pointed out that one of the biggest obstacles to agreement on welfare reform is the widely divergent views about whether or not to require welfare recipients to work. She points out two competing views on the subject. The one view suggests that poor people must and should be compelled to work by means of legal, work requirements and punitive withholding of assistance from those who refuse jobs. The other group believes in incentives which would encourage poor people to placement services. One of her conclusions was that work must be financially attractive in order to make it feasible and desirable for the welfare recipient to work.[30] To summarize, in requiring people to work, there may be negative consequences and such regulations could aggravate feelings of frustration and anger if both training and work were not readily available and financially attractive.

Myth—The public welfare atmosphere in this country is based upon a positive attribute of charity and is basically one of helpfulness.

Reality—Welfare recipients are frequently required to wait unusually long periods of time for service. They may be required to fill out long complicated forms and to undergo a form of interrogation.[32] In addition, there is a prevailing atmosphere of humiliation that exists in the welfare bureau's relationships with welfare recipients. Jacobs examined a Los Angeles welfare bureau and emphasized the lack of cooperation between the bureau and its recipients, as well as what he called "punitive intention creating policies" on the part of program administrators. A particular source of conflict within the Aid to Families with Dependent Children program were the complicated procedures for receiving assistance that were not fully explained to the welfare recipient. Jacobs called for the reevaluation of the entire welfare system in so far as the eligibility investigation was concerned with increased implementation of employees' selection and training and a positive attitude toward applicants of welfare services.[16]

Myth—Although many people talk about helping the poor and the welfare recipient, only the welfare recipient is really interested in welfare programs.

Reality—In January, 1972, the AFL-CIO testified before the Senate Finance Committee and strongly supported a full permanent program of government income subsidies that would be authorized to the "working poor." There was also indications of support from the administration through comments President Nixon's Press Secretary Ronald Ziegler made. Not only labor and government but philanthropic institutions have shown concern about welfare programs and frequently contribute heavily to the support of welfare endeavors.[28]

Myth—Family planning of programs for the poor are viewed

positively by the poor and are seen as a helpful addition to welfare services.

Reality—Rauch found family planning programs that were linked to welfare programs to be necessarily coercive and unable to reduce poverty. The Black community leveled charges of "genocide" and were generally not in favor of family planning programs. In other instances there was a lack of access to the medical services provided through family planning programs, and welfare recipients were unable to take full advantage of the program.[27]

Opposition has also been expressed by certain church groups including the Roman Catholics. Particularly, the coercive nature of the provision as found in the proposed Social Security Amendments of 1967, left such provisions open to serious debate. Requiring welfare recipients to accept family planning services in order to be eligible for federal matching funds even though it was intended to combat rising illegitimacy, was felt to be an unnecessarily harsh restriction.[4]

Myth—Other agencies cannot cooperate with welfare programs because they are impossible to work with.

Reality—Cooperation and close collaboration between schools and social welfare agencies is a necessary and desirable objective. The Catholic Welfare Services and three parochial schools in Minneapolis believed that teachers and social workers could perform complementary roles in dealing with special problems of students. A formal program has been established in the schools which provided for inclusion of social work services in the counseling program. Differential roles were prescribed for teachers and social workers, and the conclusion was that the experience had been a rewarding and successful one for both the social welfare agencies and the school. Of particular importance was the trust and confidence developed between teachers and social workers.[9]

Vocational rehabilitation agencies have developed cooperative and mutually beneficial relationships with public welfare agencies. Sharing of costs and services and mutual referral have been ingredients of the cooperative relationship between vocational rehabilitation and public welfare.

Myth—Welfare recipients do not want job training and cannot benefit from job training.

Reality—Detailed interviews were held with graduates of work experience programs. These in-depth interviews revealed significant satisfaction with their training. Of particular interest was the finding that these women enjoyed their role as helping persons far more than they did their role as dependent-welfare-recipients. It was even felt to be beneficial to the mother-child relationships in the family because it encouraged some separation. Dissatisfactions were centered around the limited choices of job training and the lack of continuing day care services for children during the period of training. Findings revealed an increase in self-esteem on the part of the women who obtained employment following training.[5]

Myth—Public welfare programs are basically meeting the needs of the poor in this country.

Reality—Millions of Americans are chained to poverty, squalor and degradation. America is far from achieving a fair, just, human, and effective program of public welfare. Martin indicated that people are entitled to the basic necessities of life without the stigmas and humiliation to which they are now submitted. He suggested that rather than frustration, repression, thrift, and efficiency, public welfare programs should be based upon faith, justice, brotherhood, and generosity.[21]

Myth—Rather than more money, what is actually needed is broader social service programs.

Reality—The President's Commission on Income Maintenance Programs has indicated, "the broadening of social services have not led to a reduction in welfare."[43] When one is hungry, it is necessary to have money to purchase food before services mean anything. Adequate social services are necessary but are an independent variable for rich and poor alike. Either social services or money without the other is inadequate.[7]

Myth—Other countries are far behind the United States in welfare provisions for recipients.

Reality—Welfare services to the impoverished in Maharashtra, India include free education, economic aid in the form of agricultural tools, seed, loans, animals, and health and housing aids. Students may live in urban areas while studying, and such programs were sponsored by government and voluntary groups.[3]

Even "underprivileged" countries do have programs and aid for their citizens who are living in poverty and unable to provide the essentials in life for themselves and their families.

The previous paragraphs have focused on several common myths and evidence to counter each of the myths. It should be remembered that this is by no means an all inclusive list of myths or realities but rather illustrative of many of the more frequently repeated myths and some information to counter each myth.

PUBLIC IMAGES OF THE RECIPIENTS OF PUBLIC WELFARE

Some have said that today is the day for questioning and challenging beliefs and values. If this is so elsewhere within our society, it is most certainly the case within public welfare programs. Specifically, beliefs regarding characteristics of welfare recipients are challenged today more strongly than any time in the recent past. Even so-called substantiated themes resulting from social and psychological research are undergoing question.

Herzog has indicated that the following themes relating to poverty and welfare are viewed today as blinders rather than beacons. These themes include the following:

"The poor do not accept the values of the middle class, but live by a set of their own.

"The poor are impulsive, living for the moment, incapable of deferred gratification and planfulness.

"Among the poor, especially the Negro poor, illegitimacy carries no stigma.

"The low income Negro family is in disarray and rapidly deteriorating.

"The broken family, so frequent among the poor, is by definition a sick family.

"The Negro woman is dominant, economically and psychologically.

"The family and sex patterns of the Negro poor are a direct reflection of the slavery heritage."

Herzog goes on to suggest that each of these themes is supported by some evidence; however, there is a small but growing number of practitioners and social scientists who are questioning and even strongly critical of such statements.[12] This is most certainly the time for additional research, further rethinking and questioning, and possible alteration of beliefs and views held toward welfare recipients.

Several of the myths connected with public welfare recipients will now be explored with some realities for each situation.

Myth—Public welfare recipients have plenty of money and are on welfare only to acquire more.

Reality—The cash assets of each welfare applicant are reported and scrutinized. In order to qualify for public assistance in Baltimore, Maryland, for example, a mother with three children must have no more than $300 in cash assets. She may have life insurance policies up to a face value of $1,000 for herself and up to $500 for each of her children. Cash assets include checking and savings accounts, stocks and bonds, property not occupied by the applicant, a car, and any other personal property. This fictitious mother would not be allowed to have an automobile unless she could prove that the car was needed for medical purposes for one of her children or for herself. Also, she would not be allowed to own a house unless she occupied the house herself.[32]

If this mother with three children has no income and no other visible means of support, and less than $300 in cash assets, and less than the maximum allowable life insurance requirement, she would be eligible for not more than $200 a month from Aid to Families with Dependent Children (AFDC) assistance. This is the maximum allowable amount for a family of four.[32]

Schneiderman indicated that current federally-financed public welfare programs supply less than enough support even for living at the poverty level. He believes that the abject poverty of welfare recipients in this nation is maintained by official policy.[33]

Nationally, the average payment to a family of four on public welfare with no other income varies from a low of $60 per month in Mississippi to a high of $375 per month in Alaska. In all but four states, public welfare payments are below the established poverty level of $331 per month, or $3,972 per year for a family of four. A state establishes its own "need standard" and such a standard may be either below or above the poverty line for that individual state. However, thirty-eight of the states pay less than their own established standard of need.[50]

Myth—Welfare families have extremely large numbers of children and have more children just to get more money.

Reality—Since 1967, the trend has been toward smaller families among those on public welfare. The typical welfare family has a mother and three children, and the birth rate for welfare families is dropping as it is in the general population. The typical payment for the additional child is $35 a month which is hardly enough to cover the cost of rearing an additional child. In addition, there are states that impose maximum payment limits which are usually four or five persons in a family, and an additional allowance cannot be obtained for more children.[50]

A survey reported in 1965, found between 70 percent to 83 percent (72% to 84% of the nonwhite patients) continued to take a contraceptive pill regularly 30 months after they came to the clinic and received their prescription. This was felt to be an astonishingly high retention rate for any procedure requiring continuous self administration of medication and was interpreted as testimony to the readiness of poor, generally, and in particular the Black poor, to respond positively to well conceived modern contraceptive programs and to voluntarily limit the size of their families.[10]

Myth—Most welfare families are Black.

Reality—The largest racial group among public welfare families was White. The percent of Whites receiving welfare payments was 49 percent. Blacks represented approximately 46 percent and American Indians, Orientals, and other racial minorities represent the remaining 5 percent.[50]

These figures were essentially the same as those reported by the United States Department of Health, Education, and Welfare in March, 1970. These figures applied to AFDC families in the 50 states and the District of Columbia. Within this jurisdiction, 49.2 percent of the recipients were White, 46.2 percent were Black, 1.3 percent were American Indian, .7 percent other, and 2.6 percent had race not reported.[45]

Myth—Public welfare recipients are basically dishonest and lie and cheat.

Reality—Jacobs reported an amazing lack of cooperation between the Los Angeles Welfare Bureau and public welfare recipients. He believed that the lack of cooperation between the two groups as well as the punishment and tension created by policies adopted by program administrators, were the basic causes for dishonesty and fraudulent activities of citizens receiving various amounts of assistance.[16]

Eighty families with dependent children (AFDC) had an extremely low rate of fraud and misrepresentation among welfare recipients. Less than 4/10 of 1 percent of the total caseload in the nation were suspected of fraud. Cases where actual fraud was established occurred even less frequently. Another 1 to 2 percent of the caseload was technically ineligible and because of a misunderstanding of rules, agency mistakes, or changes in family circumstances, these human and technical errors appeared to be instances of misrepresentation. The conclusion was offered that the overwhelming majority of recipients were not willfully misrepresenting their situations and cheating on welfare.[50]

Myth—Persons who are willfully out of work such as on strike and those who have been fired from jobs are not eligible for public welfare assistance.

Reality—In Maryland, a federal court panel recently struck down state regulations denying welfare aid to otherwise eligible families in which the father was out of work either because he had been fired or was on strike. The court further emphasized that the welfare rule conflicted with social security legislation as well as with Health, Education, and Welfare regulations. It was emphasized that fathers on strike or fired from their jobs must still meet general standards of need based upon resources and cash assets as well as income, and strike benefits paid by a union would also be classified as income.[40]

Myth—If welfare reform as recommended by President Nixon was enacted, public welfare recipients would have sufficient money to live comfortably and support their families.

Reality—A $2400 base has been proposed for a family of four with no other income. For a man heading a family of four who is working but receiving wages below the poverty level of approximately $4,000 for a family of four, he could receive supplementary income payments to boost his income. It has been pointed out in testimony before the Senate Finance Committee that $2,400 is below the poverty level in many sections of the country and a family of four without other income cannot live on that amount of money.[29]

Myth—Public welfare roles (AFDC), are full of able-bodied persons who refuse to work.

Fact—Less than 1 percent of the welfare recipients were able-bodied unemployed males. The exact figure was approximately 126,000 of the more than 13,000,000 who were on federal/state supported welfare programs. Eighty percent of the less than 1 percent who were able-bodied unemployed males wanted work and about 50 percent were enrolled in work training programs.

The largest group of working age adults on welfare was 2.5 million mothers of welfare families and most of these heads of families without an able-bodied male present in the family. Approximately 14 percent of these mothers worked and 7 percent were in work training. Thirty-five percent could be employable if job training, jobs, and day care facilities were available. Four percent needed extensive medical or rehabilitative services before becoming employable and the remaining 40 percent were needed at home to care for small children, or have a long term disability.

Of the total 13 million on welfare, 55.5 percent were children, 15.6 percent were aged and 9.4 percent were blind and disabled. This leaves the 2.5 million mothers (18.6%) and the able-bodied fathers (0.9%) who make up a total of 100 percent of welfare AFDC recipients.[50]

Myth—Welfare recipients have nice houses to live in.

Reality—The vast majority of welfare recipients do not own their own house. Of those who are renting, a recent survey reported that public welfare funds were used to support tenancy in substandard housing. Welfare departments frequently "close their eyes" to substandard housing. They reportedly felt that this was a service to the welfare recipient. It was also felt that the cost of code enforcement involving landlord expenditures, would be passed on to the tenant and perhaps rent would be increased if codes were enforced.

A cooperative project was proposed in which local code enforcement agencies would cooperate with the welfare department and encourage landlords to bring housing up to standard. In instances where landlords did not comply, the welfare department could adopt a policy of working with clients to help them find housing meeting code standards. Two approaches have been tried with some success. The first was to place rent money in escrow to be used to pay the cost of bringing housing up to code standards. A second involved taking over, by the city or county, of a below standard building owned by an uncooperative land owner and using the rent to bring the building up to standard. The conclusion drawn was that something needed to be done to assist welfare recipients who lived in substandard housing with building code violations. Clearly, adequate housing for welfare recipients was a serious problem.[25]

Myth—Welfare recipients view themselves as possessing a right to receive welfare because of their citizenship.

Reality—Briar reported a study in which 46 couples receiving AFDC were interviewed regarding their experiences with their welfare agencies. In addition, they were asked about the conceptions of its operation, perceptions of their rights and obligations, their attitudes toward welfare policies and issues, and effects of recipient status on family life. This group was nearly evenly divided between White, Black, and Mexican Americans; and they were interviewed by persons of their own ethnic background.

The findings of this study were of interest. Few of the recipients were certain of their rights including the right to appeal the denial of aid. They were not aware of the role of the social worker and judged the justifiability of others' welfare claims on the similarities between the other's claim and their own. It was concluded that because of the complexity of the welfare process, recipients viewed themselves as suppliants not citizens who have a right to receive welfare.[6]

Myth—Most welfare children are illegitimate without either a mother or a father.

Reality—Fifty-eight percent of the children in families receiving welfare payments were born in wedlock. In numbers this amounts to over four and one-half million children in welfare families who were born to parents while the parents were married. This was even all the more surprising since only in recent years has the government made a concerted effort to provide family counseling services for the poor.[50]

Myth—Once a person is on welfare, he will likely always remain on welfare.

Reality—The average welfare family (AFDC) has been on the roles for twenty-three months. The same study reported that at any given time, about two-thirds of the families on welfare have received assistance for less than three years. Only 7.3 percent on public welfare have been receiving support for ten years or more. In most of these instances, some form of disability was involved.

Surveys have revealed that the majority of welfare families were embarrassed by being on welfare. Most wanted to get off welfare roles and were discontented with welfare. It took about two years for the average family to overcome its problems and leave the roles of public welfare.[50]

Myth—Welfare is only a money handout to help the poor.

Reality—Many services were provided for welfare recipients in addition to direct payments. These services included health care advice and referrals, counseling on financial and home management, employment counseling, services to secure child support, services to improve housing conditions, and services to enable children to continue school. Although money was a very necessary part of the total welfare program, most families received several services. For example, 55.7 percent of the families received health care advice and referral, 54.2 percent received counseling on financial and home management, and 51 percent received employment counseling.

The range of social services was found to be essential in helping welfare recipients move toward independence and constructive living.[50]

Myth—Most welfare recipients have some kind of character disorder and represent a poor treatment risk.

Reality—Schneiderman indicated that there was substantial evidence, "to indicate that clinical judgment is heavily infused with middle-class bias; that diagnostic criteria have their source as much in cultural tradition as in science; that such behavior as planning ahead or being deliberate is drawn largely from middle-class society's accumulation of folk wisdom about problem solving." It was possible to look at the same data and conclude that the welfare recipient and the poor displayed a success in adapting to a reality that was impoverished in opportunities and resources. Because of the differences in environment, special adaptive patterns for sure survival have been necessitated, and these were not weaknesses or maladjustments but rather the best possible adjustment under the circumstances.

Schneiderman suggested that it was well to keep this in mind even when evaluating social science research findings. Such findings included the following characteristics of the impoverished;

1. The very poor were thought to have little interest in education and believe in spending rather than saving money;

2. The poor had a bad reputation among those persons who were socially above them in social class;

3. They were believed to have no respect for the law or for themselves;

4. They were thought to desire money, possessions, education, and favorable prestige, but they did not know how to achieve them;

5. They were thought to have distinctive patterns of speech, marriage, family life, and dress;

6. The poor were seen as unmotivated for service and lacking awareness of their problems;

7. They seemed to hold unrealistic expectations and make inappropriate requests for services;

8. The poor tended to relate problems to causes and forces outside of themselves;

9. They used different rules for ordering speech and thoughts; and

10. They were likely to be insensitive to different background experiences between themselves and their listeners.

Schneiderman pointed out that there was some research to support each of the characteristics of the impoverished, but they must not be considered deviant and to be in need of treatment even if some of the stereotypic characteristics were true in part.[34]

Significant attention has been given to myths and realities connected with public welfare recipients. Many beliefs have been stated and certain research findings support in some instances and contradict in other instances certain of the beliefs. It should be apparent now that evaluative, judgmental, and stereotype views of welfare recipients are often misleading and frequently may do damage to the recipient.

SUMMARY AND CONCLUSIONS

As rehabilitation workers sift through the many beliefs and the extensive research data available, they need to be aware that each of the myths and each of the realities have a potential of affecting their attitudes toward the public welfare recipient and in the end affect both their efforts and perhaps the efforts of others who have as a primary responsibility the rehabilitation of the public welfare recipient.

New welfare programs must be developed and existing welfare programs will require change in order for them to meet the needs of urbanization. Even in services for children, welfare serves only a particular segment of poor children and only in certain ways. Schorr has indicated that 13 million children lack the essentials of basic care. Division within our country is in part related to the disparity in income with such deep conviction about quality.[35]

Services are often fragmented and uncoordinated because patterns of living have changed radically. Families are no longer self-reliant, population density makes family problems more observable, reliance of families upon employment for income has promoted more working mothers who are not in the home full-time, and inner city poverty has exacerbated family problems. Additional day care is desperately needed and greater reliance on group services is expected. Neighborhood based services need to replace centralized agency services, and increased caseload services and income security are badly needed.[23]

Public welfare staff members need increased skill and knowledge if they are going to be able to keep up with the increasing demands and make even a greater impact upon both welfare programs and welfare recipients. Welfare workers must be committed to the enforcement of human rights for all citizens in society.[11] Rather than considering the welfare recipient as one who is in a condition of bondage, he needs to have greater respect for his right of privacy and other fundamental Constitutional guarantees. The root of the problem according to Bendich lies in the persistence of the view that access to basic necessities is not a matter of constitutional entitlement, but at the discretion of charity.[2]

One of the essential ingredients in change is to modify the criteria that are employed as measures of effectiveness in welfare programs. Even with instituting cost benefit anaylsis into social welfare programs, it is not desirable to translate all the benefits into dollars. Therefore, social-psychological outcomes as well as monetary benefits need to be measured in order to aid in evaluating welfare programs from expectations to outcomes.[19]

A more realistic view might ask whether or not it is possible to make alterations and changes in welfare programs in order to eliminate the base for many of the fallacies and myths that have been perpetrated upon welfare recipients. The answer is that it is not only possible but it is already being done. A five-year study and demonstration project has been undertaken in Massachusetts to find ways to increase the effectiveness of state programs for children and their families and to improve the coordination of these programs. In the first phase of the study, an analysis was made of the socioeconomic characteristics of each area under study including child health and medical services, family and social welfare services, recreation and group work services, and mental health services. It was discovered that coordination and planning were lacking and the services provided tended to be fragmented. It was recommended that planning be area wide and comprehensive and that services be increased and strengthened. Early evaluations indicate a valuable contribution has been made to the field.[15] Other similar studies have been undertaken and demonstration projects are under way.

It is not only possible but necessary that changes in public welfare programs be instituted. The myths that have been perpetrated upon society with regard to welfare programs and welfare recipients not only damage the programs but also the people who are providing the services and the people who are receiving the services. One needs to look no further than a report by Schur on poverty, violence, and crime in America. In this report the researchers hesitated to attribute crime to poverty but there was little question that poverty was the social and economic condition that drove many into criminality. If these conditions could be ameliorated or eliminated, crime could be reduced.[36]

Those in rehabilitation working with welfare recipients need to examine first their own attitudes relative to these and other myths, and then to bring into reality the services needed by and the rights provided for each citizen in our country.

REFERENCES

1. Ambrosino and Salvatore: New directions for the family agency. *Social Casework, 49*(1):15-21, 1968.
2. Bendich, Albert M.: Privacy, Poverty, and the Constitution, In Tenbroek, Jacobus (Ed.): *The Law of the Poor,* San Francisco, Chandler, p. 83-118, 1966.
3. Bharaskar, B. M.: Welfare schemes for backward classes in Maharashtra. *Journal of Social Welfare, 19*(7):3-6, 1969.
4. Brazda, Jerome F.: Proposed amendment to Social Security Law would expand government's role in family planning. *Medical World News, 8*(37):97, 1967.
5. Brecher, Sally L.; Kliguss, Anne F., and Stewart, D.: The participants' view of an antipoverty program. *Social Casework, 49*(9):537-540, 1968.
6. Briar, Scott: Welfare from below: Recipients' views of the public welfare system. In Tenbroek, Jacobus (Ed.): *The Law of the Poor.* San Francisco, Chandler, 1966, pp. 46-61.
7. Chaiklin, Harris: *A Social Service Team for Public Welfare.* New York, Columbia University Press, 1970.
8. Chaiklin, Harris: *Final Report: Community Organization and Services to Improve Family Living.* The University of Maryland School of Social Work and Community Planning Research Center, 1970.
9. Christie, Lyle, and Quesnell, John G.: Beyond the office interview. *Catholic Charities Review, 54*(1):10-16, 1970.
10. Frank, Richard, and Tietze, Christopher: Acceptance of an oral contraceptive program in a large metropolitan area. *American Journal of Obstetrics and Gynecology, 93*(1):122-127, 1965.
11. Hanlan, Archie: Public Welfare, Civil Rights and Human Rights. *Public Welfare, 27*(1):36-39, 1969.
12. Herzog, Elizabeth: *About the Poor Some Facts and Some Fictions.* Washington, U.S. Government Printing Office, 1968.
13. Hirsch, Carl: Kent, Donald P., and Loux, Suzanne B.: Homogeneity and heterogeneity among low-income Negro and White aged. *Gerontologist, 8*(3):27, 1968.
14. Hoos, Ida R.: Retraining of the Underprivileged: The Job Corps and programs for welfare recipients. In *Retraining the Work Force: An Analysis of Current Experience.* Berkeley and Los Angeles, University of California Press, 1967, pp. 166-194.
15. Jacobi, John E.: "Meeting the needs of children and youth in Massachusetts' communities: The local area study and demonstration project. Boston, Massachusetts Committee on Children and Youth, 1968, p. 131.
16. Jacobs, Paul: The welfare bureau. *Prelude to Riot.* New York, Random House, 1967, pp. 298, 61-99.
17. Johnson, Josie: The black community looks at the welfare systems.

Public Welfare, 26(3):205-208, 1968.

18. Levin, Herman: Volunteers in social welfare: The challenge of their future. *Social Work*, 14(1):85-94, 1969.

19. Levine, Abraham S.: Cost benefit analysis and social welfare program evaluation. *Social Service Review*, 42(2):173-183, 1968.

20. Martin, Virgil C.: Voluntary responsibility for influencing public social policy. (Conference Paper). *New Trends in Citizen Involvement and Participation*, New York, National Social Welfare Assembly, January, 1965, pp. 25-32.

21. Martin, Webster: Human Rights and the 1967 Amendments. *Catholic Charities Review*, 53(2):4-15, 1969.

22. McKenzie, Leslie H.: The citizen participates in public welfare. *Public Welfare*, 11(1):24-27, 1953.

23. Meyer, Carol H.: The impact of urbanization on child welfare. *Child Welfare*, 46(8):433-442, 1967.

24. Meyer, Lawrence: Welfare criticism clarified. *The Washington Post*, November 15, 1971.

25. Mougulof, Melvin B.: Subsidizing substandard housing through public welfare payments, *Journal of Housing*, 24(10):560-563, 1967.

26. Morrissey, Rosemary: *Strengthening Public Welfare Services Through the Use of Volunteers*. Chicago, American Public Welfare Association, 1960.

27. Rauch, Julia B.: Federal family planning programs; choice or coercion. *Social Work*, 15(4):68-75, 1970.

28. Rich, Spencer: AFL-CIO backs full welfare program. *Washington Post*, February 1, 1972.

29. Rich, Spencer: Compromise reached on welfare bill. *Washington Post*, February 3, 1972.

30. Rivlin, Alice M.: Should the poor be encouraged, or compelled to work? *Washington Post*, January 31, 1971.

31. Royster, Vermont: Thinking things over: The lysenko syndrome. *Wall Street Journal*, 171(101):18, May 22, 1968.

32. Samuel, Paul D.: The facts on welfare eligibility. *The Evening Sun*, November 12, 1971.

33. Schneiderman, Leonard: Project Head Start: Aprons to cover their dirty clothes. *Mental Hygiene*, 52(1):34-41, 1968.

34. Schneiderman, Leonard: Social class, diagnosis and treatment. *American Journal of Orthopsychiatry*, 35:99-105, 1965.

35. Schorr, Alvin L.: Responsibility for children: What does it mean? *Child Welfare*, 47(9):516-518, 1968.

36. Schur, Alvin M.: Poverty, violence, and crime in America, In Schur, E.: *Our Criminal Society*. Englewood Cliffs, N.J., Prentice-Hall, 1969, pp. 121-157.

37. Stearns, A. W., and Ullman, Albert D.: One thousand unsuccessful careers. *American Journal of Psychiatry*, 105(11):801-809, 1949.

38. Taylor, William W.: Unintended consequences of the Nixon Welfare Plan. *Social Work, 15*(4):15-22, 1970.
39. *Characteristics of General Assistance in the United States.* Washington, D.C., U.S. Department of Health, Education, and Welfare, 1970.
40. Court panel strikes down Maryland welfare stipulations. *The Washington Post,* January 30, 1972.
41. Institute for the Study of Crime and Delinquency Interaction of the Social Welfare System. In *ISCD Model Comm. Correctional Program.* S. Joaquin Co., California, II. Sacramento, Inst. Study Crime and Delinquency, 1969, pp. 83-128.
42. Pennsylvania Public Welfare Department, Planning and Research Office: *Pennsylvania Fact Book on Children and Youth.* Harrisburg, Pa., Dept. of Public Welfare, 1966.
43. *Poverty Amid Plenty:* The American Paradox-Report of the President's Commission on Income-Maintenance Programs. Washington, D.C., U.S. Government Printing Office, 1969, pp. 140-141.
44. *Preliminary Report of Findings from Mail Questionnaire-1967 AFDC Study.* U.S. Dept. of Health, Education, and Welfare, January, 1969.
45. *Preliminary Report of Findings—1969 AFDC Study.* U.S. Dept. of Health, Education, and Welfare, March, 1970.
46. *Program Facts on Federally Aided Public Assistance Income Maintenance Programs.* U.S. Dept. of Health, Education, and Welfare, June, 1970.
47. Public Welfare "Win" Program: Arm-twisting incentives. *University of Pennsylvania Law Review, 117*(7):1062-1074, 1969.
48. Texas Department of Public Welfare: Formulating preconditions to assistance. *Texas Law Review, 47*(5):909-926, 1969.
49. *United States Commission on Civil Rights A Time to Listen . . . A Time to Act.* Washington, D.C., U.S. Government Printing Office, 1967.
50. *Welfare Myths vs. Facts.* Washington, D.C., Department of Health, Education, and Welfare, 1971.
51. *Welfare Programs and Services.* Washington, D.C., U.S. Department of Health, Education, and Welfare, Welfare Administration, 1966.
52. *You're in Good Company: Millions of Americans Use USDA Food Stamps.* Washington, D.C., U.S. Government Printing Office, September, 1969.

CHAPTER VI

LEGAL PROBLEMS OF THE PUBLIC WELFARE RECIPIENT

CHARLES R. ROUSELLE

๛๛

Each Profession Has a Special Role

๛๛

A SUBSTANTIAL MOVEMENT toward provision of a broad range of legal services to the poor has occurred during the past decade. In this chapter we will discuss legal problems of economically disadvantaged people, the large population which includes the public welfare recipient. We approach this subject from a social orientation to provide the practitioner with a non-legalistic framework for aiding clients who encounter problems of either a civil or criminal character. It is not our intention here to outline the development of legal services or to engage in discourse pertaining to adequacy of a particular forensic service. We are expressly interested only in establishing a series of guidelines or benchmarks for dealing with the myriad of extralegal factors which normally confront the client who is enmeshed in an entanglement of legal difficulties.

It seems somehow incongruous that in this land of enormous economic prosperity, so many Americans can be without adequate food, clothing, shelter, and other essentials of life. President Johnson's declared War on Poverty and the crisis of American cities in the middle 1960's focused national attention on the ghetto ills that were traceable to abject poverty. Prior to that period, public policy largely had ignored the poor. In the legal profession, legal aid for the poor increasingly drew the attention of judges, lawyers,

110

legislators and law students; the Legal Services Division of the Office of Economic Opportunity, established in 1965, began funding law offices in low-income areas. The first efforts were aimed at extension of free legal services to indigent residents in areas of heavy urban density; similar services to rural communities later developed. These neighborhood legal services concentrated on civil proceedings with the recognition that unless properly administered, the law can operate as an enemy of the people who are trying to escape from poverty:

> A sudden and unexplained eviction, or an arbitrary decision by a welfare department can be the stroke that pushes a family more deeply—perhaps irrevocably—into poverty.
> An impoverished neighborhood receives inadequate public health services or refuse collection, services that are provided in other sections of the city.
> A mother receiving Aid to Families with Dependent Children benefits is subjected to unfair or arbitrary administrative decisions. She may be subjected to unlawful and harrassing investigative procedures that invade her right of privacy.
> A child is denied entry into a school for arbitrary reasons or is suspended without right to a fair hearing. The denial of education can have severe economic consequences. It can impair his attitude and ability to earn a living.

When a person of greater financial means is faced with a legal problem, he copes with it since he has easy access to a lawyer. He also sees the law, not necessarily as his antagonist. In the past, the poor man was unable to cope with the problem. Such difficulties could throw his life into a turmoil with long-term consequences. He did not know the law, was fearful of its interpretations, and did not have access to a lawyer anyway.

Before the 1960's the financially depressed person did have legal sources available but too few and frequently these were not forceful advocates of his cause. Legal Aid Societies and Prisoner Aid Societies had long established themselves as competent spokesmen but, alone, they often were mere echoes in a massive vacuum unable to reach the masses. In 1936 a landmark decision by the Supreme Court established the practice of assigning counsel in indigent cases—paid for by the government—for criminal litigation before federal courts. It was not until 1963 that another ruling extended the right to counsel concept to indigents who were accused of felonies before state courts. In many jurisdictions poor people still must fend for themselves without a lawyer in misdemeanor violations. (The overwhelming majority of cases which are presented to the courts are misdemeanors at the state or lesser levels of prosecution.)

Legal service agencies, acting as advocates for a group that has long been unrepresented, have put a new perspective on the legal problems of the poor. Judges, officials, lawyers, professors and community leaders are adopting new attitudes toward the poor and the law. Law schools have instituted courses in poverty law. The new interest of the profession in the problems of poverty is reflected by a new breed of lawyers enlisting to serve as advocates for the poor. Public Defender Services are emerging throughout the nation; large, prominent firms are assuming increasing responsibility to handle *pro bono* work in criminal courts; many nationally acclaimed attorneys have redirected considerable amounts of time and energy from lucrative practices to seek equal justice for the economically disadvantaged.

This relatively recent influx of legal services is yet not sufficient to provide adequate representation for the problems of the disadvantaged. But because of its comparatively rapid growth, adjustments have been required by the recipient, adjustments in the learning processes of how to make appropriate use of the services. The matter of confiding a personal and often embarrassing situation to an "outsider," demands time and testing by the recipient and proof of sincerity by the attorney. What types of problems are truly legal and need be remedied through such course? Can rent payment be withheld because of broken window panes or falling plaster? Should an accused defendant trustingly accept the advice of a "free" lawyer; would he be less likely to be convicted as charged with retained counsel? As questions are raised and resolved and new issues clarified, we are able to move toward a more closely aligned system of justice between the "haves" and the "have nots." However, the gap is still far too wide.

EACH PROFESSION HAS A SPECIAL ROLE

Remedial action for the legal problems of the economically disadvantaged is essentially the responsibility of the legal practitioner. The social, psychological, vocational and related nonlegal problems which frequently interface with legal issues, however, are the tasks of other professions. Cooperative and collaborative interdisciplinary efforts are mandatory in moving toward both immediate and long-range goals. The lawyer is not a social worker, rehabilitation counselor, educator, or otherwise and should not attempt to be. By training and inclination, the lawyer generally tends to look at specific and concrete problems in terms of possible, individuated solutions through the operations of the legal system and not in terms of larger social issues. The possibility that low-income people may have special problems, may be treated differently by the law and its institutions, or may require special consideration is not the lawyers major concern.

The counselor or social worker is not a lawyer. He must address himself to those areas where his skill, interest and discipline are established. He must recognize that law victories which are secured by the lawyer may prove to be short-lived or hollow, unless the extralegal problems are attacked simultaneously. This practitioner must assume an apparently different role from the lawyer, sometimes conflicting in style or approach although not at variance in goals. The practitioner must establish the position that the client's well-being is better secured by assisting him in overcoming personal and interpersonal problems which mitigate against societal functioning. He is concerned with the client's capacity and strengths for relating to his environment in a satisfying manner for longer than the duration of the particular legal issue. The lawyer, especially in adversary proceedings of criminal cases, concentrates on triumphs before the court; the counselor focuses on sustaining these triumphs. Employed in teamwork, the lawyer and the non-lawyer should provide for the best interest of the client. This interest consists of the legal, social, economic and psychological components of his situation.

We need to recognize that problems of the disadvantaged are all of a piece-connected, derivative of one another, but they are susceptible to realistic assessment only if we break them apart to view each facet separately. In this chapter we do not direct discussion to the conglomerate of sociological-psychological-cultural agents which impinge upon the individual causing him to act and to react in a certain manner to situations. It is, however, of fundamental importance that the practitioner possess a firm grasp of these factors in order that he understand patterns of behavior so as to prescribe valid and practical remedies. Of like importance is the conscious analysis of the component parts—the plan of action for resolving the problem—to be pursued by the practitioner. We consider this plan of action to be composed of five basic parts or functions: Problem Identification, Process, Selection of Services, Solution, and Evaluation and Termination.

Problem Identification

The recipient has a legal problem or problems for which he requires the effective assistance of counsel. That is his dominant concern. He may be accused of a law violation for which a fine or sentence can be imposed; he might face loss of purchased goods because of payment default or arrearage on which annual interest rate requirements were exhorbitantly and unlawfully set; he may have engaged in a family altercation which results in court action; he may claim ignorance of or be mistakenly accused of wrongdoing. Regardless of the nature of the legal situation, and obviously there are literally hundreds of situations in which legal advice and support may be required in either civil or criminal litigation, the client's immediate direction is to a satisfactory (to himself) disposition. His attention is not divided into looking on one hand at the law and, on the other, at any causative factors from a sociogenic point of view. Analogously, the family which is in dire need of food is not prone to participate in an in-depth discussion of family budget management. The priority has been established. The practitioner commences services at that point of imminency. This is not to imply that the rehabilitation counselor, social worker or other practitioner should attempt to treat the legal crisis any more than he would endeavor to diagnose mental disorder. His stance is in tandem with the legal expert (or psychologist in the case of the latter). The practitioner must at the point of entry concentrate on establishing lines of communication and upon constructing a rapport on which subsequent movement can proceed. Once the recipient has gained some assurance that his legal problem is receiving due attention, related issues can be explored.

The task of identifying the problem is frequently over-simplified. The practitioner should be aware that his and the client's frames of reference may be dissimilar. The practitioner often interprets problems as he, himself, sees them—usually in terms as proscribed by the larger "middle-class" or middle-income group. The client, economically deprived, is by definition, not a part of that group. His attitudes, standards for judgment and value systems may be either foreign or unacceptable. Additionally, racial differences, cultural and subcultural differences, and ethnic backgrounds all tend to make the task of meeting at a common point in clarifying the actual problem more complex. It is a requisite that the counselor clearly understand that which the client interprets as the presenting issue. When a uniform interpretation is meted, work on methods to be employed for the client to resolve problems should be undertaken.

Expertly laid plans in goal setting and goal achievement have often gone awry causing the counselor to question the sincerity of the client or his own judgment. In many instances failure is traceable to the mere identification of whose problem was being resolved. Is it the client's problem as he feels and lives it, or, the counselor's problem as he interprets it?

> An unemployed father is apprehended for stealing food from a supermarket. While awaiting disposition of charges he is referred to a social service agency for an evaluation of personal and family requirements. The court will consider the report of the agency before rendering a judgment in the case. After obtaining various sociobiographical information from the client, he is referred to the state employment agency which, in turn, places him onto a job. It is obvious to both workers that employment is a pressing need for the father and his family. At least this facet of the family's needs is resolved. Is it? Following three days on the job, he quits. He is returned to court and sentenced to an institution. The thinking of the judge and counselors is that the man had an adequate opportunity to demonstrate an interest in assuming family responsibility and, failing to, probably would need to continue stealing in order to support the family.

This example is purposefully simplistic but reveals much of what not infrequently takes place in our daily relationships in agencies. An attitude is reflected that the poor are "mere clients" rather than citizens, an attitude unfortunately in the hearts of many who deal with them. (If the poor person is also a defendant in a criminal proceeding and/or is of a different racial or ethnic group, he may be truly in a dire strait.) He is shuffled from place to place having had little chance to participate in the decision-making process. His need is identified for him and he is programmed. In the example cited, the father's need may have been for counseling in the nature of getting along with employers if his work history indicates this has been the reason for previous unemployment. It could have been the presence of narcotic or alcohol addiction which interferred with functioning. It might have been that the type of employment was not consistent with his expectations for the world of work—anything is not always preferable to nothing. Whatever were his needs, they were not identified through contacts with the agencies.

Problem Process

The methods used to achieve favorable results can be determined once the principal and contributing problems are identified. These methods may be modified during the process as needs change and as new problems develop and replace old ones. The practitioner must recognize the dynamics of behavior and should be prepared to shift his emphasis from one area of concentration to another when the variables of a life situation require a shift. The practitioner assumes the responsibility to work with the client. Inherent in this assumption is that he relate to the client with openness, integrity and honesty. He makes suggestions, gives advice and provides alternatives to courses of action in accord with his own professional judgment as well as in relationship to the client's right to determine that which is both realistic and practical for himself. The counselor is not performing a service *for* the client; he is providing a service *with* him.

The process of problem resolution requires that the causative factors which led to the problem are isolated. This may necessitate use of psychiatric, psychological, medical or other examinations which might expose underlying difficulties. The counselor should remember especially that he is not a diagnostician. He should not interpret every instance of slightly peculiar behavior on the part of the client as symptomatic of illness. Evaluation (by the expert), if called for, can give insight into factors which precipitated the client's action and helps the practitioner in establishing appropriate techniques for working together. Examination may reveal emotional problems, as, feelings of gross inadequacy, severe rejection or an undue fear of failure. How the client has dealt with these problems is crucial to the counseling relationship. What is the connection between his feelings and the legal difficulty which has evolved? Is it a reasonable expectation that once capable of coping with his feelings, the reoccurrence of similar legal difficulties will be minimized? The counselor should make use of his knowledge of the client in reality-based discussions. These discussions must focus on that which *is* rather than what *ought* to be. During the step-by-step process toward solution, discussions expand to include broader areas as the practitioner enables the client to move forward.

Respect for the client as a person is paramount to any successful relationship. The practitioner must share a commitment with the client that there exists the capacity to surmount present difficulties. He has to be honest in this commitment. The client may have preconceived ideas that the counselor is merely "here to do a job," that he is not really concerned. The client whose poverty is compounded by legal entanglement may feel justified in this assumption. Unless this is dissolved through conscious effort, meaningful dialogue is unattainable. Respect for the client also entails the recognition of, perhaps, varying value systems to which the persons involved in the counseling process may adhere. The counselor needs to remain cognizant of the systems so as not to necessarily impose his own either consciously or unconsciously. Is the counselor's value system superior to the client's because he is the counselor; if so, compared to what standard? Would the client achieve greater satisfactions and be able to move out of the rank of the economically disadvantaged by adopting an alternate system? Hardly, however; as he moves to an elevated income plane, he might possibly adopt values of persons at that level.

The process of problem-solving is a process of habilitation or rehabilitation. The practitioner should anticipate the inherent challenge in assisting to effect necessary progressions. Movement is usually inconsistent—two paces forward, one (or two) pace back. Achievement is the result of persistence by both client and counselor.

Selection of Services

Many clients require particular services which cannot be provided by the counselor or the lawyer. Without the additional service, other efforts may be incomplete or even futile. The lawyer assumes a responsibility to the client to provide the most comprehensive representation consistent with legal ethics. He should rely on sources which add to his knowledge of the facets of his case: statement of fact; evidence; witnesses; and psychological, social, vocational and related data. While the counselor can provide much of this information, he is not an expert in all fields. The agencies or services which are selected to augment the counselor's involvement should be chosen on the basis not only of appropriateness to client needs but also with regard to the client as a person. The counselor assumes the role of coordinator of resources. He should be aware of community services and, through his knowledge of the client, he is in a position to effectively mate one with the other. Communication between each program which is utilized to provide a particular service, as, vocational rehabilitation, employment placement programs, welfare administration and others, should be as frequent as practical to assure a continuity without fragmentation. At the same time, the counselor must remain in position to insure against an oversaturation. Services which are required at a particular stage of the working process should be the only ones provided at that time.

The service agency selected should demonstrate a concern for people and not see the client as but a number, a case to be disposed of. Of course, this may be idealistic. Recognizing this, the client should be alert that some persons with whom he must relate in agency settings will be inconsiderate, hostile, antagonistic or otherwise unreceptive. The client might be encouraged to utilize such negative encounters as a "test" of his own movement, especially if the reason for his having had need for counsel originally was precipitated by his handling of similar situations. The counselor should be aware of such experiences in assisting the client's progress. Most communities do not have such a wide latitude of service agencies to allow the client the option of selecting others (which will provide identical services) in the event that he experiences some difficulty as above. If the experience is too tense or explosive, the client should be encouraged to quit

Agency goals in working with the client must be compatible with the counselor's overall planning. Divergent interests and/or conflicting services can hardly be in the client's interest. The client is the best gauge of this compatibility; his progress is predicated on that which he receives from the sources with which he is involved.

Solution

The practitioner has achieved the goal of assisting the client to resolve difficulties at such point that the client is capable of responsibly planning his own course of action. The client who is able to make effective use of his own skill in dealing with day to day occurrences and who has a sense of personal accomplishment is prepared for discharge from the counselor-counselee relationship. At this stage, he should have a firm hold on methods for employing his own technique to adequately handle situations which were previously overwhelming. Problem solution occurs when the client feels as though he is personally respected and is accepted within his family, community, or into that which is important to him.

If the client had been determined to be a narcotics user and supported his addiction through illegal activities, would his problem be resolved solely through withdrawal from drugs? Obviously not unless, in addition to the treatment prescribed, he gained satisfactions from other areas. Part of his life style may have been the existence with fellow users, a comradeship, or a vicarious enchantment in dodging law enforcement personnel. Without substitution for this established style or manner of existence, the treatment may be short-lived in terms of success. Problems are resolved when adequate alternatives are accepted by the client.

Evaluation and Termination

Timing in case closure is extremely important. The counselor should avoid "holding on to" the client past the point of need. The client is not a dependent of the counselor and, if his problem(s)

have been handled adequately, he should not be treated as such. Counseling is a difficult process with many frustrations and failures. The counselor may have a desire to remain in close contact in order to continue to derive a personal satisfaction from accomplishment. This is not in the client's behalf. Periodic discussions may be in order following case dismissal as a review of continuing adjustment; however, contacts should be gradually decreased according to a mutually agreed upon timetable. The final phase of the counselor's activity is in assisting the lawyer or court in arriving at an equitable disposition of legal problems. This disposition should be in keeping with the client's proven abilities as demonstrated through the counseling relationship.

The counselor works toward social betterment of his client. If the client has a legal problem, the counselor moves additionally toward social justice before the court. The Hebrew prophets spoke not to lawyers alone when they said: "Justice, justice, shall ye pursue."

CHAPTER VII

PSYCHOLOGICAL ASPECTS OF POVERTY AND DISABILITY

JOHN G. CULL AND RICHARD E. HARDY

Role of Body Image in Adjustment to Disability
Factors Associated With Adjustment
Special Problems in Adolescence
Role of Defense Mechanisms in Adjustment
References

W HEN WE THINK ABOUT how an individual will react to illness or disability, we can safely say that each person reacts according to what is characteristic for his own personality. For instance, the person who has in the past shown a strong need for dependence on others, who has shown that he cannot lead an independent life, will usually react in maybe an even more dependent fashion once disability is evident. The person who has been strongly independent and mature in his own adjustment to life in general will probably make an adequate or more than adequate adjustment to disability.

Values of poor persons seem to differ from those of the middle-class person, but it should be remembered that these values do not differ in all respects. Persons living in poverty seem to have a stronger orientation in the present and in short-term perspective rather than long-term planning and goals. In addition, there is a definite feeling of fatalism and the belief in chances; impulsiveness and general inability to delay immediate gratification or make definite plans for the future. Also, there is a thinking process that could be termed much more concrete in character than abstract. There are general feelings of inferiority and an acceptance of authoritarianism; therefore, when an individual who has lived in a poverty environment during the formative years of his growth and development becomes disabled the reaction is generally substantially different from those who have been reared in a middle-class environment. To a large portion of the newly disabled from the deprived environment the newly acquired status of disability is merely one more of a long series of misfortunes which he has encountered. While those from more affluent backgrounds are concerned about the future impact of the disability, those from the ghetto areas are more concerned with here and now aspects of the disability.

When an individual accepts that his disability is of a permanent nature and that it is irrevocable, there will be a period of what can be called reactive depression and depending upon the severity of the disability there may be various suicidal inclinations. This period of extreme depression after severe injury is a normal phase of adjustment. It is at this time that often much harm is done by well-meaning individuals who offer too much hope in terms of what may or may not be accomplished by science in order to aid the individual in the future. This is a period when candid advice and information can be of great value to the individual in planning what he is able to do in reference to his particular circumstance.

Accepting disability is of paramount importance. Persons vary in their reactions to a disability. Some think they are being punished for their own or their parents' sin. Others may give the disability societal meaning in terms of their never being full members again with equal status. Still others may put sexual meanings on the disability problems. In addition, the economic aspect of the problem is often emphasized.

The meaning of disability to the family and friends of the individual cannot be overly stressed. If a child, for instance, is born disabled the family is not only grief stricken, but since the child represents the family's position in the community the disabled child is more than a disappointment. Often the families of these children can find little happiness in caring for them. Often they enter upon very expensive endeavors to ameliorate a disability which cannot be corrected. In some cases the father will completely abandon the disabled child and his family saying that the defective child is the mother's responsibility since she gave birth to it. The family often can disintegrate during arguments and disputes which center around a disabled child.

While under the best of circumstances the integrity of the family constellation is severely tested when disability occurs, the integrity of the family is definitely threatened when disability occurs in poverty families. One very important characteristic of poverty families is that they are in constant crisis. It seems that no sooner is one crisis worked out than another takes its place. There is always the financial situation; there is always the situation of the possibility of divorce due to increased stress; there is always the child in trouble; and the possibility of loss of employment. There is always the stress of insufficient nutrition; insufficient provision for activities, entertainment, etc. When these deficiencies are super-imposed upon a crisis situation in the family such as disability, the psychological reaction to the disability by both family members and the disabled is heightened. These constant crises have the effect of draining all energy from the family and its members. Such emotionality takes a high toll in terms of overall ability of a family unit or of an individual.

Moynihan (1968) has indicated that intensive family and personal rehabilitation must make up a major part of the war on impoverished conditions. He said that increased opportunities for decent and well-paying jobs are simply not enough. Moynihan maintained that for an unspecified number of the American poor, deprivation over a long period of time has caused such serious personality difficulties (personality structure problems) that many of these persons are psychologically unable to avail themselves of the various training and job opportunities which might be available to them. When these personality structure problems have a chronic or permanent physical disability superimposed upon them the reaction to the disability is severe and often devastating.

It is important for the rehabilitation professional working with disabled disadvantaged to show that he has confidence in their abilities to improve themselves not only from the point of view of poverty condition but also from the point of view of whatever handicap the individual may have. With this group of individuals the counselor needs to be particularly aware of the fact that disability does not occur in isolation from other factors in the individual. It is not adequate rehabilitation to treat the disability as a discreet event in the individual's life. Probably 85% of the major problems among persons who have physical disabilities are made up of emotional reactions to the disability. Rehabilitation personnel working with the disabled must evaluate constantly the actual limitations and freedoms associated with the person's disability, in other words what the person can and cannot do, and the importance or meaning of the disability to the person. The term "hidden disability" has been used by some persons to explain how the individual views life itself and how he has been able to cope with reality problems and experience these as his own special problems and frustrations. In other words, one individual may see the handicap as punishment for past misdeeds while another may view it as a challenge for the future. Each individual sees a disabling circumstance in his own way just as he perceives other situations in his own way. This is why we should view each person as an individual who has a special disability. This is why we must take individual approaches in social and rehabilitation services.

ROLE OF BODY IMAGE IN ADJUSTMENT TO DISABILITY

The area of study concerning body image and adjustment has become known as somatopsychology. The basis is the body image concept. The body image is a complex conceptualization which we use to describe ourselves. It is one of the basic parts of the total personality and as such determines our reaction to our environment. According to Horace and English (1966) the body image is the mental representation one has of his own body.

There are two aspects of the body image concept—the ideal body image (the desired body image) and the actual body image. The greater the congruity between the individual's two body images the better the psychological adjustment of the individual, and conversely the greater the discrepancy between these two parts of the self-concept the poorer an individual's psychological adjustment. This is very understandable. If an individual is quite short and views himself as such but has a strong ideal body image of a tall person, he is less well adjusted than he would be if his desired image were that of a short person. This is a simplistic example, but it portrays the crux of psychological adjustment to disability.

In order to adjust to the psychological impact of a disability, the body image has to change from the image of a non-disabled to the body image of a disabled person. Early in the adjustment process the actual body image will change from that of a non-disabled person to the actual body image of a disabled person; however, for adequate psychological adjustment to the disability the ideal body image must make the corresponding adaptation. Therefore, in essence the psychological adjustment to a disability is the acceptance of an altered body image which is more in harmony with reality.

During the first and second world wars, behavioral scientists noticed an increased incidence in conversion reactions. Conversion reactions are (APA, 1965) a type of psychoneurotic disorder in which the impulse causing anxiety is "converted" into functional symptoms in parts of the body rather than the anxiety being experienced consciously. Examples of conversion reactions include such functional disabilities as anesthesias (blindness, deafness), paralyses (aphonia, monoplegia, or hemiplegia), dyskineses (tic, tremor, catalepsy).

The study of these conditions along with other studies led to the development of a discipline known as psychosomatic medicine. Psychosomatic medicine is concerned with the study of the effects of the personality and emotional stresses upon the body and its functions. This psychological interaction with physiology can be observed in any of the body systems.

After the establishment of psychosomatic medicine, behavioral scientists (psychiatrists, psychologists, social workers, etc.) began observing the converse of this new field. Instead of studying the effects of emotional stress on bodily functioning, they studied the effects of physical stress on emotional functioning. Their concern was directed toward answering the question, "What are the emotional and personality changes which result from physical stress or a change in body function or physical configuration?"

FACTORS ASSOCIATED WITH ADJUSTMENT

There are three groups of factors which determine the speed or facility with which an individual will adjust to his disability. They help an individual understand the degree of psychological impact a particular disability is having on a client and the significance of the adjustment he must undergo.

The first of these three groups of factors are those factors directly associated with the disability. Psychological effects of disabilities may arise from direct insult or damage to the central nervous system. These psychological effects are called brain syndromes and may be either acute or chronic. In this instance there are a variety of behavioral patterns which may result directly from the disability. In disabilities involving no damage to brain tissue the physical limitations imposed by the disability may cause excessive frustration and in turn result in behavioral disorders. For example, an active outdoorsman and nature lover may experience a greater psychological impact upon becoming disabled than an individual who leads a more restricted and physically limited life, since the restrictions imposed by the disability demand a greater change in the basic life style of the outdoorsman. Therefore, factors directly associated with the disability have an important bearing upon an individual's reaction to disability.

The second group consists of those factors arising from the individual's attitude toward his disability. An individual's adjustment to his disability is dependent upon the attitudes he had prior to his disability. If his attitudes toward the disabled were quite negative and strong he will naturally have a greater adjustment problem than an individual with a neutral attitude toward disability and the disabled. A part of this attitude formation prior to the onset of his disability is dependent upon the experiences the client had with other disabled individuals and the stereotypes he developed.

The amount of fear a client experiences or emotion he expends during the onset and duration of the illness or accident leading up to the disability will determine the psychological impact of the disability. Generally, the greater the amount of emotion expended during onset the better the psychological adjustment to the disability. If an individual goes to sleep a sighted person and awakens a blind person, his psychological reaction to the disability is much greater than if a great deal of emotion is expended during a process of becoming blind.

The more information an individual has relating to his disability the less impact the disability will have. If the newly disabled individual is told about his disability in a simple, straightforward, mechanistic manner, it is much easier to accept and adjust to the disability than if it remains shrouded in a cloak of ignorance and mystery. Any strangeness or unpredictable aspect of our body associated with its function immediately creates anxiety and if not clarified rapidly can result in totally debilitating anxiety. Therefore, it is important for psychological adjustment to a disability that the individual have communicated to him, in terms he can understand, the medical aspects of his disability as soon after onset of disability as possible. This is a particularly important concept when dealing with the client from ghetto areas. It is an interesting observation that in our relating with clients or patients, we assume the level of intelligence which is roughly equivalent to the social status. By this we mean that the higher the social status of the client or patient the more thorough his condition is explained to him. In the case of illness the physician is much more meticulous in explaining the ideology, diagnosis, prognosis, and prescription of any disease process when working with someone from a rather affluent background than when working with someone from a ghetto area. Further, it is quite interesting to observe how professionals seem somewhat callous in informing the culturally disadvantaged of their current status whether it is medical, psychological, or vocational. In the face of newly onset disability, it is of particular importance to describe the limits of the disability and communicate quite clearly to the disadvantaged the various aspects and ramifications of his disability. It is of particular importance with this group because of the various environmental and psychological crises with which the client is confronted on a daily basis. Without this level of interaction with a professional, his psychological adjustment to the new disability will be almost overpowering.

When we are in strange or uncomfortable surroundings our social perceptiveness becomes keener. Social cues which are below threshold or not noticed in comfortable surroundings become highly significant to us in new, strange or uncomfortable surroundings. Upon the onset of disability the client will develop a heightened perceptiveness relative to how he is being treated by family, friends, and professionals. If others start treating him in a condescending fashion and relegate him to a position of less importance, his reaction to the psychological impact of the blindness will be poor. Professionals can react to the client from an anatomical orientation (what is missing) or a functional orientation (what is left). The anatomical orientation is efficient for classification purposes but is completely dehumanizing. The functional orientation is completely individualistic and as such enhances a client's adjustment to his disability.

Perhaps a key concept in the adjustment process is the evaluation of the future and the individual's role in the future. In many physical medicine rehabilitation centers a rehabilitation counselor is one of the first professionals to see the patient after the medical crisis has passed. The purpose of this approach is to facilitate the patient's psychological adjustment. If he feels there is a potential for his regaining his independence and security the psychological impact of the blindness will be lessened. While the counselor cannot engage in specific vocational counseling with the individual, he can discuss the depth of the vocational rehabilitation program and through these preliminary counseling sessions the counselor can help the newly disabled person evaluate the roles he might play in the future.

The last factor which determines the adjustment process is based upon the individual's view of the purpose of his body and the relationship this view has with the type and extent of disability. The views individuals have of their bodies may be characterized as falling somewhere on a continuum. At one end of the continuum is the view that the body is a tool to accomplish work; it is a productive machine. At the other end is the view that the body is an aesthetic stimulus to be enjoyed and provide pleasure for others. This latter concept is much the same as we have for sculpture and harks back to the philosophy of the ancient Greeks. Everyone falls somewhere on this continuum. To adequately predict the impact of a disability upon an individual one has to locate the placement of the individual upon this continuum; then evaluate the disability in light of the individual's view of the function of his body.

As an example of the above principle consider the case in which a day laborer and film actress sustain the same disabling injury— a deep gash across the face. Obviously, when considering the disability in conjunction with the assumed placements of these two upon the functional continuum, the psychological impact will be greater for the actress; since we have assumed the day laborer views his body almost completely as a tool to accomplish work and the disability has not impaired that function, the psychological impact of the disability upon him will be minimal. However, if the disability were changed (they both sustained injury to the abdomen resulting in the destruction of the musculature of the abdominal wall) the psychological impact would be reversed. In this case the actress would view her disability as minimal since it did not interfere with the aesthetic value of her body, while the day laborer's disability would be overpowering since it has substantial effects upon the productive capacity of his body.

The most obvious conclusion to be drawn from the above three factors is that the degree of psychological impact is not highly correlated with the degree of disability. This statement is contrary to popular opinion; however, disability and its psychological impact is a highly personalized event. Many counselors fall into the trap of equating degree of disability with degree of psychological impact. If the psychological impact suffered by a client is much greater than that considered "normal," the counselor will often times become impatient with the client. It should be remembered that relatively superficial disabilities may have devastating psychological effects. The psychological impact of quadraplegia is not necessarily greater than the pyschological impact of paraplegia or for that matter, more anatomically superficial physical disabilities.

SPECIAL PROBLEMS IN ADOLESCENCE

There are important reasons why traumatic experiences during adolescence can be of particular significance to the individual.

Physique plays an especially important part in how we look at ourselves and in adolescence the body is constantly changing. In addition, the adolescent period overlaps both childhood and adulthood, and it is during the period of adolescence that important self-concept changes take place. During this period an individual is making a real effort to get to know himself, his abilities, and his limitations. If traumatic injury causes disability during this period, the adjustment to such disability can be of extreme difficulty.

During adolescence, the young person is particularly concerned about his physique in terms of sexuality. The young person is very interested in learning how others will view him from the point of view of his sexual role. He has constantly heard about marriage and bearing offspring and is evaluating how he will measure up to the criteria established by society. The adolescent who sustains a disability must tolerate the frustration and psychological meaning to him as an individual of this disability plus the overlapping child-adult status which he holds. The fact that he is disabled may cause the overlapping of childhood and adulthood to persist into years beyond that of the usual adolescent period. When the person is denied adulthood status, due to disability which may retard his forward movement, insecurities increase. It should also be noted that the tremendous influence of the adolescent's peer group during this period has a great deal to do with how he evaluates himself in comparison with what he would like to be later as an adult. It is easy for the adolescent during this difficult period to develop contempt for adult authority and to become very cynical even without the added burden of a disabling circumstance.

Slums offer their own patterns, their own subcultures, their ways of behavior are determined by persons living within them. In order for an individual to maintain the level of self esteem he wishes to hold, he must be accepted by those persons who are important to him within his environment. The persons he knows within the slums or ghetto determine life goals, meanings, and social roles for him to a considerable degree. It is of prime importance for him to be accepted by them and be accepted by himself at the same time. The individual identifies himself and gives status to his "being" according to the values of those around him, especially to those important "others" who almost predetermine his present and future behavior and goals. This fact is important in understanding why many persons who live within the ghetto and within slums do not avail themselves of various training and placement opportunities and in general, the services of the rehabilitation counselor. These individuals have found their present identity and any threat to their way of life represents a threat to their "person." Proposed changes by the rehabilitation counselor bring about great feelings of anxiety. While persons in poverty are unhappy with their fate, they do not have the strength to change that which they have become comfortable with and that pattern of behavior through which they have found identity. Consequently in the face of the onset of disability, it is much more likely that the individual will seek to achieve a level of adjustment in the environment in which he lives which existed prior to the onset of disability than strike out in a new area and achieve at a higher level even though he may be fully capable intellectually and vocationally to accomplish at a higher level. The problem here is that disability had added an additional stress in the equilibrium he has established between his own personality integration and the demands and stress of the environment. The psychological adjustment to disability among poverty groups is most difficult with individuals in early adolescence up through early adulthood since they are adjusting to a life style which makes unusual and somewhat severe psychological demands upon them thereby reducing the available psychic reserves to adjust to other conditions.

Few individuals are strong enough to make an identity change on their own and changes within areas of the ghetto and slum often must come through a total community development process. Persons can change once change has begun easier than they can change on their own initiative as separate individuals. Change then within slums and ghettos must come about within individuals and groups and cannot be achieved just by moving people to new geographical areas and physical surroundings and providing rehabilitation services in these new surroundings.

In order for disabled individuals to change they must be somewhat dissatisfied with their present state—their present self-image. Disabled people in poverty, as well as people in middle and higher classes vary in their satisfaction with their self-image and this is why some are more susceptible to change than others. This is why some are more receptive to vocational rehabilitation services than others. It is important for social service workers to ask for opinions of the disabled living in poverty in order that they can evaluate the present conditions of these individuals lives and see whether or not they wish to change in their communities and in their individual physical environments. Many of these people have no idea that they could bring about a change in their lives and have given little thought to the possibilities of improving their living conditions. The concept of vocational rehabilitation in many of these instances is totally alien and incompatible with their life style. Rehabilitation workers working with the disabled in these areas must be cognizant of the fact that the most effective way to change people is to treat them in accordance with the status in life which they would like to achieve. If an individual is to change behavioral patterns he must be treated or rewarded in a manner different from that to which he is accustomed.

ROLE OF DEFENSE MECHANISMS IN ADJUSTMENT

While the three groups of factors discussed above determine the length of time required for adjustment to disability, the path to adjustment is best described by defense mechanisms. Defense mechanisms are psychological devices used by all to distort reality. Often reality is so harsh it is unacceptable to us. Therefore, we distort the situation to make it more acceptable. Defense mechanisms are used to satisfy motives which cannot be met in reality, to reduce tensions in personal interactions, and to resolve conflicts. To be effective they must be unconscious. They are not acquired consciously or deliberately. If they become conscious they become ineffective as defense and other mechanisms must replace them. For the major part of the remainder of this chapter we will look at the defenses most often employed by the disabled in the general order of their use.

Denial

Denial is an unconscious rejection of an obvious fact which is too disruptive of the personality or too emotionally painful to accept. Therefore, in order to soften reality the obvious fact is denied. Immediately upon onset of disability the individual denies it happened, but as the fact of the disability becomes so overwhelming to him that its existence can no longer be denied, he then denies the permanency of the disability. The newly disabled individual, while utilizing the defense of denial, will adamantly maintain that he shall be whole again, that there will be a miraculous cure, or that a new surgical technique will be discovered.

While there are few steadfast rules in human behavior, one is that rehabilitation at best can be only marginally successful at this point. Rehabilitation cannot proceed adequately until the client accepts the permanency of the disability and is ready to cope with the condition. This is what is meant by many professionals when they say a client must accept his blindness or his deafness. Denial is the front line of psychological defense, but it may outlast all other defenses. It is most persistently used by persons with deafness, blindness, and the plegias.

Withdrawal

Withdrawal is a mechanism which is used to reduce tension by reducing the requirements for interaction with others within the individual's environment. There are two dynamics which result from withdrawal. In order to keep from being forced to face the acceptance of the newly acquired disability, the individual withdraws. As a result of the client's changed physical condition, his social interaction is quite naturally reduced. His circle of interests as determined by friends, business, social responsibilities, church, civic responsibilities and family is drastically reduced. Thus, the client becomes egocentrically-oriented until finally his entire world revolves around himself.

Rather than functioning interdependently with his environment to mutually fulfill needs as our culture demands, he is concerned exclusively with his environment fulfilling his needs. As his world becomes more narrowed, his thoughts and preoccupations become more somatic. Physiological processes heretofore unconscious now become conscious. At this point he begins using another defense mechanism—regression.

Regression

Regression is the defense mechanism which reduces stress by avoiding it. The individual psychologically returns to an earlier age that was more satisfying to him. He adopts the type of behavior that was effective at that age but now has been outgrown and has been substituted for more mature behavior—behavior which is more effective in coping with stressful situations.

As the newly disabled individual withdraws, becomes egocentric, and hypochondriacal he will regress to an earlier age which was more satisfactory. This regression may be manifested in two manners. First he may, in his regression, adopt the dress, mannerisms, speech, etc. of contemporaries at the age level to which he is regressing. Secondly, he may adopt the outmoded dress, mannerisms, speech, etc. of the earlier time in his life to which he regressed. This second manifestation of regression is considerably more maladaptive since it holds the individual out to more ridicule which, at this point in his adjustment to his disability, quite possibly will result in more emphasis on the defense mechanism of withdrawal. This would be regressive as far as the adjustment process is concerned.

If reality is harshly pushed on him and his defenses are not working while utilizing the first three defense mechanisms, he may as a last resort become highly negative of those around him and negative in general. This negativism is demonstrated as an active refusal, stubborness, contradictory attitudes and rebellion against external demands. He may become abusive of those around him and may become destructive in an effort to act out the thwarting he is experiencing. This negativistic behavior is an indication the defense mechanisms he is employing are not distorting reality enough to allow him to adjust to his newly acquired disabled status. If, however, he is able to adjust and the defense mechanisms are effective to this point, he will employ the next defense.

Repression

Repression is selective forgetting. It is contrasted with suppression which is a conscious, voluntary forgetting. Repression is unconscious. Events are repressed because they are psychologically traumatic. As mentioned above the attitudes the client had relative to disability and the disabled has a major bearing upon his adjustment. If these attitudes are highly negative the client will have to repress them at this point if his adjustment is to progress. Until he represses them he will be unable to accept the required new body image.

Reaction Formation

When an individual has an attitude which creates a great deal of guilt, tension, or anxiety and he unconsciously adopts behavior typical of the opposite attitude, he has developed a reaction formation. In order to inhibit a tendency to flee in terror a boy will express his nonchalance by whistling in the dark. Some timid persons, who feel anxious in relating with others, hide behind a facade of gruffness and assume an attitude of hostility to protect themselves from fear. A third and last example is that of the mother who feels guilty about her rejection of a newborn child and adopts an attitude of extreme overprotectiveness to reduce the anxiety produced by her feelings of guilt. This example is seen more often in cases of parents with handicapped children.

In this new dependent role the disabled individual will feel a varying degree of hostility and resentment toward those upon whom he is so dependent—wife, children, relatives, etc. Since these feelings are unacceptable he will develop a reaction formation. The manifest behavior will be marked by concern, love, affection, closeness, etc.; all to an excessive degree.

Fantasy

Fantasy is daydreaming. It is the imaginary representative of satisfactions that are not attained in real experience. This defense mechanism quite often accompanies withdrawal. As the client starts to adjust to a new body image and a new role in life, he will develop a rich, overactive fantasy life. In this dream world he will place himself into many different situations to see how well he fits.

Rationalization

Rationalization is giving socially acceptable reasons for behavior and decisions. There are four generally accepted types of rationalization. The first is called blaming an incidental cause—the child who stumbles blames the stool by kicking it; the poor or sloppy workman blames his tools. "Sour grapes" rationalization is called into play when an individual is thwarted. A goal to which the individual aspires is blocked to him; therefore, he devalues the goal by saying he did not really want to reach this goal so much. The opposite type of rationalization is called "sweet lemons." When something the individual does not want is forced upon him he will modify his attitude by saying it was really a very desirable goal and he feels quite positive about the new condition. The fourth and last type of rationalization is called the doctrine of balances. In this type of rationalization we balance positive attributes in others with perceived negative qualities. And conversely, we balance negative attributes with positive qualities. For example beautiful women are assumed to be dumb, bright young boys are assumed to be weak and aesthetic, and the poor are happier than the rich.

The disabled individual will have to rationalize his disability to assist him in accepting the permanence of the disability. One rationalization may be that he had nothing to do with his current condition, something over which he had no control caused the disability. Another dynamic which might be observed is the adherence to the belief on the part of the client that as a result of the disability there will be compensating factors. For example, many newly blinded persons feel they will develop special competencies in other areas such as music, etc.

A paraplegic client's rationalization for his disability ran something like this: All of the men in his family had been highly active outdoors types. They all had died prematurely with coronaries. The client was a highly active outdoors type; however, now that he was severely disabled he would be considerably restricted in his activities. Therefore, he would not die prematurely. This logic resulted in the conclusion that the disability was positive and he was pleased he had become disabled. Granted, rationalization is seldom carried to this extreme in the adjustment process, but this case is illustrative of a type of thinking which must occur for good adjustment.

Projection

A person who perceives traits or qualities in himself which are unacceptable may deny these traits and project them to others. In doing so he is using the defense mechanism of projection. A person who is quite stingy sees others as being essentially more stingy. A person who is basically dishonest sees others as trying to steal from him. A person who feels inferior rejects this idea and instead projects it to others; i.e. he is capable but others will not give him a chance because they doubt his ability. These are examples of projection. With the disabled person many of the feelings he has of himself are unacceptable. Therefore, in order to adjust adequately he projects these feelings to society in general. "They" feel he is inadequate. "They" feel he is not capable. "They" feel he is inferior and is to be devalued. This type of thinking, normally, leads directly into identification and compensation.

Identification

The defense mechanism of identification is used to reduce an individual's conflicts through the achievement of another person or group of people. Identification can be with material possessions as well as with people. A person may derive feelings of social and psychological adequacy through his clothes ("The clothes make the man"), his sports car, his hi-fi stereo paraphenalia, etc. People identify with larger groups in order to take on the power, prestige, and respect attributed to that organization ("our team won"). This larger group may be a social club, lodge, garden club, college, professional group, etc.

In adjustment to his disability the client will identify with a larger group. It may be a group of persons with his particular disability, an occupational group, a men's lodge, a veteran's group, etc., but at this point in the adjustment process he will identify with some group in order to offset some of the feelings he has as a result of the projection in which he is engaging. If successful the identification obviates the need to employ the mechanisms of denial, withdrawal, and regression.

Compensation

If an individual's path to a set of goals is blocked and he finds other routes to achieve that set of goals, he is using the defense mechanism of compensation. A teenager is seeking recognition and acceptance from his peers. He decides to gain this recognition through sports. However, when he fails to make the team he decides to become a scholar. This is an example of compensation. Compensation brings success; therefore, it diverts attention from shortcomings and defects, thereby eliminating expressed or implied criticism. This defense mechanism is most often used to reduce self-criticism rather than external criticism. As the individual experiences successes he will become less preoccupied with anxieties relating to his disability and his lack of productivity.

Identification and compensation usually go together in the adjustment process. When the client starts using these two defenses he is at a point at which he may adequately adjust to the new body image and his new role in life.

In summary, it is difficult for one who has never experienced an alteration of the body to understand the traumatic reaction that persons have to such an occurrence. We must remember that in adults, the psychological body image is relatively fixed and that it is developed over a long period of time. Even when the actual anatomical body has been changed by a traumatic injury, the psychic is unable to adjust to this change for some long period of time. The long period of time in adjustment is a means of coping with an unpleasant experience. It slows down the change in order to allow the individual to adjust to it.

Our society puts great emphasis and importance on independence as a goal for all of us to strive toward. Independence generally has meaning in terms of masculinity, leadership and strength. The society very definitely devalues dependence and associates it with femininity, indecision, helplessness. Disability threatens independence, and this threat can be personally devastating to the individual especially in a society which overvalues independence.

Rehabilitation personnel see many people who respond to the stresses of disability in a pathological sense. When this has happened the psychological defenses against stresses have failed the individual. In this case, the individual has become extremely maladaptive; however, in most cases individuals will be able to adjust to their environment. Adjustment will always be made on the basis of the individual's coping ability, in other words, in terms of his own personality characteristics.

REFERENCES

American Psychiatric Association: *Diagnostic and Statistical Manual of Mental Disorders*. American Psychiatric Association, Washington, D.C., 1965.

Horace, H. B., and English, A. C.: *A Comprehensive Dictionary of Psychological and Psychoanalytical Terms*. New York, David McKay Company, Inc., 1966.

Moynihan, Daniel P.: The professors and the poor. *Commentary, 26,* No. 2, 1968, August.

Wright, Beatrice. *Physical Disability—A Psychological Approach*. New York, Harper and Row, 1960.

CHAPTER VIII

EDUCATIONAL AND PSYCHOLOGICAL APPRAISAL OF THE DISADVANTAGED[1]

JOHN J. CODY

What Does I.Q. Mean?
Mechanical Aptitude
An Inventory of Interests
Physical Skill Tests
Personality Testing
What Questions Can Test Results Answer?
Information Needed
Test Content
Norm Reference Group
Test Data and Other Information
Individual and Group Prediction
Test Results Have Value
Objective Information
Tests Can Open Doors
Tests as Diagnostic Instruments
Conclusion
References

A TRAINING PROGRAM in diesel engine mechanics initiated at the local vocational school will accommodate an additional ten candidates. This program is well-financed and is capable of providing,

---

[1]An annotated bibliography is provided at the end of this chapter. Please refer to this source for more complete information desired as you progress in this chapter.

without cost to the student, four months of technical training. Six people who appear on the welfare rolls or who are seen as needy individuals are to be recommended to take part in this training program. When the list of possible candidates is examined, the task of selecting only six out of all the potential candidates seems nearly impossible. Case histories on each person are relatively incomplete and in many cases the only consistent information is that provided by the public schools. In many cases the candidates attended school elsewhere or failed to establish much of a record while in school. Many dropped out long before the time they were supposed to graduate and others attended school as long as thirty to forty years ago.

A typical example of a school drop-out and a likely candidate is Sam, age twenty-two. Sam dropped out of high school at age sixteen. He is now married and has three children. He might be called socially different or disadvantaged. He found little success in school. He has found little satisfaction or success in his jobs. He began as a grocery store clerk stocking shelves and lasted approximately seven weeks. He was discharged because he failed to arrive at work on time for over a week. Sam was referred to the welfare office because his family had no food. He was recommended for a job as a filling station attendant. In this position he lasted four weeks and again his employer let him go. In this case Sam failed to appear at work because he could not stand the cold weather. About three months ago he took another job, this time as a maintenance worker. It was a job inside in which he was not required to go out in the weather and it did not require strenuous physical labor. His job consisted of sweeping and picking up paper in thirty offices. After three weeks of work, Sam could not be located for a period of ten days. When he was found, he indicated that this job was boring and he refused to return to work again. With this kind of record, should he be among those considered for the training program? How might a welfare worker get some assistance determining whether or not Sam might benefit from this program?

In the case outlined above, as in many others, three questions seem of major significance. First, can Sam learn the material to be presented in this training program? Second, does he have the aptitude and the skills to progress in such a training program? Third, if he can learn and if he has the aptitude and skills, will he take, and work, to hold a job as a diesel mechanic after completion of the training program? Each of these questions is of grave importance since Sam is not the only concern. What about the Joe's and the Harry's and the Tom's who will not have an opportunity to participate in this program if Sam and others like him are selected? The questions raised, then, are based on two concerns. The first of these is the welfare of Sam. The second is equally important and that is the welfare of other men who might not get the opportunity to participate in the program if Sam were selected ahead of them.

An immediate reaction to such problems might be to select some standardized test or tests to provide answers to these questions. Tests should be available that will let us know whether Sam could learn, whether he has the skills and aptitude and whether or not he has the motivation to work.

An instrument that many would select to help answer the question whether Sam can learn material to be presented in such a program would probably be identified as an I.Q. test. According to *Webster's New World Dictionary of the American Language,* I.Q. is defined as the level of mental power or ability. If it is assumed that an I.Q. test will provide the information needed, then the resulting test results can be examined to see what meaning they might have.

In order to determine if tests are available to determine whether or not Sam has the skills and the aptitude to progress in such a program, we would have to know what aptitudes and what skills are required. If it were determined that no more than normal coordination or finger dexterity or relatively simple manipulative skills are needed to perform in this occupation and that the aptitudes are those which are related to mechanics, we could then get results from tests which carry labels indicative of these skills and attitudes—a mechanical aptitude test and finger dexterity test.

The same kind of exploration might be employed in seeking answers to the third question—"Will Sam work given the training and an opportunity to take a job?" One might contend that the components of such answers would include whether or not he was interested in the job and whether or not he saw this particular kind of work as meaningful or meeting some need. An interest inventory and an inventory of personality are thought by many to provide such information. After Sam has been tested and the results are returned, a history of Sam's previous on the job performances and a set of test scores would be available.

Sam's test record is not very impressive. His score on an I.Q. test was an equivalent of an I.Q. of 75. Compare this I.Q. of 75 with failing school marks and one might conclude that Sam would have difficulty completing or competing in a class which required many of the skills required in a typical school setting. A score on the mechanical aptitude test placed him at the 45th percentile. This should be interpreted to mean that 55 percent of the population to whom Sam is compared (the norm group) scored higher on the test of aptitudes for mechanical work than has Sam or that 45 percent of the population is below him. Results of the finger dexterity test indicate that Sam scored at the 85th percentile. Only 15 percent of the norm population surpassed his performance on this instrument. Perhaps stating this situation positively, Sam scored above 85 percent of the persons in the norm population, would help point out that apparently Sam can handle objects with his fingers better than most people in the norm group.

Finally, Sam had an above average 65th percentile ranking of his interests in mechanical work. This indicates that his interests, as measured by the inventory, are more closely related to interests of mechanics than 65 percent of other people in the norm population.

WHAT DOES I.Q. MEAN?

The 75 I.Q. score tells us that Sam is below the average (mean) score. He scored approximately 25 points below the mean (100 I.Q.). It is important to note that even though the test is labeled I.Q., it is a general achievement test. It tells us how Sam responds to items for which he should have learned answers while growing up in the society. It does not tell us what his potential to learn is or whether he had normal opportunities while growing up. This is an important concept to understand. It is the one area in standardized testing that perhaps causes more trouble than any other.

I.Q. stands for intelligence quotient. It is computed by dividing chronological age (CA) into the mental age (MA). By and large, the mental age is determined by what the majority of people learn by a certain time in life. In other words, if a 22-year-old man (CA) learned what most other 22-year-old men (MA) learned, it would be 22 divided into 22 which equals 1. Multiply that 1 by 100 and the I.Q. equals 100 which would be a normal intelligence quotient (I.Q. $= \frac{\overline{MA}}{CA} \times 100$). If a 22-year-old man (CA) knows about what the average 16-year-old boy (MA) knows, he would have an I.Q. of approximately 73 ($\frac{16}{22} = .72 \times 100 = 73$).

The I.Q. score does not tell us what Sam might have learned had he been more highly motivated. It does not tell us how much potential Sam has for learning, given ideal conditions. One of the reasons there is much confusion in this area is because many people fail to distinguish the difference between I.Q. (intelligence quotient), an empirically-defined quotient, and the concept of intelligence.

Intelligence is a construct, an idea, a notion or a word invented to describe a concept, which has to do with our ability or potential to learn. Just because a test writer defines it differently does not change the generally accepted connotation of the word. About the only excuse we might provide for confusing these two terms or for looking at them as having the same meaning would be a basic assumption that the best predictor of future performance is present and past behavior. In this sense, then, an I.Q. score would be indicative of a range or level at which Sam had performed at a given point in time and also a predictor of how he would perform in the future. One must be extremely cautious in making such an interpretation, however. Despite the likelihood that the prediction of another test score from this score is reasonably sound, the generalization to include all areas of achievement such as classroom learning or success on the job is, at best, hazardous. This is especially true when the major concern is about the individual himself. If we are only concerned at a point in time with one person, perhaps this assumption is never necessary. Only when we are concerned about selecting from among many people do we become concerned about predicting. In fact, this is the only time when probability theory has much to contribute. If the selection of one man is likely to disenfranchise another man, it is better that we select from among many with the best possible and with the most objective information we can obtain. In such a case a test score becomes a valuable index of prediction, but it does not become an indicator of potential of the one selected. In Sam's case, with a poor record in school and the 75 intelligence quotient, one might conclude that he is a poor risk. In this sense "poor" is a relative term (poor compared to whom?). Are there many other people whom we might consider for this particular training position who have a higher I.Q., better background in school than Sam? This fact will probably affect how this 75 I.Q. is interpreted. We cannot tell at what level Sam must score so that success in the training program is guaranteed. Sam or someone else might achieve a 135 I.Q. and still fail the mechanics course. Too often it is concluded that Mr. X could have succeeded since he has the potential (130 I.Q.). At the same time Mr. Y (85 I.Q.) does succeed. Intelligence, or potential to learn, is something about which little is known except that test scores used alone are *not appropriate* estimates.

MECHANICAL APTITUDE

Let us move on to the next score—the 45th percentile on a mechanical aptitude test. Again, we are faced with an achievement situation. Sam has scored at a point above which 55 percent of the population who has taken this test have scored. He is again below the middle of the norm group who took the test. More than half the people who took this test scored well above him in this achievement performance. The question is, what does this performance mean? Does it mean that Sam really can't learn mechanics or does it mean that up to this point Sam has not learned as much as the majority of people in the norm group who have been exposed to the usual things in society? The latter is closest to truth. Sam has not learned up to this point what over half the other people who took it have learned in relation to mechanics. It might even be well to examine the test and see precisely what it is that Sam has not learned that other people have. We have no data which indicate that because he has scored at the 45th percentile he does not have sufficient aptitude or he has not learned enough up to this point to give him a background to learn more in mechanics. What we do know is that, by and large, on the whole, on the average, compared to most other people who took this exam and who have been followed up that Sam will probably not do as well as the people who scored much higher on the examination.

Another question that arises is whether or not Sam's score at the 45th percentile is lower than, higher than, or approximately equal to other people who may be considered for this training program. It should be remembered that it is on the basis of further comparisons that his score on the test will have real meaning. Sam may be the highest of all those who are eligible for participation. On the other hand, he may be significantly lower than others. Then, too, this 45th percentile must be considered along with the I.Q. score of 75 and match him against other applicants for the same position in the program.

Case workers should be aware that aptitude is a word used by psychologists to identify areas of special skills or knowledge. In some contexts the idea of an aptitude is related to natural or inherited talent. Even though this may be the case, there should be no confusion between these ideas and notions and the results of tests that claim to measure aptitude. Such tests measure what a person has learned just as all other achievement tests. The content of an aptitude test cannot be differentiated from items included in tests with different names. Perhaps it is best to think of aptitude tests as measuring achievement in a narrow set of skills or body of knowledge. Compare this to the contention to the notion that I.Q. tests sample a broad area of knowledge. With this comparison in mind, the advantages of measuring knowledge specific to mechanics for a person who wishes to pursue a career in a mechanical field seems reasonable. The fact that the content included in aptitude tests is not necessarily a good sampling of the field mechanics is a fault in test construction. In the future more sophisticated tests may be developed that will truly measure that which is required of persons in a special field such as mechanics.

AN INVENTORY OF INTERESTS

Now we can examine the next score—the 65th percentile on the interest inventory in the mechanical technical area. What this means is that 35 percent of the norm population indicated a greater interest in the area than Sam. On the other hand, he indicates a greater interest in this area than do 65 percent of the same population. An examination of the actual interests inventoried will indicate quite clearly that there is very little that deals explicitly with the task of being a mechanic. Although people have responded in a way to this inventory that indicates a range of responses, this does not in any way indicate that these are necessarily interests which are required for success in a specific occupation. The reliability coefficients which indicate that the people tend to respond similarly over long periods of time do not indicate that these are truly reflective of interests essential to success as a mechanic. They merely indicate that people respond similarly over time to the same statements concerning preference. However, it does tell us that Sam feels or thinks the way other people who are mechanics tend to think or feel about the topics covered in this inventory.

PHYSICAL SKILL TESTS

No matter what test is used to measure a physical skill, the results have no more meaning than the activity used to test the individual and the circumstances surrounding the testing situation. In this case the test required that small (about the diameter of a 50 cent piece and about 3/4 inches thick) pieces of metal be taken from slots (1/4 inches deep), turned completely over and inserted in the same slot (either flat side down). A person who can turn pieces in less time than most other people demonstrates that he can use his fingers, in a coordinated way, better than most other people. The results do not indicate that he will have a superior touch when it comes to "feeling" the correct contact of threads between a nut and bolt. It does not tell how well a man will be able to use a screwdriver blade and the slot of a screw head. Coordinated finger movement (finger dexterity) may be related to these skills or may even be essential. However, it is not the total composite of such skills, and it may not be the most important variable in the use of hands in an auto mechanic's job.

In Sam's case we know that he has better coordinated finger movement than most people in the norm reference group. From this

information it seems reasonable to conclude that Sam has no handicapping physical restriction that might interfere with his learning
the hand skills required in the job as a diesel mechanic.

PERSONALITY TESTING

Finally, you are probably wondering why scores on a test of
personality have not been mentioned. In a clinical situation a
psychologist, who is familiar with the theoretical constructs which
underlie the test, can relate the results to the total behavior pattern
of the client. Test results have little meaning unless they are verified
by the behavior patterns of the individual in other situations. The
use of the results of personality tests for selection purposes in a
public agency seems a questionable practice. Without carefully
controlled preparation for taking such tests and equally controlled
conditions for the interpretation of results, personality tests may be
dangerous tools. Since most personality tests have questionable
validity, the use of the results with anyone other than the client
certainly has ethical considerations. As a general rule, there is so
little information that can be gleaned from personality testing that
there seems little value in considering them further.

WHAT QUESTIONS CAN TEST RESULTS ANSWER?

What has been said here is that the three questions that were
raised initially—first, can Sam learn?; second, does he have the
skills and aptitude?; third, will he work given the training?—
cannot really be measured by a test score or a set of test scores. The
scores obtained on each of the tests (which both measured achievement) gave us some indication of what Sam had learned in relation
to the content measured by the tests administered. In the case of the
interest inventory we found out how Sam responded to different
preferences of activity. These choices of preferences may or may
not have been related to the job requirements of a diesel mechanic.
None of the scores individually told us with any degree of complete-
ness what he has really learned that would be essential for completion of a course in diesel mechanics. Even taken together, the test
scores do not give us a clear profile of whether or not Sam can
succeed. Without further investigation, we do not know whether or
not Sam compares favorably or unfavorably with others who will

participate in this same training program.

Test scores are only a part of a total picture which will have to be developed more intelligently before decisions can be made with Sam or about him. Someone might say, well, if better tests had been selected than those that were administered to Sam, then more precise statements concerning the likelihood of his success could be made. Although there may be some tests which are technically superior to a small degree than those which were employed, and there may be tests or inventories which offer a broader range of measurement in terms of labels of behavior, a different set of tests would not be of much more help. The fact of the matter is that test data are not available to answer the kinds of questions that were asked initially. The questions that test results can answer are: How well can Sam perform in comparison to other people in tests of knowledge achievement (aptitude and I.Q.)?; How much skill has Sam developed with his hands in comparison to a specific norm group? We can find answers to these questions from test scores. In addition an inventory of interest can tell us how Sam compares to a norm reference group in respect to activities that he prefers.

"Will Sam work, given the opportunity, if he completes the training program?" Perhaps the best place to seek this answer is from Sam himself. Prediction of work behavior in the next year, two years, or three years would probably be much better based on his past work performances and Sam's personal commitment rather than scores on tests. The point of this latter discussion is to indicate that the results of all tests are tenuous. At best, they are estimates of what the real situation is. Not only are they estimates, but they are inclusive of measuring error also. The best test estimate, like other estimates, is usually inaccurate and is added to by the error in the measuring process itself. There is good reason to contend that the use of test data in making decisions with people should be limited to situations when qualified and experienced help is available. It is for this reason that psychologists talk about psychological workups rather than psychological testing. What this means is that test results are taken in connection with much more personal information. All the information is considered and then some judgment is forthcoming. It is fortunate that in some cases in which the welfare worker must deal, there is no information of high quality or of an objective nature other than test data. In these situations one must admit the weaknesses of test data, and when the reason for decision making is judged significantly important so that such data are all that is available there is no question that, used with caution, achievement tests can serve a useful purpose.

At this point, let's look at Sam's case again. How could his test scores be used in a reasonable way? First, the condition imposed was that six applicants be selected. In such a situation three concerns arise with the worker in field. Sam is an important individual and he should be given every bit of assistance possible. Each of the other individuals who are to be considered are important also and they, too, deserve *just* consideration. The agency itself must maintain its reputation of competent assistance, or it will not be in a position to help anyone. It is important for these reasons to make the best selection possible.

An I.Q. test administered to each of the applicants will result in a means of comparing these candidates on how much they can demonstrate they know about the general areas the test measures (it is a test of what a person has already learned). In this way not only is a general I.Q. score available, but it can be compared with the scores of the other applicants for the same position also.

A manipulative test can be administered to each applicant also, so that it can be determined how each compares with the normal population and how they compare to one another. This measures how well the individual at this point in time can use his hands. Similarly a mechanical aptitude test can be employed to ascertain, within limits, how much the applicants have learned about this element of the mechanical field compared to a normal reference population. Again, comparisons can be made among the applicants.

Finally an interest inventory could be employed. The results of this instrument can best be used to identify extreme dislikes as compared to the normal population. Comparisons among applicants is perhaps meaningless in this case since the nature of these interests as measured apparently have little predictive value when it comes to succeeding on a job. Personality inventories are worthless without a comprehensive psychological workup and even then they are best described as experimental. The general use of such instruments even for research reasons outside a carefully controlled clinical situation is always a dubious practice.

With this kind of information, Sam can be considered along with other applicants. His past work performance, along with other factors incorporated from his case history, will aid the worker in interpreting the test results. When an evaluation of the individual is made, he can be compared to other applicants. Selections can then be based on who seems to have the best qualifications. It is important to *predetermine* those factors which are most important for selection to this program. In this way personal bias of the case worker can be reduced. Given a case worker's involvement in his client's needs, it is likely that Sam's welfare is more important than the objectivity required by a *just* selective process. If criteria for selection are identified *after* all data have been gathered, it seems that each case worker is more likely to allow his preference for a particular client to determine which data are most meaningful. In this way the value of objective data is lost because the requirements of the proposed task or program no longer contribute significantly to the selection of the individual. This is precisely the charge that minority groups now raise when they feel personal preferences have led to discrimination against them when they were truly qualified to fill a given position.

If possible, the test results of applicants could be compared with others already accepted into the training program. This would provide another index for comparison. Such a comparison may be important. Since Sam will be in a class, moving at the tempo required of other class members, it seems reasonable to see if he is equal to, above or below these people in his level of knowledge and skill related to class activities. Once all the information to be used in decision making is gathered, the decision rests with the welfare worker and perhaps his client. It is essential to know with complete accuracy what the test results really tell you. Only then is the decision based on an intelligent evaluation of facts. It should be noted that no scores have been identified as the point that might be used as minimal limits for success in a training program. Without locally determined norms (data gathered from the community and from the specific program) statements concerning scores below which success is impossible or unlikely are impossible.

Before we explore this topic further, let us briefly review some basic considerations in test utilization.

INFORMATION NEEDED

Before a test is selected, one should first establish the purpose for the testing based on what information is needed. In most cases the purpose for testing is determined by the peculiar nature of the circumstances relating to an individual's predicament. As in the case of Sam, a finger dexterity test or a mechanical aptitude test seemed most appropriate. But for most other situations diesel mechanics would not be the focus of the decision and these tests may not be deemed relevant. Tests should not be administered just for the sake of having data available. When the person taking the test is aware that there is a reason for taking it, he will be more likely to take the test in a sincere manner.

TEST CONTENT

When selecting tests to suit the purpose identified, it is not always possible to obtain the exact information desired. In fact this is the usual state of affairs. Recall that none of the questions that we wished answered in Sam's case could really be answered by results of tests. What a test is purported to measure (test validity) and what it measures are not a matter of instant discovery. It involves the time consuming practice of stating as clearly as possible the purpose of testing. Then tests must be sought that appear to measure the same attributes that will provide the data necessary to answer the questions asked, or in other words, fulfill the purpose of testing.

Three sources are recommended when the welfare worker seeks information about tests. The first is Buros' *Measurement Yearbook*.[4] An up-to-date volume of this publication should be available to case workers. The seventh edition is the last published volume. This book lists tests by title, author and test category. It is one of the best sources of all published tests. Not only are the tests identified, but they are reviewed also. Although the reviews may be helpful to some, they may be the greatest deterrent to the proper use of tests also. Reviews of tests must be written in a general context so that the information will be of interest to many people. A specific review for a single purpose might be relevant to only one reader. As a consequence, some test users ignore the specific questions they ask, or the specific purpose for testing and get lost in the generalizations of a review. This comment serves as a word of caution. The Buros resource is only one step in test selection.

A second source to consider is the manual printed by the test publisher. An examination of a few of these manuals should be very enlightening. On first reading it is easy to conclude that a particular test will provide you with just about all the information you will ever need. Read the manual again and it will become clear that even the most hopeful advertisers will limit their claims to the interpretation of the results of this test and relate them to considerably more information. Again, caution is raised. The tester must read the test manual carefully, relate this information to the reviews in Buros, and once more compare the conclusions to the original purpose for testing. Test selection is a decision-making process which must be guided by information, but the final criterion is dictated by the relationships among facts as interpreted by the test selector—you—not the test author or reviewer.

Third, the test itself should be examined carefully. This examination should include an inspection of the items, the method of responding (forced choice, sentence completion, etc.) and the intent behind the construction of the test. Only by a thorough examination, item by item, of the instrument can a determination be made as to whether it suits the purpose for which it is being considered. Try this procedure and then take the test yourself before forcing it upon someone else.

A good example to help emphasize these points is an I.Q. test. Many writers of test manuals fail to make the reader aware that I.Q. and the concept of intelligence are usually not synonymous notions. Usually mention is made that these tests will identify potential. Unless a careful examination of the intent of the test in relation to the items in the test is undertaken, a determination of the value of the test may be distorted. When it can be observed readily that the items require no more than previous learning to obtain correct responses, then the meaning of "potential" can be examined. Of course, the inappropriateness of discussing "limits" to how much can be learned will stand out. In the case of Sam, as in most other situations, the results of tests will yield some information that, if used correctly, may aid in the decision-making process.

NORM REFERENCE GROUP

Since nearly all standardized tests are based on the theory that the traits measured are distributed normally in the population, consideration of the norm reference group is critical. It is important to understand also that nearly all standardized tests are designed to discriminate. Without test items that discriminate, statistical item analysis in the usual application becomes nonsense. Take these two notions together and think about them for a minute. An achievement test has items which have been selected initially because they seem to represent desired, required or sampled areas of knowledge. Further selection occurs as the items prove useful in discriminating between people who score high on the total test and those who score low. If a test item is answered correctly by 60 percent of those who score in the highest quartile of those taking the test and only 2 percent of those who score in the lowest quartile answer it correctly, it is usually considered a "good" item. It discriminates well. So the items that make up a test are selected on the basis of how well they discriminate between those who know and those who do not know the content of the test.

The composition of the norm reference group is extremely important because they are the ones whose performance has been used to determine which are the most discriminating items. They, too, are the individuals who make up the group to whom other test takers will be compared. For both reasons norm reference groups are important. Sam's case provides an interesting illustration of these points. If Sam is being compared against a group that doesn't represent a similar geographic area or a population with whom he is not going to be compared in his work, the percentile rank may not have much meaning for the purpose intended. Comparisons have meaning when the norms represent the group with whom the individual is to be compared and when the test content is really reflective of the information required to succeed. In Sam's case neither of these conditions were met. However, with a little additional effort Sam's performance could be compared to the performances of other applicants and members of the class in diesel mechanics. In this way some value of the testing could be salvaged. Since there is little known about the relationship between the content of the tests and the content of the course, even such comparisons provide very limited information about Sam's knowledge and the requirements for success in the field of mechanics.

In order to make test scores take on more meaning, an assumption that each person in the norm reference group had an equal exposure and an equal motivation to learn the material included as content is usually made. The fact of what has been labeled as cultural difference or educational deprivation denies such an assumption. For this reason predicting rate or amount of future learning for a person when you are concerned about his or her welfare as well as efficiency in selection is always hazardous.

TEST DATA AND OTHER INFORMATION

About the highest expectations we can have for results of standardized tests is that they provide some information that will help us assist people. No single test score should be interpreted outside the context of what else is known about the individual. Since human beings are indeed complex, it seems clear that the best test gives us only an extremely small part of the total picture. If we really wished to learn whether Sam was capable of completing the mechanics courses and of taking and holding a job, we would get some insight from how he behaved in similar situations previously. If a refinement of this prediction was preferred, perhaps an in-depth interview with Sam to see how he would tell it could be added. Other than allowing Sam to begin the courses and keep observations to continually refine the prediction, perhaps the past experiences of Sam considered along with his personal evaluation of the situation would be the best indicator of what would happen, provided Sam had the basic skills to succeed.

In other situations, unlike Sam's, considerations such as physical impairments (bad hip, sore back, arthritis) could be most important. It really isn't as important to know whether such ailments are physically or psychologically based. The fact that an individual uses them as reasons for behavior may be the most important variable. Helping a client with such problems is a different kind of problem requiring cooperative action of medical, psychological, welfare and perhaps legal personnel. In such a situation tests may or may not be used by professional workers.

INDIVIDUAL AND GROUP PREDICTION

A discussion of the individuals in the process of group prediction seems essential in any coverage of testing. When discussing the kind of client with whom welfare workers are concerned, the necessity is underscored. By definition, welfare recipients are atypical of the normal population and as such the results of tests converted to standard scores based on a normal population have little application. Due to the fact that the usual generalizations do not apply, individual attention is employed to assist them in society. There is no way that prediction statistics can be applied to the individual. Prediction holds only when you make statements about groups.

In Sam's case, for example, we are unable to predict how he will do in the training course. If we have one hundred people from whom we are to select six and we apply statistical prediction, we can tell whether or not Sam ranked near the top of the group of one hundred in mechanical ability. We could also indicate that, in general, the people who score higher on the test will achieve better in the training session. At the same time we know from past experiences predicting with such tests that with a normal population our predictions about success and failures will be accurate roughly 67 percent of the time (or as an average over thousands of predictions, 67 times out of 100). Stated differently we would be wrong roughly 33 percent of the time (or as an average over thousands of predictions, 33 times out of 100). Would Sam be among those we made correct predictions about or would he be among those about whom we are mistaken? By chance alone, with no information about the people in such a situation (assuming a normal population again), our prediction would be accurate 50 percent of the time. As in the case of the test score, we know that half of the people will succeed and half fail, but we can't identify in which half Sam or George will fall. We have no statistical way of making this decision about Sam. It remains a clinical or professional decision.

When our concern is as much for rehabilitating one individual at a time as it is for the selection purpose we serve, then group prediction is no panacea. This statement is not intended to reflect negatively on situations when efficiency in selection is the major criterion. It is meant only to indicate that selection efficiency should not and in fact is not the sole concern in many cases. There are two cases then when predictive statistics provide no help: (1) when one person at a time is being considered and (2) when the purpose of testing is not selection alone.

TEST RESULTS HAVE VALUE

Discussion of the limitations of standardized testing which accent the limitations of testing are usually harked as "cry wolf." In this particular situation the emphasis on the limitations of test results is due to the situation of the welfare worker. Due to the nature of welfare work, standardized tests have value only when used with great care. To make the best use of tests in such a situation is difficult, time consuming, and subject to misinterpretation. There are three good reasons for using test data in a welfare worker's situation: (1) use tests to gather information in an objective way; (2) use tests to open doors for clients rather than to close doors for them; and (3) use tests, if possible, in a diagnostic way.

OBJECTIVE INFORMATION

A world that was simple would not require concerns about test results. But since it is not, it is common to find disagreements or conflicting evidence about common things. A group of teachers might disagree on whether Jennifer knows enough about arithmetic to hold a job as a cashier in an outdoor theatre. A group of case workers would disagree as to whether or not Mike is coordinated enough to work on high-rise apartment construction. Although tests cannot provide answers to these questions, they can provide objective data about Jennifer's math skills and Mike's coordination. The test does not like or dislike the taker. Scores are not affected by a person's looks or what he says. At a given point in time a test result is an objective evaluation of what a person has learned up to this time.

None of us will deny the value of objectivity as a criterion in appraisal. Each of us has felt the sting of what we believed to be biased judgments about ourselves. A standardized test, with its objective scoring procedures, does eliminate scoring or judging bias. The reader should be cautioned that objectivity refers only to the scoring procedure employed. A great deal of subjectivity is employed in selecting the items included in the test. Objectivity in testing is similar to objectivity in baseball. Each player is entitled to three strikes before he strikes out. The rule is objective. It is the same for short, tall, black, white, fast and slow. The subjectivity occurs when the decision is made as to what is a strike. Similarly in testing, the scoring may be objective, but the selection of test items may be affected by several forms of bias or prejudice.

TESTS CAN OPEN DOORS

Since the validity—what the test purports to measure—may always be questioned, the safest procedure is to use the results of tests as door openers only. Instead of placing the test result in a place where it is used to identify those to be selected and those to be eliminated, it might be used only to help admit people. An example should help make this point more clear. If Sam were judged ineligible for the training program in mechanics due to his apparent inability to handle tools in his previous job as a service station attendant, test results might help him. If he scored high enough on a finger dexterity test, this could be used to suggest that he could handle tools under different conditions. In this situation the test results would be used to give Sam another chance. Test scores may not be sufficiently high to roll back previous failure situations, but there is always the possibility that they might open doors.

In a similar situation George had not shown any difficulty in handling tools in previous jobs, but fell at the bottom of the scoring range on the finger dexterity test and he was made ineligible for the training program. In this situation the test was the selector and it closed a door.

When these two situations are compared, it seems reasonable to conclude that tests can be used to open doors or to close them. Since there is a great deal of error in measurement and since we know so little about what constitutes success, perhaps test results can serve welfare workers best if the data are used to open doors only. Further, it should be noted that test scores are usually a substitute for more preferred information such as observations on the job. Since this is the case, then the results of a test should never be substituted for the observation if both are available unless the individual is protected from negative evaluation (Sam's case). In the case of Sam such a substitution was made as a possibility of opening a door for Sam. In this way all advantages were given to the client. In George's situation the test results were used inappropriately. His past performance was not held in highest priority. The consideration in both cases relates back to the purpose of testing, "Can the man handle tools?". In Sam's case the test results indicate that he has skill with his hands and fingers even though he hasn't had much success demonstrating this skill in the past. At least in the test situation he demonstrated he had the skills. It might be concluded that given the proper circumstances in a job he would demonstrate these skills again.

George on the other hand demonstrated his skills on the job. He, too, has such skills, even though the test results indicate he may lack them. In this situation it is impossible to claim George can't handle tools when he already has demonstrated he can. It is more defensible to use test results to open doors for clients, as in Sam's case, rather than to close them as in George's case.

TESTS AS DIAGNOSTIC INSTRUMENTS

Up to this point tests have been discussed in relation to how valuable they are in determining how a person compares to others in relation to what he has learned. This information was used to help make decisions about whether or not the person would succeed or fail. Another use of tests is to determine what specifically an individual has learned and the things he has not learned. If a person scores poorly on a test and there are specific areas of knowledge that he lacks and these are detected, then perhaps he can be helped. Assisting an individual to gain some knowledge would not only help raise the test score, but theoretically should better prepare him for other activities. A look at a mechanical aptitude test should help illustrate this point.

In this particular test there are four items that deal with the turning direction of gear combinations and five items that require the selection of a specific kind of wrench for specific nuts and bolt heads. This total of nine items were missed by Sam when he took the test. In addition he missed three items that required discrimination between sizes and shapes. He also missed two items that required simple arithmetic functions. While missing these last five items he answered correctly seven other items. Four of these answered correctly required simple arithmetic functions and three of them required discrimination between sizes and shapes. It was impossible to define characteristics which differentiated between the content of presentation of those size and shape problems that were answered correctly, and incorrectly. The same was concluded after examining the arithmetic items missed and those correctly answered. Since essentially the same knowledge and skill level were required to answer each of the arithmetic items, there wasn't much that could be concluded from the two that were missed. Some might conclude that the errors were due to inattention or carelessness.

The items missed most consistently in the gear train problems were related to the direction gears turned. Would it be possible to teach Sam or someone else the principles behind gears and how to figure out the direction each turns? If this knowledge could be learned—in say, thirty minutes—would that knowledge increase his mechanical aptitude?

An assumption that ability to identify which way gears in combination turn is an important element in success as a mechanic may be true but it is difficult to substantiate. If such skill can be taught, it seems likely that the learner will score higher in the test. It might also mean that he has one less weak area in mechanics. Steps should be attempted to remove this weakness after it has been discovered.

If we look at the problems of selecting the best wrench for the specific kind of nut or bolt head, a similar situation is observed. Sam demonstrated almost no cognizance of a hex nut taking a hex-shaped wrench. He apparently was unaware that a pipe wrench has an open side and a closed side. If pressure is applied so the pipe can twist out the open side, this is a less efficient use of the wrench than using it to take advantage of the closed side and then applying pressure so that the grip tightens on a pipe in the closed end. Could Sam learn this given an hour or less? If he could, then would he have a "higher" aptitude? At least it could be said that if he learned these skills he would score higher on the test. Perhaps if he were taught in a reasonable way he could probably select the correct wrench and use it properly. This is how some tests can be employed diagnostically.

Not all tests can be used to analyze skills because they are not designed with enough items in specific areas to discover strengths and weaknesses. In most cases group I.Q. tests fail in this non-diagnostic category. Just because a test was usable in an analytic way for one person does not indicate it will be useful for all unless the test is designed to be used in such a way. Some people get their total score on a test by sporadic answering. That is, they answer some of every section correctly, but seem not to do exceptionally well in any single category. Ordinary tests are of little value under these conditions.

Unfortunately, no group standardized test has been developed for true analytic or diagnostic purposes. Few such tests are available since they must be designed so specifically for each case that they have little use in other situations. The content of skills and under-standings have not been well enough defined at this time so that really sound group analytic or diagnostic tests have been developed. Some attempts have been made in the area of intelligence and learning disability, but they have been restricted almost exclusively to individual testing. The value of their results has not proved sufficiently beneficial to be recommended at this time.

All the tests discussed have been group tests designed for use with adults. Tests have been designed for use with children also. In fact most tests designed to measure I.Q. that are administered individually have well-developed norm groups for children. For the most part the description of how a child solves problems in the different parts of these tests is much more meaningful than the scores on the subtests or on the total test. Use of such instruments should be restricted to those who have specialized training in their administration. The same principles that apply to the use of group tests apply to individual assessment instruments also.

An additional note of caution seems warranted. There is a strong temptation for adoption purposes, foster home placement and in institutional decisions to use the results of individual tests as the "true" measure of "ability." Such interpretations are no more justified for individual testing than for group tests. Observations of behavior during testing, medical and physiological examinations and psychological consultation may result in decisions about a child's level of intellectual functioning. No test has been published that provides data to substitute for such professional coordination. Children as well as adults should be protected against the test and tell syndrome so prevalent in our society.

CONCLUSION

One of the disadvantages of working with people is that few inventions have been brought forward to lessen the responsibility of the individual case worker. The personal qualms one has as a result of making decisions about or with other humans remain of constant concern in the task of working with other people. The fight to maintain objectivity in making such decisions finds only minimal support in the technology of testing. Test results provide specific and limited information. The true value of this information must be determined by the individual case worker. The amount of influence meaningful and nonsense test data will have in the decision process is left to the individual case worker also. With conscientious study, careful selection, administration and honest interpretation, the results of standardized tests may be helpful. The use of tests should not be taken lightly. Too frequently results of tests are used to substitute for the acceptance of professional and human responsibility. One of the most urgent pleas to the welfare worker is, "Know your client and know the test thoroughly." Use tests and their results as you would any other confidential and questionable information.

Professional judgment may include the use of tests when their content reflects the purpose for such measurement and if the results are used as one sample, along with many others, of the behavior of the individual. Results of tests should be employed as only samples of responses to specific situations which are related to the type of behavior in which we are interested. Even under these conditions tests can only be an aid to, not substitute for, professional judgment.

REFERENCES

1. Amos, William E., and Grambs, J. D.: *Counseling the Disadvantaged Youth*. Englewood Cliffs, New Jersey, Prentice-Hall, Inc., 1961, pp. 30-52.

   In this book of selected writings a chapter entitled, "Appraisal of Disadvantaged Youth," presents a logical background and some empirical data to support a position concerning the inappropriateness of testing the disadvantaged.
2. Anastasi, Anne: *Psychological Testing*. New York, Macmillan Co., 1961, pp. 105-133.

   One of the best theoretical and at the same time clear discussions of reliability has been presented by Anastasi in this edition of her writing. For those who are concerned with this notion in measurement, this selection is recommended.
3. A.P.A. Committee on Psychological Tests: Technical recommendations for psychological tests and diagnostic techniques. *Psych Bull*, Supplement, *51*:2, 1-38, 1954.

   This supplement contains the technical recommendations for psychological testing as prescribed by the American Psychological Association. It may be shocking to some to see what is considered to be unethical practice.
4. Buros, Oscar K. (Ed.): *The Seventh Mental Measurements Yearbook*. Highland Park, New Jersey, Gryphon Press, 1973.

   Perhaps the best reference for published tests and reviews that is available. This selection is a "must" for those involved with test selection and use.
5. Cronbach, Lee J.: *Essentials of Psychological Testing*. New York, Evanston, London, Harper and Row, 1970, pp. 142-144.

   Cronbach provides one of the best discussions of validity available. From a position of logical structure and technical accuracy, this is indeed a worthwhile selection for those interested in reading more about this concept.
6. Guilford, J. P.: *Psychometric Methods*. New York, Toronto, London, McGraw Hill Co., 1954, pp. 5-17.

   For those interested in the theory of testing, this Guilford selection has much to offer. It is not necessarily a simple presentation, but as far as this type of theory is concerned, it is a straightforward presentation.

7. Lien, Arnold J.: *Measurement and Evaluation in Learning.* Dubuque, Iowa, Wm C. Brown, 1967, pp. 45-59.

Perhaps one of the easiest to understand presentations on the reasons for testing is presented by Lien in this selection. It won't take long and it has some interesting challenges.

8. Rothney, John W. M.: *Methods of Studying the Individual Child: The Psychological Case Study.* Waltham, Mass., Toronto, London, Blaisdell Publishing Co., 1968, pp. 1-4, 5-19.

From one of the best writers in field comes this precise description of the case study method. Rothney uses only the necessary number of words to express concretely "Why a Case Study" and the "Contents of a Case Study."

9. Rothney, John W. M.; Danielson, P. J., and Heimaun, R. A.: *Measurement for Guidance.* New York, Evanston, London, Harper & Row, 1959, pp. 226-281.

A clear picture of how test data relate to other information is provided in this brief selection. The briefness and the preciseness of the writing simplifies the presentation.

10. Terman, Lewis M., and Merrill, M.: *Stanford-Binet Intelligence Scale.* Boston, Houghton-Mifflin Co., 1960, pp. 5-28.

Some may wonder how an I.Q. test is designed. This selection describes the historical derivations of the Binet briefly and clearly points out the strategies in the new Stanford-Binet.

11. Tyler, Leona E.: *Tests and Measurements.* Englewood Cliffs, N.J., Prentice-Hall, 1964, pp. 70-87.

An analytic presentation of personality testing is presented for those who wish to pursue this topic in more depth. Easily understandable is the nature of this solid writing by Tyler.

12. Wechsler, David: *The Measurement and Appraisal of Intelligence.* Baltimore, Williams & Wilkins Co., 1958, pp. 24-37.

For a review of an empirical approach to testing, this classic is offered for your inspection. Anyone sincerely interested in this field should read this selection.

PART III

CHAPTER IX

REFERRAL AND ELIGIBILITY: INPUT FOR THE REHABILITATION PROCESS

STANLEY J. SMITS

"REFERRAL" AND "ELIGIBILITY DETERMINATION" are technical terms for the mechanisms which feed the rehabilitation process. These mechanisms have their origins in legislative mandates, agency traditions, and the decision-making processes of the rehabilitation counselor. While seemingly clearcut, fixed phenomena, these input mechanisms vary considerably from agency to agency and within any given state rehabilitation agency.

A person is technically in a "referred status" with the state rehabilitation agency as soon as the following information has been communicated and recorded: name, address, stated disability, age, sex, and referral source. In other words, the referral mechanism is nothing more than making the agency formally aware of the existence of an individual who, in the opinion of himself or others, is a potential rehabilitation client. Once referred, a person is eligible for rehabilitation services if he is able to meet the criteria which differentiate rehabilitation clients from persons not in need of help and from persons who are the prime responsibility of other agencies. These criteria are the existence of a disability which poses a vocational handicap and sufficient residual vocational potential so that rehabilitation services can reasonably be expected to be successful, i.e. lead to employment.

To become a *bona fide* client of a state rehabilitation agency, a person must make contact with the agency; establish the fact that he has a disability; show that the disability interferes with the achievement of his vocational potential; and have sufficient residual potential that the current array of rehabilitation services will *probably* render him employable. It is the purpose of this chapter to describe the mechanisms through which a person becomes a client of a state rehabilitation agency; to clarify the responsibilities of the people involved; to pinpoint the obstacles which may eliminate people who should be accepted for services; and to suggest ways to increase the effectiveness and efficiency of the input procedures.

THE REFERRAL PROCESS

The referral process is a simple mechanism made complicated by the variety of sources from which potential clients are referred or solicited, the human elements upon which it is dependent, and the systematic obstacles which interfere with its accomplishment.

Sources

A person may be referred to the state rehabilitation agency by himself, by another person, or by an agency or organization. Self-referrals are dependent upon motivational and informational resources infrequently found among chronically unemployed, lower socioeconomic populations. When referrals are made by other people, it is typically done by a member of the prospective client's family, a neighbor, or his family physician. Public and private community agencies, schools, churches, institutions, and civic groups are the major sources which refer potential clients to state rehabilitation agencies. McGowan and Porter (1967) insist that continuous contact must be maintained with the following agencies:

> *Health Agencies*—Public and private, general
> and special hospitals, clinics, TB sanitariums,

mental institutions, physicians, public health service, nursing groups, artificial appliance companies, etc.

Employment and Guidance Service Agencies— Public and private employment offices, public and private guidance and counseling agencies such as B'nai B'rith, Urban League, and other voluntary religious, racial, and welfare units.

Welfare Agencies—Public and private assistance and relief agencies such as Red Cross, Salvation Army, Catholic Charities, and state and city public welfare.

Educational Institutions—Public, private, and denominational schools and colleges, including schools for the handicapped and business colleges.

Special Interest Agencies—Crippled children's services, heart associations, TB associations, polio foundations, and other organizations of and for the handicapped.

Insurance Companies—State workmen's compensation boards, Bureau of Old Age and Survivor's Insurance, and private and fraternal insurance companies.

Civic Service Groups—Lions, Masons, Kiwanis, Rotary, YMCA, etc.

Religious Group—Protestant, Hebrew, and Catholic social and helping organizations.

Employers—Especially those who have handicapped employees on their payroll who are good workers.

Labor Unions—Have a vested interest in rehabilitation services and will often take an active role in the rehabilitation of their members (p. 45).

Cooperative Relationships.

Many state rehabilitation agencies develop and maintain cooperative relationships with agencies known to be involved with large numbers of potential rehabilitation clients (Table 9-I). The most frequently encountered relationships are with state employment service programs, public welfare departments, sheltered workshops, and the special education units of the local school systems. When formal arrangements have been made in writing, as is often the case with agencies such as the state employment service, public welfare departments, and the Department of Labor training programs, the referral procedures are rather specific and uniform throughout the state. When informal cooperative relationships are established, the degree to which the agency or program is utilized is up to the discretion of the counselor. The best possible referral

Table 9-I

State Vocational Rehabilitation Agencies Having Cooperative
Relationships with Selected Programs

Type of Program	Per Cent
State Employment Service	95
Public Welfare Offices	93
Sheltered Workshops	90
Local School System (Special Education)	88
BOASI	85
Workmen's Compensation Agency	81
Psychiatric Hospitals	81
General Hospitals	76
Vocational Education Schools	76
Tuberculosis Facilities	75
Schools for the Retarded	71
Medically Oriented Rehabilitation Centers	69
Schools for the Deaf	68
Correctional Settings	68
Schools for the Blind	66
Vocationally Oriented Rehabilitation Centers	65
Department of Labor Training Programs	61
Comprehensive Rehabilitation Centers	47
Multiservice Centers	37
State-Operated Rehabilitation Centers	35

Source: Sontag, C., & Wilson, M. E., Jr. *Principles for Developing Cooperative Programs in Vocational Rehabilitation.* Washington, D. C.: U.S. Dept. of H. E. W., 1968. (IRS No. 70-1, p. 40)

relationship exists when (1) cooperative agreements have been developed in written form, and when (2) staffing arrangements have been made so that counselors who are employees of the state rehabilitation agency reside within the cooperating agency.

State rehabilitation agencies have received substantial numbers of referrals from public welfare. In fact, welfare has at times been the major source of rehabilitation referrals (Dishart, 1964). These referrals have had primary or secondary disabling conditions of a physical, mental, or emotional nature and often concomitant vocational handicaps stemming from their economic disadvantagement.

Non-Agency Referrals.

An individual who voluntarily seeks help from a state rehabilitation agency is a somewhat unusual, but preferred, applicant for services. By virtue of his initiative in seeking services, he indicates motivation for change, some degree of acceptance of his need for help, and a self-image which says "I am responsible for, and capable of, taking action to improve my circumstances." His situation is quite different from someone in the same technical status, i.e. "referred," who is merely a name and address sent from one agency to another.

The involvement of family, friends and/or the family physician in the referral process adds a more personal touch than is typically true when it is handled by an agency. It does not insure a higher level of motivation to participate in the rehabilitation process; nor does it indicate a willingness to accept help. It does, however, indicate to the prospective rehabilitation client that significant others in his intimate circle want him to change and that in their opinion outside help is needed. Their interest, concern, and opinion add an element of interpersonal pressure which may stimulate more active involvement on the part of the participant himself.

Responsibilities

Administrative personnel within the state rehabilitation agency generally assume the responsibility for initiating, developing, maintaining, and monitoring the formal written agreement with cooperating agencies and institutions.

The rehabilitation counselor is typically responsible for casefinding within his geographical territory. He carries out formal agreements and initiates and utilizes informal agreements with a variety of referral sources. Although he is often already burdened by an excessively large caseload, the rehabilitation counselor is given the prime responsibility for casefinding. He may discharge this responsibility in a number of ways. The responsibility for "casefinding" and for "public relations" often amount to the same thing.

During the last five years, many state rehabilitation agencies have been hiring people for positions as "support personnel" or "rehabilitation aides." These support personnel are given case-finding responsibilities and they help prospective rehabilitation clients process their applications for service. Their responsibilities in the area of "casefinding" include:

1. Routinely contacts private and public community agencies to secure likely referrals.

2. Explains services of the state agency to private and public community agencies.

3. Explains agency services to neighborhood or indigenous groups.

4. Participates in surveys. (In one instance, rehabilitation aides participated in a house-to-house survey of an impoverished neighborhood looking for disabled individuals with vocational handicaps.)

5. Makes initial contact with a referral received from some outside source.

6. When individuals fail to follow through on referrals, makes some sort of personal contact, including home visits.

7. Keeps check on referrals to insure that prospective clients are promptly and efficiently contacted (Lucas and Wolfe, 1968; p. 55).

In summary, the personnel employed by the state rehabilitation agency are responsible for casefinding activities ranging from formal agreements with other state, federal, and community agencies through door-to-door contacts in impoverished neighborhoods.

Obstacles

The "on-paper" referral may or may not want to change his current life style; he may or may not be willing to share in the responsibility for his own rehabilitation. Dishart (1964) found that 18 percent of the 84,699 people he studied while they were in a "referred" status eventually terminated as "not accepted for services" for one of the following reasons: (a) they refused to accept the services, (b) they did not respond to communications or appear for appointments, or (c) the agency was unable to locate or contact them.

There are a number of obstacles which mitigate against public welfare recipients becoming *active* referrals to the state rehabilitation agency. Many of these obstacles are also encountered by the severely physically disabled. Some of the obstacles have their origins in the population to be served; whereas others originate in the agency, e. g. its tradition, philosophy, procedures and personnel; still others exist as part of society's approach to solving the problems of the poor. There are three major obstacles which, in the opinion of this writer, prevent many public welfare recipients from making a serious attempt to secure help from state rehabilitation agencies.

Many public welfare recipients exist in a state of perpetual referral. The fact that they are referred to so many different agencies and programs with so many delays, forms, questions, and evaluations, resulting in so little actual help, tends to make them skeptical. Help-seeking behavior becomes extinguished. Their compliance with referrals is stimulated not by an expectation of help, but rather by a need to please the referring agency so that funds and/or services are not revoked. For example, welfare selects one of its AFDC recipients for referral to the Work Incentive Program (WIN); WIN refers the client to the state rehabilitation agency when they discover that she has a medical disability; the state rehabilitation agency refers the client to a voluntary rehabilitation facility to have an evaluation of work potential completed; the rehabilitation facility sends the client back to the state rehabilitation agency for recommended treatment; the state rehabilitation agency sends the client to a different rehabilitation facility to develop work habits and work tolerance in a work adjustment program; after six weeks of work adjustment training, the client is sent back to the rehabilitation counselor with the recommendation that she be placed in employment; the rehabilitation counselor, in turn, passes this recommendation on to the WIN counselor who, in turn, sends the client to the state employment service (SES) for job placement; the SES places her on a job as a maid; one week later she gets fired during an argument with her employer; she returns to the welfare office for help. Several weeks later she is again referred to the state rehabilitation agency either directly by the welfare office or indirectly through a related program. This time she fails to keep her appointment with the rehabilitation counselor, who eventually closes her case from referral status because of her lack of motivation. Interspersed in this fictitious, but entirely possible, example are numerous referrals to physicians and clinics for medical evaluation and treatment; and from one caseworker to another or from one counselor to another within the agencies involved.

There is a great deal of apathy on the part of the public welfare recipient and the rehabilitation counselor with respect to his entry into the rehabilitation process. The prospective client does not necessarily come to the rehabilitation agency of his own volition; he may be hostile, angry, and resistive to help (Kunce and Cope, 1969); he may resist the middle-class values and goals of the agency through passive-aggressive expressions of dependency (Goldin et al., 1967); he is oriented to immediate and short-term goals rather than goals achieved through lengthy treatment processes (Kunce and Cope, 1969). The rehabilitation counselor, on the other hand, is faced with a prospective client who makes irrational and angry demands and who responds to offers of help in an ungrateful manner (Goldin et al., 1970); who has "poor educational skills, low levels of occupational aspirations, poor work histories, and transportation problems (Wilson, 1967; p. 12);" and who frustrates the counselor intensely with his motivational structure which runs counter to middle-class values (Thoreson et al., 1968).

Interagency cooperation is disrupted by distrust, competition, and a lack of communication. There seems to be "a feeling of distrust between the older, established, programs and the new poverty programs (Cohen *et al.*, 1966; p. 52)." There is an alarming lack of information on the part of welfare, the employment service, and WIN personnel regarding the rehabilitation services available from facilities and from state rehabilitation agencies (Smits and Walker, 1970). "To date there has been little cooperation between community action programs and state vocational rehabilitation agencies. Each agency's view of the other is in many cases characterized by negative attitudes and stereotypes. Such attitudes have led to a lack of initiative in developing cooperative relationships and at times have resulted in direct avoidance of mutual professional contact (Feinberg and Cohen, 1969; pp. 48-49)." "The attempt to integrate or coordinate community rehabilitation services runs afoul not only of professional boundaries but also of agency domains. Agencies with overlapping areas of responsibility are often reluctant to cooperate. Agencies are frequently drawn into competition for scarce commodities—state or federal funding, community recognition and support, and even clients (Benson and Allan, 1969; p. 179)."

The three problems described above indicate an environment in which referrals are difficult to initiate and complete in a manner which would best prepare a public welfare recipient to enter into, and maximally benefit from, the rehabilitation process. Suggestions will be made in a later section of this chapter as to steps which can be taken by the practitioner and others to minimize the negative elements encountered in the referral process.

ELIGIBILITY DETERMINATION

"Eligibility" is a test to determine whether or not an applicant for services is entitled to services under the provisions of the Vocational Rehabilitation Act as amended. A person is eligible for services from a state rehabilitation agency if he has:

1. A mental or physical disability with resulting functional limitations or limitations in activity;
2. A substantial handicap to employment caused by the limitations resulting from such disability; and if there is
3. A reasonable expectation that vocational rehabilitation services may render the individual fit to engage in remunerative employment.

In making its determination of eligibility, the state rehabilitation agency must rely upon the expert opinion of physicians and psychologists to establish the existence of a disability. The rehabilitation counselor, however, is responsible for much of the judgment involving the vocational aspects of the case.

Establishing A Disability

Public Law 333 liberalized but complicated the criteria to be used in the establishment of a disabling condition. Prior to 1965, disability was a medical concept, except for mental retardation, and the physician's report either confirmed or denied the applicant's alleged problems. The 1965 amendments described "eligibility" for rehabilitation services as a certification that (1) the handicapped individual has a physical or mental disability which constitutes a substantial handicap to employment, and (2) vocational rehabilitation services may reasonably be expected to render him fit to engage in a gainful occupation. "Physical or mental disability" was defined as:

> A physical or mental condition which materially limits, contributes to limiting, or, if not corrected, will probably result in limiting an individual's activities or functioning. It includes behavioral disorders characterized by deviant social behavior or impaired ability to carry out normal relationships with family and community which may result from vocational, educational, cultural, social, environmental, or other factors (*Federal Register,* 1966, 401.1; p. 499).

The intent of the extension to include "behavioral disorders" was to make rehabilitation services available to a larger number of disadvantaged people. The traditional concept of disability as the "ticket" for admission to rehabilitation services persisted, however, and agencies felt compelled to uncover sufficient evidence to justify a diagnosis of "behavioral disorder" and to so label the disadvantaged people it decided to serve. The end result was described by the National Citizens Advisory Committee on Vocational Rehabilitation:

> It is unfortunate that individuals who are vocationally handicapped by the various conditions of social disadvantage must be 'diagnosed' as suffering from a behavior disorder to be eligible for service. It seems particularly unfortunate to stigmatize as behavior-disordered an individual whose 'deviant behavior' is an inability to hold a job because his schooling stopped at the second grade (1968, p. 29).

A disadvantaged individual may establish the fact that he is disabled by having a medical disability and following the traditional screening procedures; or he may do so by having a behavioral disorder. The procedures used to substantiate a behavioral disorder are much more ambiguous and variable than those used to substantiate a medical disability.

Medical disabilities are established by a medical examination. Medical information is needed not only to establish the disabling condition, but also to determine what rehabilitation services, if any, will help the applicant achieve a vocational objective. According to McGowan and Porter (1967), the purposes of the medical diagnosis are:

1. to establish, through competent medical judgment including psychiatric or psychological evaluation as appropriate, that a physical or mental impairment is present which materially limits the activities which the individual can perform, as one aspect of determining the individual's eligibility for services as a disabled person;
2. to appraise the current general health status of the individual, including the discovery of other impairments not previously recognized, with a view to determining his limitations and capacities;
3. to determine to what extent and by what means the disabling condition can be removed, corrected, or minimized by physical restoration services; and
4. to provide a realistic basis for selection of an employment objective commensurate with the disabled individual's capacities and limitations   (p. 56).

Many public welfare recipients have medical disabilities stemming from inadequate health care, nutritional deficiencies, and unhygienic living conditions. Mental retardation rates are excessively high in urban and rural slums (WICHE, 1969). People with serious medical problems are less mobile, often becoming trapped in rural and urban low income areas from which their healthy peers have greater opportunity to escape.

The process of establishing a behavioral disorder involves either a psychiatric or psychological evaluation. The typical process begins with the rehabilitation counselor whose responsibility it is to accumulate evidence of a *pattern* of maladaptive behavior on the part of the applicant. This information, or evidence, usually comes from people in the community who have had a chance to observe the applicant, e.g. friends, relatives, teachers, employers, etc. If the counselor is able to gather observations which reflect a *pattern* of behavioral problems over a period of time, he refers the applicant to a psychiatrist or psychologist with a summary of the evidence. The psychiatrist or psychologist is then responsible for indicating whether or not the applicant has a behavioral disorder.

At least one agency employs people with a minimum of thirty hours of graduate study in psychology who are called "vocational rehabilitation counselor psychologists" to determine whether or not a behavioral disorder exists by reviewing the evidence, but without face-to-face contact with the applicant (Benedict, 1967). Table 9-II presents examples of the behaviors which the counselor may

Table 9-II

Examples of Evidence Used in Establishing Behavioral Disorders

In the Home

A. Shy, withdrawn, lack of communication with other family members
B. Home psychologically broken with conflict, quarreling and fighting
C. Family chronically dependent upon public assistance and community
D. Staying out very late at night or all night against parental rules
E. Persistent disobedience
F. Persistent lying
G. Lack of social experiences, so that behavior is socially innappropriate

In the Community

A. Immaturity—unable to adjust to responsibility in community
B. Arrest for theft, vagrancy, petty crimes, etc.
C. Chronically unemployed
D. Destruction of property, cruelty, and other anti-social acts not detected by law
E. Dropped out of school
F. Persistent quarreling, fighting or other unacceptable acting out
G. Excessive drinking, drug abuse, etc.
H. Dishonorable discharge from military service (pattern of bad conduct)
I. Destruction of property (two or more instances)
J. Repeated blow-ups under pressure
K. Will not compete with others
L. Difficulty in most interpersonal relationships
M. Very poor personal appearance

In the School

A. Reports of School Misbehavior
   1. Excessive shyness and withdrawn behavior
   2. Excessive tardiness
   3. Fighting and quarreling
   4. Disobedience
   5. Stealing
   6. Destruction of property
   7. Cruelty
   8. Daydreaming
   9. Poor interpersonal relationships
   10. Poor attitude
   11. Evidence of truancy

   Source: Georgia Office of Rehabilitation Services, Personal Communication, March, 1972.

use to substantiate a behavioral disorder. The key concept is that of a *pattern* of maladaptive behavior. A single incident of disruptive or inappropriate behavior is not sufficient evidence to establish this type of disability. The maladaptive behavior must persist over a period of time and have existed in two or more social settings.

Establishing an Employment Handicap

The disability, established through the procedures described above, must constitute an employment handicap in order to qualify the applicant for services using the second criterion. The employment handicap may be the direct result of the disability, as say in the case of the recently blinded accountant. In other cases the employment handicap may be related to the disability through attendant medical, psychological, vocational, educational, cultural, social, or other environmental factors:

> Examples of attendant factors are a lack of marketable skills, low-educational level, community and employer prejudices and attitudes concerning disability, long-term unemployment, unstable work record, belonging to a disadvantaged group, residence in ghetto areas or pockets of poverty, long history of dependency and poor attitudes toward work, family, and community (McGowan and Porter, 1967; p. 87).

In other words, many of the same behaviors (Table 9-II) which are used to substantiate the existence of a behavioral disorder also affirm the employment handicap. Chronically unemployed public welfare recipients have little or no difficulty meeting this second criterion for eligibility for rehabilitation services.

Expectation of Employability

The final hurdle for our disabled, employment-handicapped applicant for rehabilitation services has to do with establishing a reasonable expectation that the outcome of the services will be a gainful occupation. "Gainful occupation" is defined to include:

> employment in the competitive labor market; practice of a profession; self-employment; homemaking; farm or family work (including work for which payment is in kind rather than in cash); sheltered employment; and home industries or other gainful homebound work (*Federal Register,* 1966, 401.1; p. 499).

The determination of the applicant's potential for gainful employment after receiving rehabilitation services is a counselor judgment. In arriving at his decision, the counselor should consider all of the information about the applicant which he has been able to gather, e.g. medical, psychological, sociocultural, and vocational.

Applicants with severe disabilities or complicated problems make the judgment of potential a "tentative" decision on the part of the counselor. Public Law 333 provided for extended evaluation in cases such as these. A rehabilitation counselor may delay a final decision on employment potential until after vocational services have been provided for a period of no more than six to eighteen months. The regulations state that necessary services:

> may be provided during a period not in excess of 18 months in the case of an individual whose disability is (1) Mental retardation, (2) deafness, (3) blindness, (4) paraplegia, quadriplegia, and other spinal cord injuries or diseases, (5) heart disease, (6) cancer, (7) stroke, (8) epilepsy, (9) mental illness, (10) cerebral palsy, or (11) brain damage, and not in excess of 6 months in the case of an individual with any other disability (*Federal Register,* 1966, 401.21).

The public welfare recipient, if sent for extended evaluation, would probably be referred to a rehabilitation facility for vocational evaluation, work evaluation, and work adjustment training. (These services are described at length in Chapter 10.) "Vocational evaluation" is the process of assessing an individual's physical, mental, and emotional abilities, limitations and tolerances in order to predict his current and future employment potential and adjustment. It is different from, but complements, "work evaluation" which is any assessment of strengths and weaknesses which uses work as the means, vehicle, or focal point of the evaluation (Roberts, 1970; p. 13). "Work adjustment training" refers to a series of structured activities designed to develop work tolerance and to establish a concept of oneself as a worker.

Other Considerations

State rehabilitation agencies have limited financial and personnel resources. They are unable to serve all of the possible applicants who would be eligible for services using the above criteria. The regulations state that:

> The state plan shall set forth the criteria to be used in selecting eligible individuals for services when services cannot be provided to all eligible persons who apply. Such criteria shall be designed to achieve the objectives of the vocational rehabilitation program to the fullest extent possible with available funds (*Federal Register,* 1966, 401.26).

Therefore, it is possible that public welfare recipients may be eligible for services through a behavioral disorder in financially limited states and still not receive them. They may be given a low priority within the state plan, with the result that their services may be delayed or actually denied.

SUGGESTIONS FOR PRACTITIONERS AND ADMINISTRATORS

Throughout this chapter, the writer has overtly and covertly described variables which often interfere with the public welfare recipient becoming accepted for services in state rehabilitation agencies. In this section, several suggestions are offered which hopefully will offset some of the problems.

The starting point in serving the public welfare recipient is an *attitudinal commitment* to doing so. Unlike other applicants who may actually seek out the rehabilitation counselor, the disadvantaged applicant must be actively pursued by the agency. It is easy to avoid service to people who are themselves avoiding the services. Administrative mandates will not be met until individual rehabilitation counselors commit themselves psychologically to working with this difficult population. Probably the best way to obtain a commitment of this sort, is to identify counselors who want to work with this caseload and assign them to it as specialized counselors. Attitude change is difficult, sometimes impossible, to achieve. However, there are many rehabilitation counselors who would enthusiastically accept the challenge of working with public welfare recipients.

Rehabilitation counselors, selected because of their interest in working with the disadvantaged, should be given specific information through inservice training programs to help them (a) understand the characteristics of the disadvantaged; (b) relate to other professionals and agencies which have direct contact with the public welfare recipient; (c) identify behavioral disorders from interview, observational, and consultative information; (d) acquire techniques for behavior management and for motivating self-improvement; (e) maximize the usefulness of support personnel as outreach and liaison workers, and (f) develop appropriate placement sites for rehabilitated public welfare recipients.

Administrators can help the counselor by providing the emotional and logistic support he needs when working with a caseload of difficult clients. Improved supervision and an accurate accounting method which credits counselors for the amount of work they do would help reduce the threat felt by counselors entering new service areas.

Administrators can help develop referral sources by following the suggestions of McGowan and Porter (1967):

—Maintain an open door policy for new referrals to agency. Let referral sources know your agency would like more referrals.

—Make periodic examination of sources of referrals to assure a continuing flow of cases from all potential community resources.

—Assign each counselor responsibility for maintenance of contact with certain agencies and potential sources of referrals.

—Prepare formal referral forms for use by referral sources.

—Develop prompt and cordial reporting back procedures to referral sources on referrals made.

—Give prompt attention to referrals; some people are seeking help at the time they apply.

—Maintain a record of referrals by date of referral, source, and actions taken for evaluation and followup purposes.

—Provide for preliminary evaluation as basis for acceptance or rejection of referrals. Advise the client, referral agency or other interested parties of decisions and reasons (p. 45).

Counselors can improve services to public welfare recipients by *accepting the challenge of using their professional skills.* The professionally-trained rehabilitation counselor has been equipped with communication skills; he has been taught how to motivate specific behaviors; to set realistic goals; to reinforce achievement; to establish supportive relationships; etc. The public welfare recipient who passively resists being processed through a social change system, whose value system and linguistic skills impede communication with middle-class representatives of social and rehabilitation agencies, and whose motivation for self-enhancement has long ago approached extinction, presents the type of challenge that the rehabilitation counselor has been uniquely prepared to meet.

In essence, the challenge to the rehabilitation agency, especially to its counselors, is to engage in two rehabilitation processes: *personal* and *vocational.* They must engage in a "personal" rehabilitation process in which the client is given the necessary motivational sets and personal attributes which will allow him to enter the "vocational" rehabilitation process the way the traditional physically disabled person has entered it, i.e. motivated to become employed. For many years the referral and eligibility determination stratagems of the state rehabilitation agency have systematically screened out the person with low motivation for self-enhancement, especially if he had behavioral problems. The success of the vocational rehabilitation process has, in part, been predicated on the motivation of the physically disabled individual to regain his role as a worker. Counselor successes were based as much on their diagnostic skills as on their treatment skills. The vocational rehabilitation process relied upon diagnostic testing and screening, medical and educational remediation, and job placement as its major ingredients. These services were sufficient because the disabled person was psychologically predisposed to succeed. The rehabilitation counselor's task was to help the client use the process and community resources to his best advantage. The initial tasks are quite different with the clientele who will enter the vocational rehabilitation process through the *recruitment* efforts of the state rehabilitation agencies' counselors and support personnel from public welfare referral sources.

CONCLUDING COMMENTS

Excerpts from a paper by Wilson (1967) summarize very clearly the referral and eligibility determination mission of the state rehabilitation agency with reference to the disadvantaged:

> Aggressive case finding can be instrumental in identifying and bringing disadvantaged persons—into the vocational rehabilitation process.—vocational rehabilitation services must be sold through action rather than words to the disadvantaged and to community referral resources (pp. 11-12).
>
> State vocational rehabilitation agencies have been conducting programs which tend to screen-out rather than screen-in questionably motivated persons.—To meet the challenge of rehabilitating the culturally disadvantaged, applicants must be qualified for services rather than disqualified.—the applicants with poor educational skills, low levels of occupational aspiration, poor work histories, and transportation problems must be screened-in rather than out.—*Only screened-in applicants can be helped* (Italics added.) (p. 12).

REFERENCES

Benedict, T.: Preparing diagnosticians for working with the culturally disadvantaged. In Ayers, G. E. (Ed.): *Rehabilitating the Culturally Disadvantaged*. Mankato, Minnesota, Mankato State College, 1967, pp. 37-42.

Benson, J. K., and Allen, D. L.: Organizational structure and rehabilitation of the disadvantaged. In Kunce, J. T., and Cope, Corrine S. (Eds.): *Rehabilitation and the Culturally Disadvantaged*. Columbia, Missouri, Regional Rehabilitation Research Institute, University of Missouri, 1969, pp. 172-201.

Cohen, J. S., Gregory, R. J., and Pelosi, J. W.: *Vocational Rehabilitation and the Socially Disabled*. Syracuse, N. Y., Syracuse University, 1966.

Dishart, M.: *A National Study of 84,699 Applicants for Services from State Vocational Rehabilitation Agencies in the United States*. Washington, D. C., National Rehabilitation Association, 1964.

Federal Register (Part II, Vol. 31, No. 9). Washington, D. C., The National Archives of the United States, January 14, 1966.

Feinberg, L. B., and Cohen, J. S.: *Rehabilitation and Poverty: Bridging the Gap*. Syracuse, N. Y., Syracuse University, 1969.

Georgia Office of Rehabilitation Services. Personal communication, March, 1972.

Goldin, G. L. et al.: *Dependency and its Implications for Rehabilitation*. Boston, New England Rehabilitation Research Institute, Northeastern University, 1967.

Goldin, G. L. et al.: *Psychodynamics and Enablement in the Rehabilitation of the Poverty-Bound Client*. Lexington, Mass., Heath Lexington Books, 1970.

Kunce, J. T., and Cope, Corrine S. (Eds.): *Rehabilitation and the Culturally Disadvantaged*. Columbia, Missouri, Regional Rehabilitation Research Institute, University of Missouri, 1969.

Lucas, H., and Wolfe, R. R.: *Use of Support Personnel in Vocational Rehabilitation*. Washington, D. C., Social and Rehabilitation Service, 1968, (RSS 69-13).

McGowan, J. F., and Porter, T. L.: *An Introduction to the Vocational Rehabilitation Process*. Washington, D. C., Vocational Rehabilitation Administration, 1967 (Revised Edition) (RSS 68-32).

National Citizens Advisory Committee on Vocational Rehabilitation. *Report of the National Citizens Advisory Committee on Vocational Rehabilitation*. Washington, D. C., U.S. Government Printing Office, 1968.

Roberts, C. L.: Definitions, objectives, and goals in work evaluation. *Journal of Rehabilitation, 36*(1): 12-15, 1970.

Smits, S. J., and Walker, R. A. (Eds.): *A Comprehensive Manpower System: The Work Incentive Program and Rehabilitation Facilities*. Washington, D. C., International Association of Rehabilitation Facilities, 1970.

Sontag, C., and Wilson, M. E., Jr.: *Principles for Developing Cooperative Programs in Vocational Rehabilitation.* Washington, D. C., Social and Rehabilitation Service, 1968 (RSS 70-1).

Thoreson, R. W. et al.: *Counselor Problems Associated with Client Characteristics.* Madison, Wisconsin, Regional Rehabilitation Research Institute, University of Wisconsin, 1968.

WICHE: *Disability and the Disadvantaged.* Boulder, Colorado. Western Interstate Commission for Higher Education, 1969.

Wilson, M. E., Jr.: Rehabilitating the culturally disadvantaged: A challenge for State Vocational Rehabilitation Agencies. In Ayers, G. E. (Ed.): *Rehabilitating the Culturally Disadvantaged.* Mankato, Minnesota, Mankato State College, 1967, pp. 1-16.

CHAPTER X

THE REHABILITATION PROCESS: A DESCRIPTION OF THE SERVICE DELIVERY SYSTEM

RALPH R. ROBERTS, JR. AND LARRY R. DICKERSON

COOPERATION BETWEEN vocational rehabilitation agencies and welfare agencies for the benefit of the person being served is not new, but neither has it been extensive. The reasons most likely include the welfare worker's failure to see any vocational potential in his clients, the vocational rehabilitation counselor's preference for working with those clients who give greater promise of quick closures, and the welfare recipient's understandable reluctance to trust services that may or may not bring employment, and even if they do the financial advantage might be insignificant.

Today there is a thrust to make such cooperation between welfare and rehabilitation more extensive. Probably the reasons for the new emphasis include the rapidly rising costs of welfare services, the greater numbers applying for welfare rolls, the desire to make taxpayers out of tax-consumers, and the suspicion that many welfare recipients are clever frauds. Indeed, present proposed legislation contains an evaluative program that would exclude many poor "non-disabled" from receiving income assistance, as well as provide rehabilitation services for the poor who are "disabled" on a high priority basis. Some of the details of the proposed legislation will be discussed later in the chapter.

Regardless of the intent, it seems apparent that high level decisions and program planning have set the stage for large numbers of public assistance recipients to appear in the caseloads of vocational rehabilitation counselors. For some who have already worked with welfare clients it may represent only a more complex caseload and a greater effort, but for those who have not it will represent a new and relatively unknown venture. For these counselors we would like to discuss some aspects of providing rehabilitation services for welfare recipients.

WHO IS THE PUBLIC WELFARE CLIENT

Initially, it seems important to identify the person on welfare and look at him from the viewpoint of his unique characteristics and those characteristics that he shares with the general population of rehabilitation clients.

There appears to be many ways that he is like other rehabilitation clients. It goes without saying that he is poor, too poor to support himself and his family, lives in very deprived circumstances and often suffers from chronic illness that reduces further his ability to cope with a very difficult life situation. In the past, when a welfare recipient received services it was due to some accompanying disability since being "just poor" or "just disadvantaged" did not constitute a sufficient reason for providing rehabilitation services. Such thinking has changed, at least theoretically, with the passage of Public Law 333 in 1965, which essentially extends rehabilitation services to the large number of culturally and socially disadvantaged who could not previously qualify for services. It is this group that encompasses the people on welfare, who can be regarded as simply a special subgroup, one that has turned to any of a number of financial support programs that are lumped under the general heading of *welfare.*

To get a clearer picture of the welfare client, we should first take a closer look at the larger population of the poor and disadvantaged. Campbell, Kaplan, and Mahoney (1969) summarize the personal and social characteristics of the group as follows:

Income. Any United States citizen with an annual per capita income of $590 or less, or belonging to a family with an annual income of less than $3,000 could be defined as poor. In 1962 these people comprised 20 percent of our national population, or about 35 million citizens; the number is larger today.

Location. The crises of our central cities have focused attention upon poverty in these areas; however, while 8 million of the poor (referring to 1962 figure above) may live in the central cities, some 12 million live in surrounding suburbs and 15 million live in rural areas (about 5 million being rural farm poor, 10 million being rural non-farm poor).

Sex. Deprivation has greater incidence among women, who generally earn less than men in the same jobs, and who are less apt to find jobs in the top pay and/or prestige brackets. The problem is especially acute for female heads of households.

Education. The hard-core poverty of rural areas and ghettos is intensified and perpetuated by inferior educational facilities, by indifferent use of the facilities available, and possibly by the self-excusing conviction of poverty area teachers that their students are "incapable" of substantial achievement in learning.

Many children of low-income families drop out of school relatively early despite a high regard for education by some parents. The parents seem to have trouble communicating their esteem for education. Of those qualified, fewer low-income family children enter college than children of higher-income families. Recently there seems to be more interest in higher education among disadvantaged youth; often their inability to meet admission standards of colleges is a direct heritage of the crippling ghetto educational experience and contributes to frustration and even civil unrest.

Not only is the quality of ghetto schools, urban or rural, low— it is frequently of the wrong kind. Vocational training, instead of an academic general education, would prepare disadvantaged youth for realistic, accessible opportunities. Part-time high school study, coupled with trade apprenticeships, plus more advanced vocational training in community colleges and technical institutes is a pressing and neglected need.

Employment. Technological change in industry most affects the young with little education, especially dropouts, and older workers whose generation had even less formal education. Without marketable occupational skills, the poor often turn to criminal activity or welfare for assistance, but such resources rarely enable them to improve their lot.

Workers may be laid off and unable to find work for a long time, or they may be subject to repeated layoffs, when only short-term insecure jobs are available.

Furthermore, inadequate income caused by unemployment or irregular employment is associated with excessive and unnecessarily widespread health problems. Disability is prevalent among the poor, a condition caused, intensified, and made chronic by inadequate diet and poor or non-existant medical treatment.

The middle-class worker, temporarily unemployed, usually can draw upon savings or a loan to tide him over until things are better; being out of work is a serious but manageable problem. For the disadvantaged, unemployment is a disaster, it wipes out savings, if any; and loans at reasonable rates of interest are unavailable.

The economic insecurity, familial instability, and general frustration generated by unemployment tend to have negative effects upon the occupational aspirations and decisions of the children of disadvantaged families, perpetuating a cycle of misery.

Age. Panic and despair are especially potent when the aged succumb to a "spirit of poverty." This "spirit" is a frame of mind which apparently paralyzes initiative, perseverance, ambition, and other qualities useful in extricating oneself from poverty. The young share this "spirit" also, made especially vulnerable by lack of education, skills, self-discipline, and a stable home life.

Housing. Housing, especially in restricted areas, is frequently used as a means to exclude "social inferiors" and to symbolize higher status. Concomitantly, this means residential segregation of disadvantaged and minority groups regardless of their economic condition. The realization that well-educated, highly-paid minority group members may still be forced to live in ghetto areas adds to the hopelessness of the disadvantaged, who have one more possible motivation cancelled.

A recent housing census indicated that 9.5 million dwelling units were seriously substandard, with an additional 5.2 million units needing substantial repair or modernization. Slums, characteristic of the urban disadvantaged, are seen to result in serious medical, social, economic, and moral problems.

Family. The family is considered the primary institution in the transmission of social attitudes and values to the next generation and in the development of an individual's personality. In this sense, the family may function as an important mechanism for perpetuating poverty when its social values and attitudes are those of the disadvantaged, and especially when the family structure is strained and unstable. Female-headed families (mothers divorced, widowed, deserted, unwed) and families with six or more children have a high incidence of poverty.

Surprisingly, relatively few families of the total disadvantaged population receive assistance from AFDC (Aid to Families with Dependent Children), the largest public assistance or welfare program. Reportedly, 30 percent of the non-white poor receive such welfare. Since census figures for the non-white poor are notably inaccurate and incomplete, the percent receiving welfare may be considerably less.

Lack of a male figure is a major factor influencing family instability, i.e. personal, social, and economic insecurity, illegitimacy of children, and inadequate total household income. Where there is some sort of liaison with a man in a female-headed household the male figure may well come across as a weak, free-loading nonentity adversely influencing the children as well as creating other problems.

Obviously, within this general description of the poor and disadvantaged there are numerous subgroups, especially the racial subgroups which constitute the loudest and most articulate voices of today's disadvantaged. Included would be the Blacks who comprise 90 percent of the non-white population, the Chicano's, or Mexican Americans, who are a growing force in the Southwestern part of the United States, the American Indians, Puerto Ricans, Oriental-Americans, and the large number of rural poor who have been identified with Appalachia but who populate rural areas throughout the nation.

Among this large group of socially- and culturally-deprived people, which may approximate 20 percent of our population or more than 35 million people, is the public welfare recipient. Burnside (1970) estimates the number of persons on public welfare rolls as more than 12 million people whose annual maintenance costs are more than 9 billion dollars. What distinguishes this group from the larger group of the poor and disadvantaged? Apparently nothing except that they have elected to cope with their impoverished conditions by turning to any of a number of programs that come under the general heading of welfare. Four prominent programs which are referred to as federally aided public assistance programs are as follows:

1. AFDC (Aid to Families with Dependent Children). Three-fourths of all recipients receive aid to families with dependent children, a program designed for the purpose of encouraging care of dependent children in their own homes or in the homes of relatives. States furnish financial assistance and rehabilitation and other services to help the parents or relatives to obtain or retain capability for the maximum self-support and personal independence consistent with the maintenance of continuing parental care and protection. Contrary to the popular stereotype of a large household overflowing with illegitimate children, the average AFDC family consists of just four persons, a mother and three children. The average AFDC mother is fairly young (median age 32 years). There is a father in the home of less than one-fifth of all AFDC families and most of these men are either incapacitated or unemployed. The average incapacitated father is considerably older (median age 49 years) than one who is unemployed (35 years).

2. OAA (Old Age Assistance). In terms of number of recipients (17 percent of the total) the second largest program is Old Age Assistance, designed to help needy individuals who are sixty-five years of age or older. The median age of OAA recipients is seventy-seven years; over one-third are eighty and over. The longer life expectancy of women is probably one of the factors accounting for the fact that over two-thirds of OAA recipients are female. However, the prevalence of females in the population of OAA recipients is much greater than in the U.S. population age 65 and over in which 55 percent are women.

3. APTD (Aid to Permanently and Totally Disabled). The third largest program is Aid to the Permanently and Totally Disabled (7½% of all recipients). Under this program financial assistance is given to needy disabled persons eighteen years of age or older, and states are encouraged to furnish rehabilitation and other services to help such individuals attain or retain capability for self-support or self-care. The median age of APTD recipients is fifty-five years and just over half of all recipients are women.

4. AB (Aid to the Blind). The fourth program and by far the smallest (less than 1 percent of all recipients) is Aid to the Blind, that is, needy persons who meet the specific definition of blindness in terms of ophthalmic measurement of the state in which they live. In addition to money payments, states are encouraged when practical, to furnish rehabilitation and other services to help such individuals attain or retain capability for self-support or self-care. There is no age limitation in this program and although there are AB recipients under eighteen and over eighty-five years of age, the median age is sixty-one years.

In addition to these federally-assisted programs there are many other state, county, and local agencies to whom the poor and disadvantaged may turn for aid. Names and responsibilities of these agencies will vary from state to state, but often include agencies such as Child Welfare Services, Medical Assistance Programs, General Relief, or General Assistance Programs, and often Veterans' Relief Commissions or Programs, which are specifically designed to provide resources for veterans. In addition, there are many agencies that provide help and finances on a temporary basis, such as the Salvation Army, Catholic Charities, Humane Society, Jewish Welfare, Volunteers of America, Lutheran Welfare Society, and St. Vincent de Paul Society.

Why have some of the socially and culturally disadvantaged turned to these types of public assistance programs in order to meet their daily needs, while others, the large majority of the disadvantaged, have chosen other methods of coping with their situation? The reasons are undoubtedly complex, but would include some of the following: First there is the continuing stigma to the receipt of welfare funds for some individuals which seems to indicate that they have somehow failed in supporting themselves and their families. For others just the procedure of applying for welfare funds probably represents too much of a hassle for too little income for them to be bothered. Still others would undoubtedly like to be the beneficiaries of some welfare program but are prevented from being so by eligibility rules and restrictions. In many states, until quite recently, residency requirements of up to one year or more prevented individuals entering that state from applying for and getting any kind of welfare benefits. Today many such restrictions are being removed by the federal courts and there is considerable pressure to standardize welfare payments throughout the nation rather than have states set the schedules of payment for persons applying within their jurisdiction. In addition, the stigma attached to receiving welfare payments seems to be on the wane, particularly among the poor and disadvantaged in the urban areas and they are quite ready to apply for and accept any benefits they can get in order to meet their needs. These reasons along with the generally heightened feeling of social responsibility for the less fortunate in our society have resulted in many more persons applying for and receiving public assistance funds. With such ever increasing numbers of applicants and the constant pressure for greater expenditures of funds it is not surprising that there is a current emphasis on rehabilitating as many public welfare recipients as is possible.

The variety of public assistance programs makes it obvious that there is considerable heterogeneity among the people served. However, since the greatest number are receiving AFDC assistance the following characteristics would seem to represent a "typical" welfare client: (1) female, (2) an urban dweller, (3) white or black (there is a slightly larger number of white persons on welfare rolls, but the difference is so slight as to be insignificant), (4) is head of the household with at least three dependent children, (5) has little education (an average of 10th grade or less), (6) has no marketable skill, (7) has a spotty or non-existent prior work record, (8) may be physically or mentally handicapped (approximately 1 in 8 AFDC recipients has such a handicap), (9) lives in substandard housing, and (10) is not presently married (the majority are separated, divorced, widowed, or have never been married).

Psychological Characteristics of Welfare Recipients

While it is important to have a "picture" of the welfare client it seems more important to know something about the way he perceives the world, interacts with others (including counselors), and the coping mechanisms he employs—in short, his psychological make-up.

One of the terms most frequently used to describe the welfare recipient is dependency. Goldin and Perry (1967) have done an extensive study of dependency as it relates to the rehabilitation process, and take the position that it is such a prominent characteristic that it should be regarded in categories such as social, emotional, financial, institutional, and psycho-medical. Obviously there is similarity between these areas of expression but the authors feel that they are sufficiently independent to warrant different types of intervention by a rehabilitation counselor. They further tie dependency in with such qualities as suggestibility, conformity, and the need for structure which also have implications for working with clients that will be discussed a little later.

Another quality often ascribed to the public assistance recipient is lack of motivation. Perhaps it relates to the frustration that stems from the knowledge of the many barriers that stand in his way to achieving employment or some level of personal independence. Even when employment seems possible, the realization that the low level of remuneration will constitute little financial gain over his welfare income and often entail undesirable working conditions, makes it easy to understand a client's reluctance to be rehabilitated. In addition, many clients apparently have some other sources of income from friends, personal enterprise, or illegal activities so that the appeal of a job is further reduced. Undoubtedly there are those who have, after several generations of public assistance, become accustomed to their situation and don't care to make any changes. And, for some, the thought of long-range planning or long-term commitment to a job holds little appeal because a sense of powerlessness is the pervading feeling that they live with. When one lumps such reasons together with a variety of others that surely are operating, it is not difficult to understand the unmotivated client.

Passivity, too, is generally associated with the welfare recipient.

His willingness to tolerate, if not accept, his life situation seems to result in his putting himself in the hands of the system and silently complying with those demands he feels he must meet, while anxiously avoiding those that represent too great a threat or too much difficulty. This trait is often linked to a passive-aggressive personality factor where the surface behavior may appear similar to simple passivity, but may really represent a mask for underlying frustration and resentment which the client is unable to express either because the feelings are unacceptable to him, or he fears some sort of retaliation (usually loss of money) by the agency if he is critical or hostile.

The tenor of the welfare recipient's life is undoubtedly insecurity and there are many personality characteristics that one might expect to accompany this ever-present feeling. For instance, suspicion that the agency is going to cut off his income, or that someone is going to exploit him, may quickly lead a client to become more withdrawn and anxious. These feelings may in turn cause a further loss of self-esteem and depression which reinforces the view that the client is truly powerless to alter his life situation.

Since many of the welfare clients are also minority group members, they generally develop a set of values and aspirations that represent a subcultural norm, or life style, and significantly influence their relationship to the larger society. For example, the language of the minority cultures often seriously impedes communications with white, middle-class counselors. With Chicano's (Mexican-Americans) it is frequently true that they rely heavily on Spanish within their own groups so that it is difficult or impossible for them to converse with English-speaking counselors. American Indian groups, too, often have a rather limited use of English so that communication is not easy with people from the agencies.

In a different way the ghetto Blacks (Negroes) have their own language that has developed over a long period of time in relative isolation from the mainstream of society. Their special idioms and grammatical transformations represent a colorful and meaningful mode of communication that is usually completely unintelligible to outsiders. Indeed, such usage often represents

a status symbol within the group and protection from the un-
wanted interference of outsiders or agency representatives.

All of these psychological characteristics, plus many others
that have not been mentioned, should be understood and appre-
ciated by the rehabilitation counselor if he is to have any chance
of working successfully with the deprived and disadvantaged in
general, and the welfare recipient in particular. Later we will
try to provide some suggestions and guidelines for working with
this population.

HOW EFFECTIVE ARE REHABILITATION SERVICES FOR PUBLIC WELFARE RECIPIENTS

Obviously many public welfare recipients have been receiving
rehabilitation services. These services have been provided to the
physically disabled recipient through the "traditional" service
program and to selected recipient populations, such as mothers
receiving aid to families with dependent children (AFDC), by
special government sponsored projects. The critical question becomes then, not whether services are offered, but how successfully
are they offered and what form should services take to be maximally successful. A review of the available research should give
a perspective on these questions.

A glaring shortcoming of the available research becomes immediately evident. While many statistics on, and discussions of,
the various services offered welfare recipients are available, little
systematic study or controlled experimentation has occurred which
evaluates the effectiveness of comparative methods of offering
rehabilitation services to welfare recipients. Government figures
indicate that since 1961 (when routine reporting of such data
began) the number of disabled public assistance recipients who
have received rehabilitation services has steadily increased, as one
might expect from the attention given to welfare programs by government reports and news media. Yet, in analyzing these statistics
we find the percentage of persons receiving rehabilitation services
who are public welfare recipients has decreased roughly from 15
percent to 10 percent during the decade 1960-70. This suggests the
rehabilitation movement is not moving forward in expanding its
services to meet the increasing national need. There are indications,

however, that the trend of the past decade is reversing itself, based on recent developments which are focusing on public welfare recipients. We shall discuss the reason for this new outlook a little later.

As mentioned, statistics reveal that while services are being offered, the state-federal programs are not meeting the national need. Is the service system so ineffective or ill-defined that services cannot be offered to this special population with complex problems?

Truax, Lawlis, Clardy, Bozarth and Rubin (1968) analyzing client data reported by the 54 general state agencies for 1967 in an effort to determine uniformities and the lack thereof in services offered, found that the percentage of an agency's rehabilitants receiving public assistance correlates only slightly or nonsignificantly with other client and caseload characteristics. The investigators believe this lack of relationship between receiving public assistance and other rehabilitation variables suggests that public assistance recipients could be handled in greater numbers by state agencies without special programs and without greatly affecting average costs for rehabilitation.

Eber (1966) developed a weighted system for predicting successful rehabilitation of clients by analyzing various records kept by the Alabama and Georgia Vocational Rehabilitation Agencies. Using client characteristics, case material, counselor variables and community information, a factor analysis revealed one factor representing the acceptance by the client of welfare or public assistance services.

Four primary variables contributed to this factor including the amount of public assistance received at acceptance, during rehabilitation, at closure, and at follow-up, respectively. A secondary contribution appeared from number of dependents. The failure of other variables to contribute to this factor made the pattern the clearest one in the entire analysis. A significant outcome was the failure of the "welfare acceptance" factor to correlate with other factors in the analysis. The investigator felt this provided strong evidence that the receiving of welfare benefits by a rehabilitation client presents no special problems to the successful provision of services.

From these two studies one might conclude that by simply expanding the current services many more public assistance clients could be successfully rehabilitated with few additional considerations. One shortcoming of studies dealing with analysis of agencies' records, and thus the above conclusion, is the lack of adequate data regarding public welfare recipients who are *not* referred for rehabilitation services or fail to become an "active" case when referred—a tendency among this population.

A more adequate picture of services to public welfare recipients may be provided by a controlled longitudinal study of services to both the culturally disadvantaged (another label applicable to the public welfare recipient) and the medically handicapped. Reagles, Wright, and Butler (1968) report such a study where culturally and medically-handicapped clients received expanded traditional rehabilitation services (experimental) in a Wood County, Wisconsin agency. Medically handicapped clients received services in a control agency operating with traditional resources. The objectives of the study involved the identification of correlates of rehabilitation gain and the development of a scale to measure client gains.

An unexpected result of this effort was the discovery that culturally handicapped clients, not only show positive gain on the developed Rehabilitation Gain Scale, but actually scored higher (larger gain) than the medically handicapped in either the experimental or control groups. The investigators concluded that traditional rehabilitation services were as effective, indeed if not more so, in rehabilitating the culturally handicapped as in rehabilitating medically handicapped clients. They suggested that rehabilitation services be extended to the culturally disadvantaged on more than an experimental basis even though their handicap is not defined in medical terms as is current practice for provision of services. While these results are promising, little mention is made of an apparently serious limitation to the delivery of traditional rehabilitation services, which is the failure of clients to be aware of or interested in services. Many eligible persons fail to get services because of their lack of knowledge about rehabilitation services, reluctancy to participate, and limited availability of the services. The significance of this last factor is pointed out in a study done preliminary to a Research and Demonstration project by the Massachusetts Rehabilitation Commission (1968) which found that rehabilitation agencies paid less attention to disabled public assistance recipients than to disabled persons who were not on public assistance, rejected more welfare recipients as applicants for services and subjected them to much longer delays in the processing of their cases. Additionally, the professional persons offering services seem to have thought this client group was less likely to succeed in rehabilitation. If the rehabilitation staff exhibits behavior and attitudes consistent with those expressed above, it is likely many public assistance recipients who might be eligible for rehabilitation services will never be offered such services. In addition, limited knowledge of the rehabilitation process by caseworkers may compound the situation through failure to refer potential clients. These persons are not reported in most research studies of the rehabilitation process.

Even when a client is successfully engaged in the rehabilitation process, not all of the problems are solved. Kunce (1969) found in reviewing the reported effectiveness of poverty programs through expanded traditional rehabilitation services in California, Vermont, and Missouri that large numbers of individuals labeled as unmotivated, and dependent on welfare typically drop out of the process between referral and acceptance for services. Between 45 and 50 percent of those referred drop out, not unlike the 46 percent dropout rate Dishart (1965) reported for physically disabled referrals to the traditional service program. Kunce concluded that while special problems arise in servicing this population, including the requirement of extended client services and training in conjunction with parallel counseling, a significant number of individuals who are often considered as hard-core unemployed and unmotivated can be effectively served and placed into stable employment within traditional rehabilitation programs.

Kunce (1969) also reports a very comprehensive statistical analysis of the effectiveness of programs for the disadvantaged. Noting that many special programs for this population simply do not keep adequate records for meaningful evaluation, he drew heavily on the Los Angeles County Vocational Rehabilitation Administration and Office of Economic Opportunity Cooperative Project, where records were fairly complete. Of 19,648 referrals, he reports that 1,068, or 5.4 percent were successfully employed after services. This is the type of statistic that is often referred to by opponents of such programs. Another way to evaluate the program is to look only at the group who received significant services and were then terminated. Of this group 1,068 were employed and 351 were unemployed, so that a proponent of such programs could readily point to a 75 percent success ratio.

Wisely, Kunce points out that neither of these statistics accurately reflects the impact of the program. Many of those referred for services were either ineligible or dropped out of their own choice. Additionally, many clients, at any given time, are either waiting for services to begin or are actively engaged in training. For the Los Angeles project these two groups comprised approximately 9,000 clients. Assuming that these groups do complete services and have the same successful placement ratio as those already closed (75 percent), there is a marked increase in the number who have benefited from services. Kunce concludes that approximately 49 percent of the referred group would be successfully closed using his analysis, but he points out that even such a refined evaluation may misrepresent the true impact of rehabilitation services since it is based solely on the criterion of employment and does not take into account the tendency for difficult clients to accumulate in caseloads on a long-term basis.

Evidence of the effectiveness of rehabilitating welfare clients is reported by Grigg (1969) who evaluated fourteen research and demonstration projects. Of 7,694 applicants in all projects, 2,786 were accepted for services and data is available on 2,614. Of this group, 1,146 were closed as rehabilitated, while another 879 were still being served. All but 6 percent of the rehabilitated clients were employed as compared to 78 percent who were unemployed before services. In addition he reports that welfare payments were reduced on the average by $48 a month for each client and that each client's weekly earnings increased $46 when compared to their earnings before receiving services.

Other writers (Levitan, 1966; Horton, 1967; Bullock, 1966) tended to be critical of programs designed to meet the needs of the poor, calling them ineffective and inefficient, but, as mentioned earlier, biased or missing data often makes it difficult to assess such programs. In general, it appears that programs for the poor are as effective as other rehabilitation programs when they get clients to enroll and remain for services. Shortcomings seem to be that only a small percentage of the potential population of clients is reached and these are served with greater difficulty and with a greater expenditure of resources. New approaches are obviously needed in reaching the welfare recipient, and some of the current attempts will be reported in the following section.

A TREND TOWARD COORDINATION OF WELFARE AND REHABILITATION SERVICES
New Programs

Following extensive experience gained in previous efforts the federal government has provided supplemental funds for expanding rehabilitation services to the culturally deprived welfare recipient through a cooperative effort between rehabilitation and social services. The emphasis of this program is to offer immediate services to persons applying for welfare with diminishing emphasis on a medically defined handicap. All jurisdictions have this supplemental funding available, but currently only slightly over half have committed themselves to a program. Of those agencies with grant approval the services to be offered vary extensively, from the development of evaluation and work adjustment facilities in the "core" section of a metropolitan area to provision of evaluation and training services with emphasis on individual and innovative approaches in rural areas where such services have not been previously available.

A specific example of this approach is the Arkansas Public Assistance-Vocational Rehabilitation Expansion Project, with which one of the authors is associated, and which has developed a team diagnostic and service unit in five areas of the state selected by the great need (large welfare rolls) and available resources (medical services, community college, on-the-job training opportunities, etc.). Each unit consists of five staff members including a rehabilitation counselor, a social service caseworker, a social services' aide, a placement specialist, and a secretary. This staff is to receive referrals from the local social service (welfare) office and provide all necessary services to the members of

AFDC families in the area to allow successful rehabilitation. Potential clients are rated on eleven variables related to successful rehabilitation outcome and categorized as having "excellent" (above average), good (average or below), or guarded (nil) rehabilitation potential. Services are provided to clients of all groups which show potential, with all area recipients eventually having the opportunity to be served. Emphasis is placed on serving the most recent applicants.

This approach to services allows local centralized control of services with minimal duplication and the expectation that all recipients will have the opportunity to receive services. It provides an additional source of information previously missing from studies of services to this population that is critical to any future planning based on the requirement that all able bodied recipients be available for training and employment. The information provided by the built-in screening process is the percentage of recipients who actually have rehabilitation potential, i.e. are trainable and employable. The program is also truly an expansion of the traditional service system, as the referral process allows continued maintenance of previous caseloads among the state agency counselors.

Additional information about this program and all others developed from this funding source is available through the specially developed Research Utilization Laboratory Information Center for Public Assistance-Vocational Rehabilitation projects at the Institute for the Crippled and Disabled in New York City.

Other efforts at coordinating social and rehabilitation services for the effective rehabilitation of the welfare recipient and culturally disadvantaged client include model cities programs, low rent housing projects and welfare grant extensions to provide client motivation and decrease problem areas.

The "model cities" programs mentioned above, include cooperative efforts in Atlanta, East St. Louis, Cleveland, Baltimore, and Hot Springs, Arkansas. Each of these projects is an attempt to extend rehabilitation services to an area and population which previously had not been able to receive help because of limited community resources. Each project developed unique approaches to providing these extended services.

The Atlanta project focused on the development of the Atlanta Employment Evaluation and Service Center (AEESC), a comprehensive center which was so located as to be easily accessible to the physically handicapped and culturally disadvantaged individuals of the metropolitan area. All services necessary for the transition of a client from underemployment or unemployment to appropriate remunerative employment is provided at the center including counseling, medical, psychological, work evaluation and adjustment, vocational evaluation, placement and follow-up. The provision of services is based upon a cooperative partnership between the social and rehabilitation programs and exemplified by the assignment to a "team" (rehabilitation counselor and caseworker) of each client coming in to the center.

The Hot Springs project parallels Atlanta's program except that the focus of services is on the rural welfare recipient (AFDC only) who because of no physical handicap would otherwise be ineligible for rehabilitation services. All services are provided at a comprehensive rehabilitation center. This program requires all clients to move from their home area (15 central Arkansas counties) to the Center thus eliminating daily transportation problems, environmental distractions, and scattered services. An extension of the "traditional" center service program includes a didactic instruction program focusing on special problems of this group, i.e. community resources, family planning, grooming, etc., and an experimentally based differential group activity that includes group counseling, cultural enrichment activities and economic action activities. Joint social and rehabilitation responsibility encompasses funding, referral of clients and provision of project staff.

Possibly the most innovative project, in terms of expanding the traditional service system to this untrusting and hard-to-serve population is the Baltimore project. This effort focuses on eliminating obstacles to such services. This is done by using indigenous case aides to initiate client contacts, make referrals, and aid in the implementation of services. The use of such aides is not new in itself, but their use in implementing services is. One of the aide's responsibilities is to drive a specially provided bus which transports clients around the city for necessary appoint-

ments. A second innovation is the provision of a "mobile diagnostic unit" which contains a medical and psychological examination laboratory. This unit is staffed by a physician and a psychologist, and provides the required general medical examination and
psychological evaluation, if necessary, at the client's front door,
eliminating unnecessary travel and the tendency toward unkept
appointments among the disadvantaged. The project thus offers
several practical solutions to difficult problems in engaging the
urban-culturally disadvantaged client. There are no special eligibility guidelines for this project. All services are processed through
the local state agency counselors.

The other two "model cities" programs in Cleveland and East
St. Louis have been equally effective in meeting the problems of
the culturally disadvantaged population but have tended to focus
on neighborhood activity needs, including medical care, recreational facilities, and hot lunch programs rather than vocational
needs.

The Oklahoma Department of Social Services in conjunction
with the state rehabilitation agency has recently developed an innovative program aimed at providing the necessary rehabilitation
services to welfare recipients and an incentive program to insure
rehabilitation success. The program is based on referral of public
welfare recipients to the state rehabilitation agency. Referred recipients receive an increase in their monthly living expense grant.
Ordinarily based on 80 percent of the families' estimated need,
this grant becomes 100 percent of the estimated need. Any additional expenses incurred during, and related to, vocational training are provided. The real innovative and incentive aspects of
the project result from a provision for continuance of the full
grant for three months after initiation of employment and a decrease of one-third of the grant each month thereafter, so that
at the end of six months the client is no longer on welfare. The
hope is that this grant extension period will allow the client to
handle any large debts incurred during his extended period on
welfare, and allow him to feel more secure in taking advantage of
training possibilities thus increasing the client's motivation for
services and the likelihood of a long-term rehabilitation success.

The provision of rehabilitation services to the economically disadvantaged has focused on the development of low income housing projects in St. Louis, New Haven, Connecticut, Pittsburgh, California, and other areas. For a full discussion of the services provided and their effectiveness in reducing dependency of the persons receiving such services it is suggested that the interested reader consult the "Northeastern University Studies in Rehabilitation" which provide a very comprehensive discussion of these efforts.

From the above discussion of past and present rehabilitation services and projects it is evident that much attention is being focused on the welfare and disadvantaged population in an effort to serve them better. Much remains to be done and learned. One thing that is apparent is that no one simple approach exists for providing effective rehabilitation services to the public welfare client.

Current Proposed Legislation

In addition to the innovative projects just discussed, there is legislation (H.R.-1) presently before Congress that directs its attention to providing better services for welfare recipients who need them, and, at the same time, preventing public assistance funds from going to those who will not cooperate with employment or training planning. Since rehabilitation counselors seem destined for a prime role in implementing this legislation, a brief summary of its provisions (as it now stands) might be helpful.

Currently before Congress, H.R.-1 offers several innovative changes to the current services offered the needy (culturally deprived, welfare recipient) family. This welfare reform legislation amends the Social Security Act by adding Title XXI which establishes the Opportunities for Families Program and the Family Assistance Plan to provide assistance to needy families with children, to encourage work, training and self support, and to "improve" family life. An additional provision, Title XX, establishes a federally-administered assistance program for needy aged, blind, or disabled individuals replacing the current state-federal program which provides aid to this population.

The eligibility requirements and services offered by this amendment include the provision of a guaranteed annual income for families with monthly income less than the benefits payable and resources of less than $1500. The monetary benefits follow a schedule which starts at $800 per year for each of the first two family members with decreasing amounts awarded per individual up to the eighth member ($200 per year) for a maximum per family of $3600 per year. Employable adult family members are required to register with public employment offices for manpower services, training, and employment. Benefits are reduced following the above increment schedule per person if any *employable* family members fail to register or accept services for employment or training or rehabilitation services. Unemployable family members are not required to register. However, persons not required to register may do so voluntarily. Those not required to register are: (1) ill, incapacitated, or aged persons (the incapacitated will be referred for vocational rehabilitation, which they will be required to accept and for which a $30 per month incentive is payable); (2) mothers of a child under age 3 (age 6 until July 1, 1974); (3) mothers if the father works or is registered for work; (4) a child under 16 or a full-time student under 22; and (5) the caretaker of an ill household member.

The services offered include manpower services, training, and employment programs including counseling, testing, coaching, program orientation, institutional and on-the-job training, job upgrading, development and placement, relocation assistance, and public service employment programs. A $30 per month incentive allowance, plus transportation is provided for all family members who register for the available services. Child care services will be provided to allow registrant participation.

Public service employment is intended to provide transitional employment when other jobs are not available or the beneficiary cannot be effectively placed in a training program. Federal financial responsibility is decreased 25 percent each year of such employment from full sponsorship the first year to 50 percent the third, to encourage moving people onto regular payrolls.

Upon application and registration for services by the members available for employment, all eligible families will be paid benefits by the Secretary of Labor, who coordinates all parts of the Service program, under the Opportunities for Families Program. Families which have no member available for employment will be paid by the Secretary of Health, Education, and Welfare under the Family Assistance Plan. Each family receiving benefits will be required to report its income and significant changes every quarter.

Under Title XX needy persons 65 years and older, blind or disabled will be eligible for monthly payments if their resources are not more than $1500 and their monthly income was less than the full monthly benefit payment. Full monthly benefits for an individual will be $130 per month for the fiscal year 1973, $140 for 1974, and $150 thereafter. For a couple the benefits will be $195 a month for 1973, and $200 thereafter. Some income will be disregarded in determining eligibility for full monthly benefits to provide a work incentive.

These new measures should provide some services not readily available to the needy interested in working, such as child care and transportation. It should also provide some interesting and complicated problems in planning and delivering services and developing necessary jobs.

As stated, H.R.-1 is presently under deliberation and there is no way to know its provisions at the time of passage. The authors feel that most of the presented information will prove accurate, but the reader should exercise caution until such time as it becomes law, a law that hopefully will be a boon to the needy.

GUIDELINES FOR WORKING WITH WELFARE RECIPIENTS

There are undoubtedly many shortcomings in our approach to working with the public welfare recipient, and with the current emphasis on providing more and better services for such clients, it may be useful to examine the deficiencies and recommend more effective ways of proceeding.

There are several levels at which we can err, and Gross (1967) points out that many errors occur in our assumptions about dealing with the disadvantaged. For example, he feels that it is a mistake to assume that clients, for the most part, come voluntarily and really want agency help. In many instances they present themselves for services under pressure from legal authorities or welfare agencies and are actively resistant to help. They may view the agency as just another arm of the bureaucratic system and reject any authority of either the counselor or the agency. If a counselor is not sensitive to such client attitudes, it is very unlikely that he will be able to work effectively with the individual. On the other hand there is no basis for generally ascribing such qualities to welfare clients so that failure is justified in advance.

Another assumption that Gross challenges is that the counselor accepts the client. Too often he feels that hidden bias and prejudice are active when counselors work with minority group members whose values and behavior they do not understand or approve. When such attitudes do exist in the counselor, they usually assure an ineffective relationship, since clients tend to be very sensitive to subtle rejection.

Rusalem (1970) is also critical of the present system of service delivery because of its centralized, bureaucratic approach that rests heavily on client conformity, while most disadvantaged and welfare clients seem to prefer a more informal and personalized approach. Taylor (1970) is sufficiently critical and dissatisfied with traditional efforts for the disadvantaged that he proposes a new model of service delivery that emphasizes advocacy as the initial counselor responsibility, followed by immediate placement into meaningful activity so that the usual "lag time" is largely eliminated and the client can benefit from early rewards, which in turn should provide motivation for continuing utilization of agency services. Only later would a plan be written and additional services provided so that suitable placement and follow-up would result.

In summarizing the conclusions of the final reports of twenty-four Research and Demonstration projects which offered cooperative welfare and rehabilitation services from 1962 to 1968, Kramm (1970) cites numerous problems in servicing this population and offers some interesting recommendations for improving services. The problems encountered in the various projects included (1) lack of formal referral procedures, (2) staff turnover which complicated referral and service continuity and compounded intrastaff communication problems, (3) recipient characteristics and problems including extensive deprivation, dependency on the welfare grant and general resistance to services, (4) welfare system rules which allow provision of services only when the client's resources are totally depleted, (5) staff attitudes that communicate pessimism or bias toward the potential of this population to the recipient and (6) lack of community resources such as day care centers, training facilities and adequate transportation.

As a result of the experience of dealing with this myriad of problems various project staff were able to recommend several innovations aimed at more effective services. Suggested were (1) a team approach to offering services (social and rehabilitation service coordination) which help alleviate client fear, accelerate services and aid interagency communication, (2) early referral to minimize the developing dependency, (3) small caseloads to allow adequate staff time for dealing with the client's complex problems, (4) restoration of hope through extensive personal contact, supportive counseling and reassurance regarding the client's ability to succeed, (5) changes in grant policy to allow incentive supplements during and after rehabilitation, (6) diagnostic and work adjustment services which contribute significantly to successful placement, (7) follow-up services up to six months after placement to insure sustained motivation and interest in the client and (8) experienced and trained staff who are more able to provide skilled and knowledgeable services to the complex needs of this clientele group.

Other writers (Margolin & Goldin, 1971) have pointed out some needed changes if rehabilitation services are to effectively reach the public welfare recipient. Primary among their recommendations are improved referral services, cross-professional training between rehabilitation and welfare workers so that each understands the viewpoint and difficulties of the other, and the mobilization of community resources to aid in the rehabilitation process. Anderson (1969) addresses himself directly to the special problems involved in working with welfare recipients and the disadvantaged and points out that the counselor can expect to meet:

1. *Hostility*—either direct and expressed or indirect and manifested by manipulation of the counselor or a lack of cooperation.

2. *Lack of Motivation*—due to feelings of frustration and powerlessness in overcoming employment obstacles, satisfaction with a long-term welfare role, or the inability to see any personal or economic advantage in working at a minimal-pay

job that often represents a drudgery.

3. *Communication Problems*—either because the client is from a foreign cultural background and converses primarily in the language of that culture, or because he is from a cultural subgroup such as the ghetto where a highly specialized and idiomatic use of language develops that is all but meaningless to the uninitiated. A worse kind of communication impasse results when the counselor resorts to complex English or professional jargon that leaves the client confused or feeling he has been "put down."

4. *Client's Lack of Understanding of What Counseling Is—Or What Is Expected of Him*—since counseling services are largely an outgrowth of middle-class values with its emphasis on ideas, concepts, and talk, and the welfare client is the product of lower class values where the emphasis is on action and immediate rewards.

From the foregoing criticisms, recommendation, and enumeration of special problems, the authors have tried to distill a set of guidelines for the practicing rehabilitation counselor in dealing with public welfare recipients as clients, and for rehabilitation agencies as they prepare to meet the considerable challenge of providing services for ever-increasing numbers of such clients on their caseloads. To be effective the counselor should:

1. Examine his attitudes toward the public welfare recipient and the disadvantaged generally, and be sure that he sees them as worthy clients who can benefit from services.

2. Expect to meet with some hostility and help the client to work it through constructively.

3. Expect to meet a lack of motivation, often economically justified, and explore it with the client in order to help him consider long-range financial advantage and personal satisfaction.

4. Know as much about the cultural and language background of the client as possible so that communication is made easier. It is not necessary for counselors to be fluent in a foreign language or ghetto dialect, but close familiarization is very helpful.

5. Be an active advocate for public welfare clients by publicizing and interpreting programs to other agencies and community resources.

6. Be prepared to deal with immediate, practical problems that often interfere with a client's continuing with services. A lack of transportation or a sick family member may result in a client's dropping out of a program because he can find no easy solution.

7. Recognize that traditional counseling approaches may be inappropriate with disadvantaged clients and be flexible enough to try new approaches, or call upon other persons or resources to facilitate meaningful contact.

To be effective in rehabilitating public welfare recipients, agencies should:

1. Modify the typical agency bureaucratic structure in the direction of a less formal, more personal approach that is more attractive to disadvantaged clients.

2. Locate agencies in areas accessible to clients. Particularly in large urban areas, offices should be placed in the ghetto to minimize transportation difficulties.

3. Utilize outreach workers who represent the cultural group being served and can facilitate the client's understanding and utilization of agency programs.

4. Speed up, significantly, the delivery of services so that clients feel like something is happening.

5. Strive to minimize staff turnover in delivery of services, since public welfare recipients and the disadvantaged are more likely to interpret a change in counselors as delay and lack of concern.

6. Actively attempt to educate employers about the disadvantaged and solicit a commitment to employ clients at levels commensurate with their ability, not just for menial tasks.

7. Support programs to abolish discrimination against disadvantaged clients and help develop government sponsored programs to provide jobs in areas of high unemployment.

SUMMARY

Within our society there exists a large group of people (approximately 20%) who do not have the resources or the opportunities to effectively cope with their life responsibilities. These are referred to as the poor and the disadvantaged. Within this large group there are those (approximately 30%) who have sought help from a variety of programs intended to supplement their income, which are lumped together under the general heading of welfare or public assistance. Typically, these individuals are females who are heads of households with dependent children, have little education, few marketable skills, live in an urban ghetto, and seem powerless to improve their lot.

Some of these welfare recipients have been referred for vocational rehabilitation services in the past, but the success ratio has not been good because many were not motivated for services; counselors felt there was little potential in this group of clients, or severe disability suggested that they were infeasible. Presently there is a strong emphasis by the federal government to provide more and better services for such clients who need and will accept such help and a corresponding emphasis on withdrawing welfare funds from those who do not need or will not accept services. Since traditional programs failed to reach large numbers of welfare clients, several innovative approaches have been tried which tend to emphasize better referral systems or means of taking the services directly to the client rather than waiting for the client to come to the agency. Such programs hold considerable promise for improved services, but it should be pointed out that traditional services have been effective for those clients who received services and remained in a program until its conclusion.

Estimates on the anticipated values of vocational rehabilitation services for the public welfare populations range from nearly all to 5 percent to 10 percent (Kunce et al., 1969). But even if only a relatively small percentage of the group receive and benefit from services, the number of persons helped would be enormous, probably resulting in double the number of persons being rehabilitated in any given year.

Both counselors and agencies need to become very knowledgeable about public welfare recipients and the circumstances in which they live. The counselor needs to understand their psychological make-up that can result in resentment, dependency and lack of motivation, recognize the subcultural values, and try to honestly accept and be the clients' advocate. The agencies need to reform the usual bureaucratic system, strive to get services to the client, and utilize outreach people when it seems necessary. If both counselor and agency can squarely meet these responsibilities and gain effective cooperation from other helping organizations, then the considerable challenge that lies ahead can be met, and for many public welfare recipients the quality of life will be considerably improved.

REFERENCES

Anderson, W.: Special problems in counseling the disadvantaged. In Kunce, J.T., and Cope, C.S. (Eds.): *Rehabilitation and the Culturally Disadvantaged*. Regional Rehabilitation Research Institute, University of Missouri—Columbia, Research Series No. 1, 1969.

Arkansas Rehabilitation Research and Training Center: Rehabilitation of the rural hard-core welfare client utilizing rehabilitation center services. Project progress report. Mimeographed paper, University of Arkansas, 1971.

Bullock, P.: Fighting Poverty: The view from Watts. Industrial Relations Research Association, 1966.

Bureau of Economic Research: The Perth Amboy Diagnostic and Employability Center, Report 4, *Guidelines from Other RSA Projects,* Rutgers University, 1971.

Burnside, B.: Who are the recipients of public assistance? *Rehabilitation Record,* 1971, May-June.

Campbell, R.R., Kaplan, B., and Mahoney, R.J.: The Poor: Social and Personal Characteristics. In Kunce, J.T., and Cope, C.S. (Eds.): *Rehabilitation and the Culturally Disadvantaged*. Regional Rehabilitation Research Institute, University of Missouri—Columbia, Research Series No. 1, 1969.

Dickerson, L.R.: Arkansas welfare expansion project—An evaluation proposal. Mimeographed paper, Arkansas Rehabilitation Research and Training Center, University of Arkansas, 1972.

Dishart, M.: Vital issues and recommendations from the 1965 Institute for Rehabilitation Research. Washington, D.C., National Rehabilitation Association, 1965.

Eber, H.W.: Multivariate analysis of a vocational rehabilitation system. *Multivariate Behavioral Research Monographs.* Monograph No. 66-1, Society of Multivariate Experimental Psychology, Texas Christian University Press, 1966.

Goldin, G.J., and Perry, S.L.: Dependency and its implications for rehabilitation. *Northeastern Studies in Vocational Rehabilitation,* 1967, Monograph I.

Grigg, C.M.: *Vocational Rehabilitation of Disabled Public Assistance*

Clients: An Evaluation of Fourteen Research and Demonstration Projects. Institute for Social Research, Florida State University, 1969.

Gross, E.: Report on problems of counseling special populations. Paper prepared for the meetings of the Panel on Counseling and Selections of the National Manpower Advisory Committee. Washington, D.C., Springs, 1967.

Horton, F. (U.S. Representative—New York): Report on the Job Corps made to the House of Representatives. *Congressional Record,* November, 1967.

Kramm, E.R. Vocational rehabilitation for disabled public assistance recipients. *Welfare in Review,* March-April, 1970, pp. 11-23.

Kunce, J.T.: The effectiveness of poverty programs. A review. In Kunce, J.T. and Cope, C.S. (Eds.): *Rehabilitation and the Culturally Disadvantaged.* Regional Research Institute, University of Missouri—Columbia, Research Series No. 1, 1969.

Kunce, J.T., and Cope, C.S. (Eds.): *Rehabilitation and the Culturally Disadvantaged.* The University of Missouri—Columbia, Regional Rehabilitation Research Institute, Research Series No. 1, 1969.

Kunce, J.T., Mahoney, R.J., Campbell, R.R., and Finley, J.: *Rehabilitation in The Concrete Jungle.* The University of Missouri—Columbia, Regional Rehabilitation Research Institute, Research Series No. 3, 1969.

Levitan, S.A.: An anti-poverty experiment: The Job Corps. San Francisco: Industrial Relations Research Association, December, 1966.

Margolin, R.J., and Goldin, G.J.: The integration of welfare and rehabilitation efforts for the rehabilitation of the public assistance client: An attainable goal. *Rehabilitation Literature,* 1971, Vol. 32, No. 11.

Massachusetts Rehabilitation Commission: *Vocational Rehabilitation of Disabled Public Assistance Clients.* Final Project Report (RD-1494), Boston, 1968.

Reagles, K.W., Wright, G.N., and Butler, A.J.: *A scale or rehabilitation gain for clients of an expanded vocational rehabilitation program.* Wisconsin Studies in Vocational Rehabilitation, Monograph XIII, Series 2, The University of Wisconsin, Regional Rehabilitation Research Institute, 1970.

Rusalem, H., and Baxt, R.: Delivering rehabilitation services. National Citizens Conference, Social and Rehabilitation Service, Washington, D.C., 1970.

Truax, C.B., Lawlis, F., Clardy, F., Bozarth, J., and Rubin, S.: *Uniformity and differential rehabilitation practices in the state-federal vocational rehabilitation program.* Arkansas Rehabilitation Research and Training Center, University of Arkansas, 1968.

Wright, G.N., Reagles, K.W., and Butler, A.: *The Wood County Project: An Expanded Program of Vocational Rehabilitation.* University of Wisconsin Regional Rehabilitation Research Institute, 1969, vol. 1.

CHAPTER XI

COUNSELING THE DISABLED DISADVANTAGED

BROCKMAN SCHUMACHER

❀❀

References

❀❀

As A PREFACE, it will be useful to reflect upon some of the more general issues that are still of concern to the field of counseling. The reader may then understand the frame of reference from which later assertions are made. Since the literature in rehabilitation counseling has given heavy attention to counseling issues (Bozarth, 1972; McGowan and Schmidt, 1962; Patterson, 1969) there will be no attempt to treat such issues exhaustively; however, a brief consideration of the writer's position on these issues will be given.

Counseling as a Specialty

Counseling has long been considered a professional specialty intended to help the client become more aware of himself and to discover the means by which he can make use of more inner and outer resources. The term, however, is also used to refer to a broader array of helping functions: Vocational Counseling, Guidance Counseling, Marital Counseling and Recreational Counseling, are a few terms from a long inventory of special areas of human adjustment. It is the writer's view, however, that what is being talked about between two persons at a particular time cannot determine the growth process that must occur. All problems, vocational, marital, or educational are, in fact, personal problems. The client's concerns in many ways are similar: He, the client, is concerned about being understood. He is concerned about whether others consider him of sufficient worth to merit their attention. He is attempting to sort through many of his needs and expectations that help him set priorities and direct his energy. The point of view held in this chapter is that the realities of information getting or deciding on practical moves are always attended by a highly personal component that involves the way the individual sees himself and others, and the way he feels about himself and others. It is this personal aspect that influences growth and is of concern in the counseling process.

Work of the Counselor

The day-to-day activities of the counselor involve many activities regardless of the setting in which he works. He is expected to do more than counseling. Training, research, job placement, public relations, case management and clerical tasks may sometimes account for a fair percentage of his daily work. Further, the counselor often finds himself in a decision making and problem solving role with the client. Such functions are especially demanding when he is working with the disabled disadvantaged. There are few positions where the counselor is expected to do only counseling. In fact, he engages willingly in many activities, and the evaluation of his work is often based upon the success with which he carries out activities other than counseling. In short, it is not possible to consider the functions of counseling by way of the particular problem the client presents at a given time or by the variety of duties the counselor must undertake.

"Types" of Counseling

A first consideration here is that counseling is, of course, not the only way to change. Many factors lead to change and personal growth. A good marriage, a job choice, a change in living conditions, or simply thinking about one's problems are some of a collection of activities that may lead to personal growth. Clearly, all clients need not be sent for counseling. The particular concerns in the course of giving services, such as vocational or training choice, sexual problems, or social alienation need not supply reasons for automatic referral to counseling, or for the delineation of a particular *type* of counseling for him. By the same token, there is little basis for assuming that there are special skills and unique training required for particular types of clients. The idea that there are unique age groups or diagnostic categories, each requiring a special counseling skill, would make the overall task unmanageable. It is the writer's point of view that the basic values and skills underlying counseling with any group are similar. Perhaps the counselor's approach and style may vary, but he must still promote a safe and secure learning relationship and afford the client freedom to discover the alternatives by which he can grow.

This point of view is especially important in light of the opinion held by some that there is a "culture of poverty." It has been proposed that the poor have a life style, language and view of the world that is fundamentally different from the goals and way of life of the broader culture. It is this writer's contention that to place the client in another culture makes him inaccessible to any attempts to ameliorate his condition. Many of the daily behaviors that are seen among the disadvantaged are a function of what they do not have rather than what they have in common as members of a culture. The often described problem of punctuality of the disadvantaged person can be a result of the fact that there has never been any reason for him to be punctual. Motivation is lacking because there is seldom anything to work toward. It is hardly necessary to codify these kinds of behaviors within a framework of a culture of poverty. The goal for rehabilitation and counseling is to aid the person in his search for maximum productivity and personal satisfaction. Experience has shown that this can be carried out without the assumption by the counselor that he is dealing with a member of another culture. Whatever the culture or set of practices we are confronted with, there is still a need to allow the client an opportunity to search within himself for his own choices, decisions and a sense of personal value that belongs to him alone. Isolating and embedding the non-adjustive behaviors at the level of a separate culture may impair this process.

The Process

When we speak of processes, what do we mean? We are talking about a communication of values between counselor and client pertaining to the client's essential worth. That there is a rightness in his attempting to discover the many ways that he can look at himself in order to feel and behave at his best. Briefly, what are some of the values the successful counselor carries to this relationship? These are really simple points of view that are a part of many productive human relations. The first is the idea that there is an inherent worth in the other human being, a built-in dignity that is independent of his behavior. What the individual does may be good or bad or even alarming, but it can be looked at as part of his attempt to find the best available solution to his problem.

A second value involves the right of the individual to take direction of himself and of his life. This goes with his understanding that his freedom of choice carries with it a responsibility to himself and to others. The counselor may simply afford a relationship with the client from which he comes to know more fully what his beliefs, attitudes and capabilities are. Clearly the client cannot be free to look at all aspects of himself if he expects to be judged and admonished. But even more, he must feel free to explore himself and his own feelings in an atmosphere of acceptance. Obviously, we are not proposing unconditional approval. The counselor might even express alarm or surprise at unusual behaviors. The important thing here is that the counselor is guided by a sense of the individual's potential value irrespective of his behavior at any given time.

Generally, the counselor encounters certain common attitudes in the client whatever his special condition. The client may have the belief that he will not be understood and cannot expect to be really listened to. The client may feel that he cannot really be himself but instead must project a picture that is really shaped by the agency and its expectations. The client may feel that he must hide what he feels is not acceptable or admirable. With such beliefs, the client, when he attempts to negotiate the day-to-day world and meet the expectations of many persons, diverts himself from his search for constructive ways of living. This leads us to the counselor's task.

The Tasks

The first task is to make sure that time is available. Somehow within the agency context, requirements of referral, paperwork and followup, a moment here or a longer period there can be found. A second need is for the counselor to allow somehow for unrestricted communication from the client. This does not mean a passive and permissive attitude but an expressed readiness to listen and understand. He reflects a responsiveness and enthusiasm about the client and whatever the practical limitations of the situation gives the client his total attention. He gets over to the client that he is attempting to understand and appreciate the personal world within which the client is moving. He also demonstrates, as he listens, that he can tolerate the contradictions and alternative views that the client is communicating. Finally, he makes the client understand that his relationship with him is safe and secure. The client must know that he has the rare opportunity of talking about himself without being watchful and defensive. He must come to see that he will be heard out but at the same time that he need not become dependent or feel that he is owned by the counselor because he has revealed himself. Such encounters are often too brief to make a lasting impression by themselves. The assumption is instead that the counseling encounter is a sort of exercise where the individual learns ways of looking at himself and communicating with himself that he may continue on his own.

The Counselor as Agent of the Client

From what is said above, the counselor who is working with the disabled disadvantaged, perhaps more than with others, cannot escape two approaches to his work. On one hand, he must make decisions and take a problem solving approach to such problems as employment, medical care, financial support, training and a myriad of other details. On the other hand, when he counsels, he is an agent of the individual. Whatever the practical outcome of the agencies' efforts, he is committed to the client's personal growth. In this respect, he is concerned about the client bringing out the best in himself by way of attending to what the client himself sees as his problem. In this role, he is less in search of his own practical solutions and more concerned about the kinds of solutions the client himself is searching for. Counseling the disabled disadvantaged is described less by differences in outlook and values than by the particular tactics imposed upon the counselor by the special realities of this work and by the conditions of life that the client faces. The following discussion can be taken in that light.

Before Counseling

Often, before there is any contact with the client on a counseling basis, there has already been a kind of interaction. The counselor has before him notes of the client's previous agency contacts and previous referrals. There are opinions in the case folder of other agency personnel and a record of the client's response to services. The counselor knows whether the client has kept appointments, continued in a training referral or was able to keep a job. There may also be an atmosphere of opinions and attitudes about the client shared by other members of the agency. On the client's side, as a disabled disadvantaged person, there is a greater likelihood that he has been exposed to a variety of agencies and has received assistance from social workers, doctors, lawyers or any number of social agents. He has a background of being helped. In all likelihood, he has a fair idea of what is going to happen in counseling. He also knows that the counselor's duties include considerably more kinds of services, such as the dispensing of funds, arranging support or emergency assistance. Both parties then have a greater than usual variety of experiences that may shape their expectations in the counseling relationship.

From these expectations it can be said that the client may interact with a *phantom counselor* and the counselor with a *phantom client* before either gets to know or work together on personal terms. As the client approaches the session, he may have already gleaned the approach the counselor will take, and from other experiences, he may have a fair idea of the words and approach the counselor will use. In such a situation, both counselor and client may be trapped in the expectancies of the agency as well as in the differences that their own backgrounds bring to the experience. No one in this situation is wrong in the ordinary sense. Clearly, as the session occurs, the first step for the counselor is to put mutual expectations on the table. "Well, sometimes it is wise to clear the air on what we might be expected to be doing, so let's kick that around first." Often this can occur pretty early in the encounter. It will probably be necessary to reaffirm the purposes of the relationship as the client goes through the ups and downs of receiving services.

When Counseling Starts

It is not necessary that the counseling interaction occur in a formal setting. It is just as likely that counseling may grow out of brief remarks in the course of other activities. Referral for evaluation, discussion of the purposes of testing, employer contacts, planning for an employment interview or training, or perhaps discussing difficulty with class or attendance are topics from which personal issues emerge. The counselor who may be preoccupied with another activity must learn to become easily interruptable. Often the client will bring up deeper personal issues in bits and snatches. This may be a very human attempt to find out how ready the counselor is to listen.

How Counseling Starts

Practical problems of daily living will often be a background and starting point for counseling. The client cannot leave her children alone in the neighborhood. Family difficulties may stem from impossible living conditions. Subtle, discriminatory practices on the job can create interpersonal problems for the black client. Language difficulties may limit the Mexican-American's ability to utilize technical training. It is obvious that all of the client's problems cannot be dealt with within the context of the counseling relationship. The agency as a whole may deal with broader matters such as discriminatory hiring practices, need for day-care centers, local birth control clinics, or other problems. From the beginning the counselor must guard against communicating the idea that he can take the full burden of the client's problems on his shoulders. The client may often be in dire need and can easily come to expect that the counselor will solve all problems. In other words, the many needs of the client which must in fact be dealt with in the larger social arena, can become traps in the counseling relationship. The counselor on his part can be stampeded into an approach that seems to say, "put yourself in my hands and we'll see if we can't beat the system." If he allows the client to believe that he is in powerful control of many resources and decisions, he will probably become a constant source of disappointment and his credibility will be considerably weakened.

At the same time the counselor must guard against the communication of hopelessness to the client. He can easily become caught up in the real dificulties the client is experiencing to the point where he unintentionally adds to the client's feeling of paralysis and impotence. The counselor can do this by passing over difficult problems or taking a matter-of-fact approach to a situation that is a real source of concern for the client. In the following example the counselor avoids a routine reply and tries to help a young adult drug abuser become more open about his feelings of being trapped.

Cl. How about calling my parole officer? He's always worried about my getting back on the stuff again. It's all he ever talks about.

Co. Makes you feel as though he doesn't trust you, is that it?

Cl. That's what I said.

Co. Oh, I see, and if I call maybe he'll believe me?

Cl. Every little bit helps. You two are more trouble than my friends.

Co. That's a rough one, everyone seems to be on you—your friends are giving you trouble too?

Cl. They got better reasons for me going back on the stuff than you have for staying off. I come in to talk about school with you but I'm around them all the time. You haven't got anything for me.

Co. They're pushing you to get back on and you can't depend on anyone else anyway.

A number of possibilities may occur to the counselor. Has the client already gone back on drugs and is he now building a justification in case he is caught? Is it worth withstanding pressures from his friends when he senses the distrust of persons trying to help? Is all this to get the counselor to confirm that society has released him from jail with no basis for defending himself from his environment? Such a guessing game would be endless for the counselor. At the beginning it is more important for him to get over to the client that he is trying to accept his stated concerns as is.

Therefore, whatever the client's intentions they are a part of his search for effective ways of dealing with the problem. Though the counselor does not take over the client's problem he tries to let the client know that theirs is a safe relationship where some of his problems might be worked out.

Issues Arising During Counseling

Language

The use of language with the disabled disadvantaged deserves some comment. Some counselors have felt the need to have detailed knowledge of particular language usages or even to learn to talk to the client in his own *non-standard dialect*. However, the use of slang phrases, in-group terms or language structure is fraught with danger. It can only come through to the client as artificial and contrived and only succeeds in creating more distance in the relationship. The counselor gains little except to communicate the feeling that he is unsure of himself and make the client guarded and suspicious. At best, the counselor will appear to be attempting to ingratiate himself with the client in ways that do not make sense.

It is better for the counselor not to allow himself to be intimidated by words or gestures that are strange to him. He can ask openly when he does not understand. At the same time he can take the attitude that he will not allow differences in communication to deter him from trying to follow the client's concerns.

Counseling Goals

At this point, it is useful to consider the goals of counseling. The counselor needs to keep in mind that self-actualization and self-esteem for the disabled disadvantaged is especially a function of the overall rehabilitation counseling process rather than of the counseling experience *per se*. A change in values and the search for maximum personal potential is only possible under conditions that allow a search for alternatives to take place. Immediate goals for the client involving employment and training should not be linked to middle class expectations of self-fulfillment or even gratifying employment. Work for many will remain a necessary evil rather than a source of fulfillment. Is is certain that the counselor will encounter a more complex value system than the traditional nobility of work when often, in the client's background, survival itself has been an accomplishment.

In working with the client towards building self-esteem, a less obvious factor must be kept in mind. Many programs involving multiple services such as training, counseling, work readiness, grooming, family planning and the like really imply that it is the client who is basically responsible for his condition. Such multiple programs seem to say, "If we change you, Mr. Client, you will indeed improve your life conditions because the problems of social and vocational ineptitude are within your own skin." In other words, the offerings of many programs translate into the idea that his condition is his own fault. When the client sees this, he will resist most aspects of the program, including those that are helpful to him. The counselor then finds himself in a peculiar situation. If he implies that he knows that it is the society that is responsible for the client's difficulties, then he opens the question of whether it is worth doing anything at all in a counseling relationship. At the same time, if he communicates the idea that he knows that the client's economic condition is essentially responsible for his problems but still insists on focusing on the client, he may come through to the client as insensitive to his day-to-day predicament.

Sooner or later, the counselor must respond to this issue. He can point out to the client that it must look as if the client is expected to do all the changing. He must leave the way open for the client to express some resentment at constantly finding himself in the center of the stage. The counselor should try to promote a sense of mutual responsibility with the client, to search for issues when talking things out will be of help.

Client Problems

The counselor must also keep in mind that some of the intense problems brought up in counseling may be crucial but short-lived. The welfare mother is distraught after an argument with her husband. She has two sick children and constant babysitting problems. She did not receive her check and is afraid someone stole it from the mailbox. Further, she is becoming frightened of herself because she cannot stop beating her oldest child. She may spend some time with the counselor discussing her resentment towards the children and anger at her husband. Shortly after, however, emergency funds are arranged and some special arrangement for child care is made. It may be that the client will never raise her feelings about her children again. The counselor can only tentatively raise these issues himself since other problems will become more salient. What is also important here is that the counselor have the client understand that such problems are also their mutual concern and can be raised at any time.

This example about the transitory nature of some problems leads to another observation. Experience has shown that the counselor cannot always expect consistency in the themes and issues that the client brings up. This is because the client's day-to-day life may be a succession of major and minor crises. The amputee may have a constant problem getting transportation for physical therapy sessions. The psychiatric referral has nowhere to go except back home to a tense situation. There may not be an alarm clock in the home, or sufficient toilet facilities. This can mean that much of the client's talk will revolve around more immediate pragmatic issues that will allow little time for long-term consideration of personal growth. Again, the counselor must work toward being accessible to the client. In the course of assisting the client in these crucial daily problems, he must guard against communicating the idea to the client that these are his only concerns.

There is always the problem that programs giving multiple services are more likely to foster dependency. If the client has not participated in the decisions and plans, there may be no commitment to them. Perhaps the only clients that remain in some programs are those who are the most cooperative and dependent. The counselor must be careful not to mistake an apparent cooperativeness for personal growth. The counselor would do well to observe himself and be sure that he is not too eager to help, that he does not, in fact, enjoy giving direction and assistance. The best control for this is the counselor's awareness and continued monitoring of his own feelings. Does he have a genuine liking for his clients and does he experience pleasure when the client does more and more on his own. It is certain that the client will detect the counselor's preoccupation with his own agenda and will then avoid a counseling relationship or simply become passively cooperative and dependent.

Summary

The point of view in this chapter has been that the counseling process for the disabled disadvantaged involves the same values and commitment to personal growth as with counseling other groups. The attempt here has been to point to ways in which the client's condition, the agency and the counselor impose special considerations for working with the disabled disadvantaged.

REFERENCES

Bozarth, J. D.: *Models and functions of counseling for applied settings and rehabilitation workers.* University of Arkansas, 1972.

McGowan, J. F. and Schmidt, L. D.: *Counseling: Readings in theory and practice.* New York, Holt, Rinehart and Winston, 1962.

Patterson, C. H.: *Rehabilitation counseling: Collected papers.* Champaign, Stipes, 1969.

CHAPTER XII

TRAINING AND
VOCATIONAL OPPORTUNITIES

C. D. AUVENSHINE

It HAS LONG BEEN RECOGNIZED that the best way to enhance one's self development and social status is through education, job training, and a "good job." The need for both academic and vocational training and the implications of the lack of training are well documented (Levine, 1965; Moynihan, 1964; Reed, 1965; Rothney, 1966; Wolfbein, 1964). While the majority of people in this country use educational and vocational achievement as a means of personal and social fulfillment, many others are unable to do so for a variety of reasons.

It has been estimated that there are 40 to 50 million (or

approximately one out of every four or five) people in this country who would be classified as victims of poverty. This number varies considerably depending on the criteria used for inclusion in this category. Within this segment of our society resides a multitude of social ills. Among them are illiteracy, joblessness, chronic mental and physical illness, disability, broken homes, drug abuse, delinquency, and violent crimes. These conditions are fostered by economically-related conditions associated with poor nourishment, poor and over-crowded housing, and inadequate medical attention. Also, the schools serving this group are frequently inferior in many aspects, making career preparation extremely difficult. So our social system is failing this large and ever-increasing proportion of our population in areas of health, education, and jobs. It is from this large pool of poverty victims that our welfare recipients come.

Hunt (1970) has indicated that there are approximately 60,000 fathers and 1,500,000 mothers who are unemployed recipients of Aid to Families of Dependent Children. He suggests all the fathers could presumably accept jobs. Some 432,000 of the mothers are already working or are waiting to enter work or training programs. Another 900,000 have to be counted out of the labor market because of being physically or mentally incapacitated, having no marketable skills, and being homemakers. However, he estimates that between 200,000 and 700,000 of the AFDC mothers can become employable. These figures point to a sizeable manpower pool if these workers can be mobilized. Inversely, this large group of persons constitutes a heavy drain on the economy in their present status as AFDC recipients. Of course, these figures pertain only to AFDC recipients and do not include any other category of welfare recipients.

This chapter represents an attempt to examine some work-related characteristics of poverty clients including attitudes toward training and employment. Evaluation for training and employment are also considered. Some specific relevant training programs are described. The placement process and some barriers to employment are included. Finally, the counselor's role and contributions as they relate to welfare recipients are considered.

THE NEED FOR TRAINING

In recent years America has experienced a great deal of prosperity. Yet, unemployment is steadily rising. Mali (1963) has suggested that some of the reasons for this are increases in technological complexity, technological changes and shifts, the profit squeeze, upgrading educational standards (causing dropouts), and insufficient counseling and guidance.

Reed (1965) has cited unemployment percentages at three levels of school completion. The figures indicated that the group having attended school for the least time had the highest unemployment rate and inversely the group having attended school most showed the lowest unemployment rate.

Wolfbein (1964) has pointed out that among the unemployed one out of three never went beyond grade school and that two out of three dropped out of high school. He went on to say ". . . we are faced with the fact that there is a compelling relationship between the lack of educational attainment and success in the labor force [p. 51]."

Rothney (1966) has followed up a sample of trained workers and a comparison group of untrained workers. He compared 179 trained males and 142 nontrained males ten years out of high school. Several differences were found between the two groups. The trained persons had a much higher proportion of counseled subjects. Members of the trained group had more frequently left their home town, married later, had fewer children, earned more money, were more optimistic, looked back more favorably on their high school experiences, reported more educational and vocational plans for the future, belonged to more organizations and held more offices in them, were more pleased with military service experiences, and reported fewer job handicaps.

In view of the above comments, it seems abundantly clear that those persons who have some training fare better in the labor force than those who have little or none. This means that the likelihood of getting a job is better, the job obtained is likely to be better, and job security and income are better. With the increase in industrial technology, job training is becoming increasingly important. The number of entry jobs which don't require training is shrinking rapidly. At the same time there is an increasing need for workers who have some training and technical skills to offer. It appears that training enhances entry, advancement, and security in the labor force and is to be recommended in all cases where feasible.

THE MEANING OF WORK

Values enhance or hinder one's achievement, depending on the strength, direction, and consistency among them. While the importance of adequate education and employment are recognized by many of our disadvantaged clients, the tasks required to achieve them often seem piddling, childish, effeminate, irrelevant, or otherwise distasteful. Whereas physical prowess is valued highly among lower-class persons, intellectual, artistic, and esthetic activities are devalued. To achieve in education, and to an increasing extent in employment, one must be adept in the use of symbolic and verbal skills. This is one example of a very basic conflict of personal values which may create resistance and defensiveness in welfare clients when the need to change is communicated or implied by the counselor.

Tyler (1967) has pointed out that we assume that something is wrong with a person who does not work. She suggests that perhaps our assumption is fallacious and that the more natural condition is the preference not to work. If this premise is valid, then she suggests ". . . that only persons conditioned to it through an appropriate course of training from early childhood on find holding down a job really congenial [p. 63]." (When viewed in this way, lack of "appropriate" attitudes toward work might be considered as a deficiency in the developmental process.)

Neff (1967) has pointed out that poor people are lacking in role models and need for achievement. The role model available to many welfare recipients is often inappropriate in relation to the formation of effective work-related attitudes. That is, to the extent that there has been a role-model present, it has been instrumental in internalizing attitudes which are negative to education, training, and employment. Specifically, these include attitudes of dependency, self-doubt, antagonism toward school or training, and even hostility toward the "white collar" society.

Neff and Helfanc (1963) have compared a group of "successful" with a group of "unsuccessful" handicapped workers on their attitudes toward work. Successful workers were fairly homogeneous in their attitudes toward work and resembled the average male industrial worker. Unsuccessful workers did not resemble the adjusted worker or even each other in their attitudes toward work.

Once developed, meaningful attitudes toward work exert a profound influence on behavior and endure to an old age. Rusalem and Speiser (1964) have studied workshop performance of older retired workers (mean age 82). The work seemed more important for some than for others. For some of them, ". . . it became a predominant theme in the lives of those who were vocationally oriented, regardless of their age [p. 120]." The authors go on to say that the workers reported that the employment ". . . was a revitalizing experience, giving them a chance to live again as a functioning member of society and to resume filling a role that was more consistent with their self-concepts [p. 120]." This seems to indicate that for those persons who had developed a wholesome respect for work and found it gratifying, positive attitudes and work-related behaviors continue into very old age. Also, these workers seemed happier and had more positive attitudes toward themselves when they were working.

MOTIVATION FOR TRAINING AND EMPLOYMENT

One of the most challenging and frustrating problems a counselor has to deal with in marginal workers and hard-core unemployed is that of motivation. The construct of motivation is basic in the behavioral and social sciences. It is a nebulous and elusive concept to define. There are many elaborate and scholarly definitions of the term. However, grossly oversimplified for our purposes, it means a force within the human organism which compels it toward a goal. For the most part we as psychologists, counselors, caseworkers, teachers and others in the social service professions, use the concept to convey the idea of a desire or striving to achieve along certain lines. Most frequently motivation to achieve implies goals of higher education, better job, better house, more material possessions, and a higher standard of living in general. These achievement strivings characterize the large American middle class and constitute a part of middle class values. On the other hand, these values of striving for economic gain are essentially absent among our poverty class. Since this kind of striving or motivation is believed to be essential to success in basic education, work evaluation, skills training, and employment, it warrants some attention in this chapter.

Barry (1965) suggests that the notion of poor client motivation masks many more specific meanings. He notes that Sinick (1961) has listed thirty-four such meanings. In his paper Sinick states that all clients are motivated. He states several reasons why the client may appear unmotivated. If one assumes that each client is motivated, the responsibility of the caseworker for understanding the client is great. Thus, if the counselor assumes this responsibility it is much more difficult for him to write off the client as "unmotivated."

Frequently associated with the lack of motivation is the characteristic of dependency. Dependency is antithetical to motivation. Several different types have been identified by Goldin and Perry (1967) according to the stimulus in the setting which precipitates it. They identified the categories of social, emotional, financial, institutional, and psychomedical. Coburn (1964) has suggested that independence has been overstressed in our society and that dependency has been equated with weakness. He makes a case for an optimal level of dependency and appropriate spread among the sources of support. All persons are somewhat dependent normally. Presumably there is a range of dependency level which would be considered normal or even desirable in most people. However, persons who are handicapped physically, socially, or emotionally by disability, poverty, or other ills of our society are necessarily more dependent than most people and in ways different from other people. One of the things a disabled or disadvantaged person has to learn as a part of his total adjustment is how to be *effectively* dependent.

To allow oneself to become, or more precisely, to teach oneself to be dependent requires a change in the way he thinks about himself. Since most middle-class people value independence so highly, it means developing the values of the person in such a way that selective dependence becomes important. Also, it involves incorporating the idea of being dependent into the self concept. The persons who can be effectively dependent are those who are realistic, objective, and comfortable in appraising their dependency status and its physical, social, and emotional meaning to them.

Ehrle (1965) has developed the idea that some of the problems attributed to lack of motivation may be problems associated with attaining one's identity. Also, the process of "validating" the identity is a continuing one. This idea has some relevance here. For our disabled and disadvantaged clients, values which in effect say that they are worthy of attention and services, that they should try to develop themselves as much as possible, that they can and should work, and that one should be as independent as possible may be foreign to their ideas about and expectations for themselves. While some of these may be meaningful to the client, some may not be consistent with the way he perceives himself, and others may be contradictory to his existing values. So, in this context, it is easier to understand how the client may be confused, resistant, and perceived as passive or lacking in motivation.

Although motivation is important at all stages of the rehabilitation process, it becomes essential when the client enters evaluation, training or employment. Up to this point in the client's rehabilitation program, he may have been a rather passive and indifferent participant in the process. The counselor considers client involvement very important and usually works hard trying to achieve it through counseling during the preliminary stages of case development. Yet, it is difficult to know the extent to which the client is committed to a course of action or the extent to which the client will persevere in implementing a plan. This is especially true of our poverty clients. As mentioned earlier, there may be conflicting or competing values or there may be other sources of resistance. Sometimes the client is not aware of the sources of his resistance because they are operating unconsciously. In fact, he may think he is cooperating and in some ways behave as if he is until he has to assume greater responsibility for himself or produce in some ways which create a threat to his personal adequacy.

Entry into evaluation, training, or employment creates some stress for poverty clients which tests the level of motivation. If a client is not highly motivated to follow through on a program of services, it is likely that he will terminate the services or offer resistance to following through on rehabilitation plans at this stage. For a person who has little education, a poor work history, and few skills in finding and applying for a job, the process of getting a job is a big hurdle. Also, if the person feels insecure he is likely to develop anxiety, defensiveness, or even symptoms of physical illness. Some people may have sufficient motivation to enable them to complete a program, but be incapacitated by personal adjustment or a mental illness. There are times when the counselor should distinguish between poor motivation and motivation which is adequate, but negated by underlying personality problems.

Clients who have been recipients of checks from welfare, social security, workmen's compensation, or unemployment insurance benefits have been relegated to a dependency status. In effect, they have been rewarded by society for being ill, disabled, and idle. Viewed in this context, the disability which rendered the client eligible for financial benefits under one or more of the programs is a saleable resource. As such, it is usually exploited to the fullest extent. In the perception and attitudes of the client he is being paid for being unemployed and disabled. To present the client with an alternative which suggests that he relinquish the security and comfort of his dependency status with an assured income to enter a job which offers little or no financial advantage, which makes demands on him, which has the frustrations accompanying employment, and which threatens his adequacy as a person, frequently does not make much sense to the client. Therefore, the counselor should realize that there are some reinforcing agents including financial gains, sympathy from others, and freedom from the frustrations and restrictions from work, all of which operate in opposition to the counselor's efforts to return the client to employment. The effects of secondary gains from disability, poverty, and unemployment are well documented (Allen, 1970; Finney, 1969; Goldin & Perry, 1967; Harrington, 1969; Mahoney, Cope, and Campbell, 1969).

Along a similar line, Margolin and Goldin (1970) have taken the position that poor motivation of the client considered alone is not sufficient to account for all the difficulty in rehabilitating disadvantaged clients. They believe that the whole environment including the client must be understood in order to provide solutions to the problems involved in the rehabilitation of this group. "Confining treatment to the counselor-client dyadic relationship without cognizance of the swirling sociological, cultural, and psychological currents in the community is inadequate for motivating the disadvantaged [p. 23]." The authors do not deny the role of the client's motivation in his rehabilitation. They believe that even with adequate motivation there are societal forces which operate against some clients being integrated into the mainstream of society. This is particularly true of minority groups against whom discrimination is widespread. So their point here is that for rehabilitation to be complete, forces both in the client and in the community must be understood and mobilized.

CLIENT EVALUATION

Evaluation is a basic and integral part of the rehabilitation process. It is continuous from the first counselor-client contact throughout the entire sequence of services. The client must be evaluated for eligibility, for restoration services, for counseling needs, and for training and placement needs. The process of evaluation serves to answer basic questions about the client, the answers which in turn point to client needs and suggest a course of action appropriate to those needs.

Typically and traditionally the counselor has relied on other professional specialists to provide certain kinds of evaluation services for his clients. These services usually obtained from specialists include medical, psychological, visual, and audiological as well as other kinds of technical services and equipment. The counselor has the responsibility for purchasing the services, interpreting the reports, integrating the information, and relating it to the client's needs. Beyond the point where the client needs evaluation primarily regarding restoration services, the counselor himself directly provides the evaluation regarding counseling services, training, and job placement.

The instruments which the counselor has available to him for his personal evaluation are the interview, case study including medical, social, educational, and vocational history, educational and psychological tests, and the counselor's own observations. These sources usually provide sufficient information on which to base a "vocational diagnosis" and project a case plan for rehabilitation. The instruments stated here have been effective to a large extent only because we have been able to make certain assumptions about our clients. Some examples of these assumptions are at least a low level of literacy, some ability to communicate, at least minimum interpersonal skills, some work experience, and some ability to follow directions. As we undertake to rehabilitate welfare, poverty, or hard-core unemployed we find that these assumptions are frequently not met or met to a lesser extent than for other clients. This is particularly true with the counseling interview where communication between counselor and client is difficult. It is also a problem with psychological testing where the client does not have an experience base comparable to the standardization group and where the norms provided with the test are not appropriate.

In recent months, there has been an increasing emphasis on the use of workshops for disadvantaged persons. This approach has much to offer for a number of reasons. It provides for constant observation of behavior in a simulated work setting over a period of several days. It provides some of the conditions found in the real world of work. Unlike psychological tests, work evaluation incorporates actual samples from the criteria it purports to predict. The work samples, because they are usually taken from real work, are more interesting to nonverbal adults than putting pegs in holes in a pegboard, marking between the lines on an answer sheet, or responding to an inkblot on a projective test.

The work-samples method referred to above involves the actual use of miniature job samples. The oldest and best known system in existence is one which was developed several years ago in New York at the Institute for the Crippled and Disabled. It is known as the "TOWER" system. TOWER is an acronym for "Testing, Orientation, and Work Evaluation in Rehabilitation." It's major objective is to assess a client's skills, aptitudes, and potentials for training or job placement. This original system includes job samples from a wide variety of areas. This system has been copied and adapted in many hospitals, rehabilitation centers, and workshops across the country. This general approach to client evaluation offers a great deal of promise, not only to disabled persons, but to disadvantaged as well.

Nadolsky (1971) has conducted a rather extensive study in an attempt to develop a model for vocational evaluation of the disadvantaged. The study involved a workshop consisting of vocational evaluators which focused on the nature of the evaluation process and related methodology as they pertain to the disadvantaged. Also, site visits were made to programs of evaluation for the disadvantaged which had been identified as effective for this target group. The above approaches combined with a review of related literature enabled the author to develop a model for the vocational evaluation process. That model is described briefly below.

The primary objective of vocational evaluation as derived from Nadolsky's study was ". . . to determine the vocational potential of each client evaluated and to establish vocational goals that were consistent with this potential [p. 40]." The study also indicated that the same general techniques and procedures constitute the substance of the evaluation for most programs. Ten techniques were identified which are commonly used and the sequence of their use was established. Here are the techniques in the stated sequence (p. 41):

1. *Biographical Data*
2. *The Evaluation Interview*
3. *Psychological Tests*
4. *Work Samples*
5. *Occupational Information*
6. *Situational or Workshop Tasks*
7. *Informal Conferences with Other Staff*
8. *Job Tryouts*
9. *The Formal Staff Conference*
10. *Vocational Counseling*

The model is based on a logical narrowing of vocational choice at each step by eliminating some untenable possibilities. So as the client progresses through the sequence he presumably learns about himself and the work world. By the time he has completed the sequence through vocational counseling, the ideal occupation should emerge. The author points out that the model is structural in nature. It was his opinion that, as such, it should be applicable to any population of clients. Whether or not one agrees with the selection of components or the sequence in which presented by the author, it appears that this conceptualization of the vocational evaluation process has considerable utility for all clients. It seems especially appropriate for a population of disadvantaged clients.

TRAINING PROGRAMS

At the beginning of this chapter a statement was made that training is one of the best known ways of upgrading one's general status and standard of living. Training also serves another function in the gamut of rehabilitation services. It is an important link in a chain of events in the rehabilitation process for many individuals. It is the link which connects the client's resources to gainful employment. So, viewed from the angle of the rehabilitation specialist, the many varieties of training constitute a very important tool in the services repertory.

Most of our welfare recipients have to be ruled out as college attenders. A large proportion of them have not succeeded in high school and have no desire to continue in formal education programs. However, there are a number of programs which are appropriate for welfare recipients. Several research and demonstration projects are currently under way and some have been completed. The evidence is conclusive that welfare recipients, when provided the appropriate services, can be rehabilitated. Varying degrees of success have been reported among the projects depending on the design, subjects, variables studied, services provided, and criteria for success. Particularly, rehabilitation efforts seem to have been moderately successful in projects for AFDC recipients (Friedman, 1966; McWhorter and Antoinette, 1967).

Several categories of training appropriate for many disadvantaged clients are provided by the Manpower Development and Training Act, the Economic Opportunity Act, Vocational Education Act, Vocational Rehabilitation Act, and Veteran's Readjustment Act. Some specific programs which have been made possible by these acts are described below. These are descriptions of some of the larger and better known government programs. As might be expected, this is not an exhaustive coverage of programs now in existence. Limitation of space dictates that the number considered be kept to a minimum and that the description of each be rather cursory. Private training schools and programs were excluded. Also, programs of purely basic education and those serving coordinating functions rather than direct training were excluded.

The information included for each program consists of the legislative base or authorization, the target population, the services provided, funding and enrollment levels where available, administering agency, and where to apply for training, employment, and related supporting services. The information pertaining to the training programs was taken from the *Manpower Information Service* which is published by the Bureau of National Affairs, Inc.

Apprenticeships

The original apprenticeship authorization was the National Apprenticeship (or Fitzgerald) Act of 1937. It was intended for persons under 26 years of age in occupations considered apprenticeable. It provides for technical assistance to employers, labor unions, and community organizations in developing and administering apprenticeship programs. Under this provision the employer pays the worker's wage. It is administered by the U. S. Bureau of Apprenticeship and Training and state apprenticeship agencies. There are about 350 apprenticeable trades. In 1968, there were 115,236 persons registered in apprenticeship programs. A more recent version of apprenticeship training has been developed under the authorization of the Manpower Development and Training Act of 1962. This program is called "Apprenticeship Outreach" and is intended for minority youth. It provides minority group organizations, building trade councils, and employer associations with reimbursement of costs involved in recruiting, motivating, and helping minority-group members to meet requirements for apprenticeship programs. This program is administered by the Manpower Administration and Bureau of Apprenticeship and Training of the Department of Labor. Inquiries for either type apprenticeship should be directed to the local Employment Service office.

Concentrated Employment Program (CEP)

This is an approach rather than a separate entity. It was authorized by the Manpower Development and Training Act of 1962 and the Economic Opportunity Act of 1964. Its purpose is to coordinate federal and state manpower efforts to make an impact on the total economic condition of the community or neighborhood. It attempts to involve local businessmen and labor groups and provide full-scale personalized help to disadvantaged persons. Primarily the target population is disadvantaged persons age sixteen and above in high unemployment areas. The specific services include outreach and recruitment, appraisal, counseling, job orientation, medical and social services, basic education, skill training, work experience, job development and placement, follow-up, and continued counseling for job adjustment. It is administered by the Regional Manpower Administration through subcontracts with local employment service offices, community action agencies, or local government. For the fiscal year 1970 the funding level was $209 million and at the beginning of that year 75,900 were enrolled. Applications should be made to an Employment Service office or a community action agency in those communities which have programs.

Job Corps

The Job Corps was authorized by the Economic Act of 1964. It was transferred to the Department of Labor effective July 1, 1969. The target population was school dropouts age sixteen to twenty-one years whose family financial resources placed them in the poverty category. It was also intended for youth from areas with no training opportunities and those who need complete training service. The program provides both residential and non-residential training in rural and urban areas. The services include basic education, job-skills training, counseling, job placement and related services. The program is administered by the Manpower Administration of the Department of Labor. The centers are operated by a variety of federal and state agencies such as employment services, conservation agencies, and universities. Some are also operated by private non-profit agencies. A training allowance is provided. The funding level for fiscal year 1970 was $180 million and enrollment that year was 19,000. Applications should be submitted to local offices of the employment service.

Job Opportunities in the Business Sector (JOBS)

This program was authorized by the Manpower Development and Training Act of 1962 and the Economic Opportunity Act of 1964. It is designed for unemployed and underemployed disadvantaged persons, sixteen years of age and older and for upgrading low income workers. Services of the program include counseling and related services, minor medical and day care, training, job placement, and job upgrading. The program is administered by the Department of Labor Manpower Administration in conjunction with private or nonprofit organizations, boards of trade, and chambers of commerce. Employer pays at least minimum wage. During the years 1967 through 1969, 432,000 disadvantaged persons were hired by 25,000 firms. Of the number hired, 90 percent were members of minority groups. Of the total minority group members hired, 73 percent of those were Negro. Fifty percent of all hired were under twenty-two years of age. The average JOBS employee had been unemployed for an average of 21.5 weeks out of the last 12 months and had only 10.5 years of schooling. Application should be filed at an Employment Service office.

Neighborhood Youth Corps (NYC)

The Neighborhood Youth Corps began in January of 1965. It was authorized by the Economic Opportunity Act of 1964. It is a program of paid work experience for young people between fourteen and twenty-one. There are actually two separate programs. One is in-school and summer for persons still in school. This is for poverty persons ages fourteen through twenty-one. It provides part-time employment, work experience and some counseling. The other program is for out of school poverty youth ages sixteen through twenty-one. It provides skill training, remedial education, work experience, counseling, and health care. The work experience in these programs usually includes jobs such as aides in schools and libraries, cafeterias, museums, offices, factories, and hospitals. The program is administered by the Manpower Administration of the Department of Labor through contracts with local sponsors. In fiscal year 1969, the funding level was $313 million total for the three programs. In-school programs received $51 million, summer programs received $138.3 million, and out-of-school programs received $124 million. During that fiscal year enrollment for each of the three programs in the order listed above was 81,600, 336,-000, and 46,000. Application should be made to the local sponsoring agency where the program exists.

Manpower Development and Training Act

This act was approved March 15, 1962. It has been amended in 1963, 1965, 1966, and 1968. The original purpose of the act was to combat unemployment and manpower problems. There has been increasing emphasis on the "hard-core unemployed" with each amendment. Manpower training is for any unemployed or under-employed person who needs education and training services, although the highest priority is given to the disadvantaged (defined to include the poor, minority group members, dropouts, handicapped, welfare clients, and low-income farmers). A person may enter training at age sixteen but will not be eligible for allowance benefits until age 17. Residents of Redevelopment Areas (under ARA) automatically qualify for training allowances. No training allowance will be paid to a high school dropout unless he has been out of school for a year or unless authorities determine he cannot benefit from regular school programs. Unemployed professionals may receive brief refresher courses. Inmates of correctional institutions may be provided MDTA education and training. The provisions of the act included both basic education and skills training, training allowances, transportation and subsistence, testing, selection, and job placement. There is no cost to the trainee. For on-the-job-training, the employer pays a wage. For institutional training there is a training allowance. The act specified the use of public educational vocational agencies except under certain conditions where it would be deemed advantageous to use private schools. Administration of different parts of the program is by the Manpower Administration, Department of Labor, the Bureau of Vocational and Technical Education, Office of Education, and Economic Development Administration, U. S. Department of Commerce. For fiscal year 1970, appropriations for institutional training was $196 million offering 98,000 training opportunities. For on-the-job training (exclusive of JOBS) the appropriation was $56.4 million and provided 65,000 training opportunities.

Operation Mainstream

This program was authorized under the Economic Opportunity Act of 1964. It was aimed at the chronically-unemployed poor who were twenty-two years of age and older. Particularly the emphasis of this program is on the older poor in rural areas. The services provided include counseling, basic education, work training, and job creation in community improvement and beautification projects. The program is administered by the Office of Employment Development Programs of the Department of Labor. Services are provided by community action agencies or other non-profit organizations. The minimum wage is paid for this work. For fiscal year 1969, the appropriation was $41 million funding 200 projects in 46 states. Application should be made at a local Employment Service office.

Public Service Careers

This was authorized by the Economic Opportunity Act of 1964 and the Manpower Development and Training Act of 1962. It was directed to disadvantaged and "near poor" persons eighteen years of age or older. There are five plans under this program, A, B, C, D, and Supplementary Training and Employment Program (STEP). Plans A, B, and D provide on-the-job training in public service jobs. It anticipates and assists the employee to upgrade through on-the-job training. Under these plans, employers are reimbursed for released time for basic education. Plan C is the "New Careers" program. It provides on-the-job training and upgrading to subprofessionals or even professionals in the general area of human services. The program under this plan provides remedial and advanced education, counseling and other supportive services for career advancement. STEP provides short-term public employment for manpower program graduates who cannot find jobs. Plans A and C are administered by the Office of Employment Development of the Department of Labor. Plan B is administered by federal agencies operating grant-in-aid programs. Plan D is administered by the U. S. Civil Service Commission and the Employment Service. STEP is administered by the Employment Service. Remuneration for plans A, B, and D are minimum wage at the beginning with increases as the person upgrades. The wage is paid by the employer. For plan C, the New Careers program, the federal contract pays 100 percent of the wage for the first year and 50 percent for the second. The employer assumes full wage at the beginning of the third year. For STEP, Employment Service pays minimum wage rate. For fiscal year 1970, the total funding for all programs was $95.6 million making available 40,000 opportunities. Application for any of these programs may be filed either with an Employment Service office or at the particular agency involved with one of the plans.

Veterans Administration

The authorization for rehabilitation services as such to disabled veterans was first provided in the Soldier Rehabilitation Act of 1918. At that time the program was placed under the Federal Board for Vocational Education. It was transferred to a newly created "Veterans Bureau" by an act of Congress in August of 1921. The Veterans Bureau was reorganized and became the "Veterans Administration" in 1933. The program was further expanded under Public Law 16 in 1943 and under the Servicemen's Readjustment Act of 1944. The current act under which services are provided is the Veterans' Readjustment Act of 1966. In general, these and additional legislative actions have continued, expanded, and refined programs of services to veterans since the original act. The present system of services includes not only services to the veteran but to widows and orphans who meet the eligibility requirements. A wide range of vocational rehabilitation and education services are available to qualified veterans. Apprenticeships or on-the-job training with an employer or in an approved apprenticeship program are provided for non-disabled servicemen for a limited time after discharge. This is at no cost to the veteran. Subsistence allowance is provided to the veteran. For disabled veterans who have service-connected disabilities, hospitalization, treatment, medication, and restorative services including prostheses and therapy are provided. The total range of services including medical, psychological, social, educational, and vocational are applied in the process of restoring the disabled veteran to his most complete usefulness. Services specific to training efforts include payment of costs of tuition, books, supplies and equipment, counseling, placement, and referral to other appropriate programs or jobs. The program is administered by the Veterans Administration through a network of Assistance Centers and hospitals located in selected cities. Application and inquiries should be directed to the local center.

Vocational Education

The original act which established vocational education as such was the Smith-Hughes Act of 1917. It provided for the establishment of a system of vocational education in the states and made appropriations for them. Several other acts have expanded the program, particularly the three George-Barden Acts (1946, 1956, 1958). Beginning with the Manpower Development and Training Act of 1962, legislative attention has been increasingly given to programs for the unemployed, underemployed, and persons whose skills are technologically outdated. Continued efforts under Smith-Hughes and George-Barden Acts were required. The Vocational Education Act of 1963 authorized vocational education programs for persons in high school, for those out of high school available for full-time study, for persons unemployed or underemployed, and for persons having academic or socioeconomic handicaps that prevent them from succeeding in the regular vocational education program. The Vocational Education Amendments of 1968 provided, among other things, for cooperative and work study programs emphasizing training in areas of high rates of school drop-out and youth unemployment. Training for employment is offered in a wide variety of semi-skilled, skilled, and technical areas. The program is administered nationally by the Office of Education of the Department of Health, Education, and Welfare. At the state level they are administered by departments of education and vocational education agencies. Federal funding for fiscal year 1969 was $248 million. There were 3.5 million high school enrollees in vocational education programs that year. Inquiries should be made to a vocational school, Employment Service office, or state department of education.

Vocational Rehabilitation

Services under this program were first authorized under the Vocational Rehabilitation Act of 1920. Major amendments since the original act have generally expanded the program to include additional client groups and additional services. Also both federal and state appropriation of funds have steadily increased. Special cooperative programs with several agencies have been established in recent years. This enables the agency to better reach the mentally ill, mentally retarded, school dropouts, welfare recipients, selective service draftees, public offenders, alcoholics, and narcotic addicts. It provides counseling, guidance, restoration, training, placement, and followup. It may provide for transportation, maintenance, tools, and supplies. Also, where restorative services such as treatment and prostheses are needed it may provide those. The program is administered at the federal level by Social and Rehabilitation Services of the Department of Health, Education, and Welfare. At the state level, the programs are administered by state rehabilitation agencies. Usually area or local offices deliver the direct services. For fiscal year 1969, federal appropriations were $650 million. During that year, 785,000 cases were in process. There were 240,000 cases declared "rehabilitated" for that year. Inquiry or application should be directed to the local office of vocational rehabilitation services or to the state office in the state capital.

Work Incentive (WIN)

This program was authorized by the Social Security Amendments of 1967. It was designed for recipients of Aid to Families with Dependent Children. It provides counseling, training, work orientation, basic education (including preparation for the GED certificate if desired), work experience, and job placement. Some examples of areas of training are business and office occupations, health occupations, printing, sales, commercial foods, or manufacturing occupations. The Labor Department administers the training and incentives through the Office of Employment Development Programs. Contracts are awarded to state employment service offices, but referrals are made by state welfare agencies (AFDC). The funding level for fiscal year 1969, was $33 million. As of July 1971, there were 108,951 trainees enrolled and the number is steadily increasing. Families receiving AFDC benefits should direct inquiries to their caseworker.

THE PLACEMENT PROCESS

Getting appropriate jobs for handicapped workers has always been one of the major objectives of vocational rehabilitation. Appropriate placement of the handicapped worker essentially means getting the worker in a job which maximizes his chances for success in a particular job or broad area of work. Successful placement, in turn, means that the worker uses his personal resources optimally and is suited for the job by virtue of the configuration of his unique characteristics as they relate to a job. This set of characteristics is often referred to as the "work personality." Successful employment or "work adjustment" as defined by the Minnesota Studies (Dawis, 1967) encompasses both satisfaction (i.e. by the worker) and satisfactoriness (i.e. satisfaction of the employer with the worker). So, in the placement process, we are attempting to place the worker in a situation where he will be happy with his work and the work setting and the employer will be satisfied with his work.

Perhaps the most essential part of effecting job placement is preparing the client for "job readiness." Job readiness actually includes all those services which have been brought to bear on the client's problems throughout the entire process from the initial interview until placement efforts are begun. However, in its usage among rehabilitation specialists it has taken on a narrower meaning. The expression usually refers to those activities which transpire between the counselor and client in specific preparation for employment interviews. Frequently topics discussed include scheduling appointments, manner of dress, how to present oneself, filling out application forms, how to answer questions, the kind of material to present, why the client thinks he is qualified for the job, the kinds of questions the client might want to ask, how to respond to questions regarding the disability, etc. Methods used in this preparation include coaching, role playing, visits to industry, group guidance, and individual counseling. These are sometimes used individually or in combination with each other depending on the individual client's needs. The important thing is that the client be well prepared before attempts at job placement are made.

Helfand (1967) has described a phenomenon of "employment shock" pertaining to entry into and adjusting to work. "The phenomenon of 'employment shock' is the reaction suffered by a trainee who has difficulty in facing, conforming, or adjusting to realities about him in relation to the current work world. It is usually experienced by the youth who has never been employed and who lacks the particular work skills and social skills needed to obtain and hold a job. He generally knows little about the world of work, because he has never been in it. He frequently does not expect success for the role models in his environment of poverty had more experience at failure than success [p. 111]." This set of conditions typifies our disadvantaged clients and clearly indicates the need for effective "job-readiness" strategies.

Negative attitudes of the employer and the public are frequent obstacles in placing clients in jobs. Employers often believe that disabled or disadvantaged clients cannot maintain the required production rate, that they will be absent from the job frequently, that they might be a disruptive influence among other workers, or that they are unpleasant in their associations with others. These attitudes are negative to employment, but they are even worse if the disabled-disadvantaged happens to be a member of a minority racial or ethnic group. Rehabilitation services and other social services agencies have done a great deal to alleviate negative attitudes and discriminatory practices toward disadvantaged persons. Yet, we still have a long way to go to achieve equal employment opportunities for equally qualified workers.

There are certain generally accepted practices which most counselors use in placing clients in jobs. These pertain to client readiness, complete knowledge about the client in the relevant dimensions, ways of approaching the employer, and amount of responsibility the counselor should assume as the client goes for an interview and enters a new job. Because of some of the characteristics of welfare recipients there are special considerations we should make. Some of the characteristics common to most welfare recipients are low educational achievement, poor work record, minority group status, poor grooming and personal hygiene, physical and mental disability, negative attitudes toward self, and feelings of inadequacy in interpersonal relations and educational and vocational tasks. Often they have attitudes of defeatism and believe they have little or no control over circumstances in their lives. All of these things are sufficiently different from the usual rehabilitation clients that the counselor needs to adopt an approach which is different from that customarily used by the rehabilitation counselor. The role of the counselor as he relates to members of this special group is considered in the following section.

THE ROLE OF THE COUNSELOR

As we reflect on the needs of welfare recipients or all poverty clients for that matter, we inevitably must ask ourselves the questions, "What are the special needs of the members of this group?" "What services do they need mostly and in what amounts?" "Are the needed services substantially different from those of other client groups?" "What should the counselor *be* and *do* in working with this group?" Especially for the rehabilitation counselor who serves as the link between the agency and the client, these are questions of some concern.

Some authors (Acker, 1967; Calia, 1966; Stone, 1971) have suggested that other roles be considered. There is some agreement among the various positions stated that the counselor can be more effective with this group by a more aggressive and supportive "advocate" role than is usual with the therapeutic model. Also, as a part of his function the counselor must be a procurer and co-ordinator of community services. He should be a consultant to other personnel who work with the client. He may need to train and supervise support personnel. Specifically, with regard to training and employment, the counselor needs to involve himself maximally with his client in evaluation and job readiness. Each person will require a considerable amount of time in those activities. Also, the counselor needs to work closely with potential employers to combat discrimination and enhance more positive and tolerant attitudes toward our clients who happen to be "different."

If the counselor is to be effective with these clients, there are several "musts." Most importantly, the counselor must continually explore his own attitudes and examine his behavior. He must be genuine in his relations with his clients. He must believe in them as worthy and unique individuals who have self-enhancement potential. He should remember that much of the observed behavior is a function of a life style of being poor and of the stark reality of poverty rather than a personality characteristic. Some observed patterns of adjustment may appear to be maladaptive. Yet, given the possible alternatives that the client has, the particular pattern he manifests may be the lesser of the evils.

For the counselor who can work effectively with these clients, they offer a real challenge. The outcomes of counseling, evaluation, training, and employment can be very rewarding. If the counselor is willing to commit himself to and involve himself with these clients, he can make a substantial contribution in working with this large and important segment of our population.

CONCLUSIONS

Job training is becoming increasingly important for entry into and advancement in a job. It not only helps to get better jobs with higher pay, but enhances job security, promotions, and working conditions. Also, available evidence indicates that training is associated with greater geographical mobility, greater social involvement, and a more optimistic outlook on life.

Training should be individualized and based on the unique configuration of client needs as determined by thorough evaluation procedures including medical, psychological, social, educational, and vocational studies. Welfare recipients and the larger pool of disadvantaged persons they represent often are not oriented to traditional methods, requirements, or tasks associated with evaluation, training, and employment. That reason, combined with lack of verbal skills and self-defeating attitudes constitute difficult problems in evaluation, training and job placement for this group. Workshops offering work evaluation and work adjustment have shown a great deal of promise in these areas. There are several manpower development programs operating now, some of which are available in most communities. Some of them are especially geared to the background and needs of disadvantaged persons. Offices such as welfare, employment service, vocational education, rehabilitation services, and community action programs can provide information on programs existing in a particular community.

Counseling can play a very important role in developing self understanding in clients, evaluating clients, providing information, assisting in finding jobs and in many other activities. However, it is a generally held notion that counseling of the traditional one-to-one variety which emphasizes personal adjustment cannot be generally effective with this population. Recommended instead is the role of client advocacy where the counselor assumes most of the responsibility for his client's progress from one stage to the next. Also, it probably needs to be rational or cognitive rather than dynamic or affective. It will likely be most effective if kept at a very concrete and unambiguous level. Also, counseling should be directed at job readiness in order to maximally prepare the client for entry into training or employment.

Job placement is the critical step in the rehabilitation process that "puts it all together" and ultimately determines whether or not the entire vocational rehabilitation process has been successful. Client-related characteristics make a great deal of the difference in whether or not a client is successfully placed. However, discrimination is still a serious problem. When the supply of workers exceeds the demand, employers can exercise their priority options such as white versus black, male versus female, and nondisabled versus disabled even when ability to perform the job per se is equal in both groups.

This chapter has identified and offered some reflections on several issues related to training and employment of welfare recipients. While there are still many problems to be solved in reaching full employment and equal opportunities, we have made significant strides in recent years. It appears that there is reason for considerable optimism for the future in this area.

REFERENCES

Acker, M.H.: Rehabilitation and the anti-poverty programs—A comparative view of counselor roles. *Rehabilitation Counseling Bulletin, 11*(1 SP): 79-84, 1967.

Allen, V.L. (Ed.): *Psychological Factors in Poverty.* Chicago, Markham, 1970.

Ayers, G.E. (Ed.): *Rehabilitating the Culturally Disadvantaged.* Mankato, Minn., Author, 1967.

Barry, J.R.: Client motivation for rehabilitation. *Rehabilitation Record, 6*(1):13-16, 1965.

Calia, V.F.: The culturally deprived client: A reformulation of the counselor's role. *Journal of Counseling Psychology, 13*:100-105, 1966.

Coburn, H.H.: The psychological concept of dependency. *Rehabilitation Record, 5*(2):37-40, 1964.

Dawis, R.V.: The Minnesota studies in vocational rehabilitation. In Moses, H.A., and Patterson, C.H.: *Readings in Rehabilitation Counseling.* Urbana, Ill., Stipes, 1971.

Ehrle, R.A.: Motivation, identity, and counseling. *Rehabilitation Counseling*

Bulletin, 8:130-135, 1965.

Finney, J.C. (Ed.): *Culture Change, Mental Health, and Poverty.* Lexington, Ky.: University of Kentucky Press, 1969. (Republished: New York: Simon and Schuster, 1970.)

Goldin, G.J., and Perry, S.L.: Dependency and its implications for rehabilitation. *Northeastern Studies in Vocational Rehabilitation,* 1967, 1.

Harrington, M.: *The Other America.* New York, The Macmillan Company, 1971. (Republished: Baltimore: Penguin Books, Inc., 1971.)

Helfand, A.: Group counseling as an approach to the work problems of disadvantaged youth. *Rehabilitation Counseling Bulletin, 11*:110-116, 1967.

Hunt, J.: Social welfare programs and vocational evaluation and work adjustment services. In Pacinelli, R.N. (Ed.): *Vocational Evaluation and Work Adjustment Services in Manpower, Social Welfare and Rehabilitation Programs.* Washington: International Association of Rehabilitation Facilities, 1970.

Levine, L.: Implications of the anti-poverty program for education and employment. *The Vocational Guidance Quarterly, 14*:8-15, 1965.

Mali, P.: Retraining the unemployed. *The Vocational Guidance Quarterly, 11*; 286-291, 1963.

Mahoney, R.J., Cope, C.S., and Campbell, R.R. (Eds.): *Rehabilitation and the Culturally Disadvantaged: A Digest.* Columbia, Mo., University of Missouri, 1969.

Margolin, R.J., and Goldin, G.J.: Motivation of the disadvantaged: Is that the problem? *The Journal of Applied Rehabilitation Counseling, 1*:23-29, 1970.

McWhorter, C.C., and Antoinette, L. Special help for special people. *Rehabilitation Record, 8*(1):26-30, 1967.

Moynihan, D.P.: Morality of work and immorality of opportunity. *The Vocational Guidance Quarterly, 12*:229-236, 1964.

Nadolsky, J.M.: *Development of a Model for Vocational Evaluation of the Disadvantaged.* Auburn, Ala., Auburn University, 1971.

Neff, W.S.: The meaning of work to the poor. *Rehabilitation Counseling Bulletin, 11*(1 SP):71-77, 1967.

Neff, W.S., and Helfanc, A.: A Q-sort instrument to assess the meaning of work. *Journal of Counseling Psychology,* 139-145, 1963.

Reed, H.J.: Training opportunities other than four-year colleges. *The Vocational Guidance Quarterly, 14*:16-20, 1965.

Rothney, J.W.: Trained and non-trained males ten years after high school graduation. *The Vocational Guidance Quarterly, 14*:247-250, 1966.

Rusalem, H., and Speiser, A.: The meaningfulness of work. *The Vocational Guidance Quarterly, 12*:119-122, 1964.

Sinick, D.: The unmotivated client. *Rehabilitation Counseling Bulletin, 4*:119-122, 1961.

Stone, J.B.: The rehabilitation counselor as a client advocate. *The Journal of Applied Rehabilitation Counseling,* 2:46-54, 1971.

Tyler, L.E.: The encounter with poverty—Its effect on vocational psychology. *Rehabilitation Counseling Bulletin,* 11(1 SP):61-70, 1967.

Wolfbein, S.L.: The role of counseling and training in the war on unemployment and poverty. *The Vocational Guidance Quarterly,* 13:50-52, 1964.

PART IV

Rehabilitation of the Disabled Welfare Recipient:
Virginia's Experience

Attitudes Among Professionals Which Affect Services

CHAPTER XIII

REHABILITATION OF THE DISABLED WELFARE RECIPIENT:
VIRGINIA'S EXPERIENCE

WM. HEYWARD McELVEEN AND JOHN H. WADE

Personnel Orientation and Development

Training

Procedures for Service Delivery

Research

Economic Benefits

Summary

IN 1970-71, THE CULMINATION OF AN historical trend occurred when the Department of Health, Education, and Welfare established as one of its chief priorities the vocational rehabilitation of 35,000 disabled welfare recipients by June of 1971. What to do about the plight of the public assistance recipient who is doubly damned by the fact of disability has emerged as a suitable and unique challenge to the resources of the Commonwealth of Virginia. Accordingly, the responsible state agencies, the Departments of Welfare and Institutions, and Vocational Rehabilitation, and the Commission for the Visually Handicapped, responded to this challenge by entering into an agreement to coordinate their resources on behalf of this group of disabled persons. At a point in time simultaneous with the conclusion of this agreement, means for assessing past program performance were developed, together with suggestions and projections for innovative approaches to problem solving. The objects of our observations were the identification of concrete activities which would improve and strengthen joint services to the disabled welfare recipient.

Necessarily, the conclusions presented here will be tentative. In most instances, observations made are not empirically based, but will, nevertheless, reaffirm the validity of prior research efforts and findings. In this chapter, the authors explore and analyze the impact of Virginia's experience to date based on the joint approach outlined above.

PERSONNEL ORIENTATION AND DEVELOPMENT

The Department of Welfare and Institutions and the Department of Vocational Rehabilitation cooperative agreement resulted in an Integrated Action Program which specified precisely the services each agency would contribute toward a coordinated and improved method of service delivery.

Planning Conferences

The first major activity undertaken by newly appointed welfare-rehabilitation coordinators was the development of a comprehensive series of state-wide joint agency conferences. These conferences served to clarify for local staffs the intent and purpose of the Integrated Action Program, as well as to solicit ideas for its implementation. The coordinators secured firsthand information from local staff, and this facilitated an appropriate assessment of the existing programs which, according to conventional practices, has been employed to serve the ends of rehabilitating clients. In relation to particular localities, for example, the coordinators were able to focus attention on situations where disruptions in effective communication had occurred. In addition to helping pinpoint needs for further training concentration, the conferences aided the coordinators in defining solutions responsive to the concerns voiced by the conference participants.

At this point, it was recognized that the effort to achieve a more compatible coordination of service delivery between the two agencies had acquired an increased impetus. It was further realized that fundamental service concepts, operational philosophies, and day-to-day procedural practices of the two agencies will require constant and continuing assessment and reexamination. From this activity, a more complete understanding of what constitutes a truly integrated, effective method of service delivery for the target population will be developed.

Obviously, there is a fundamental need for intensive interagency concentration on the joint target population, i.e. the disabled client, but the careful and orderly delineation of the precise character of the dynamics involved in assisting the welfare rehabilitant, for the purpose of replication and system building, is a far more elusive process. Nevertheless, in the following pages an attempt to focus on and define those agency resources that foster and promote the rehabilitation of the disabled, disadvantaged, welfare recipient will be explored.

Interagency orientation and staff development is the primary force for bringing about mutual awareness of what services are available to the target population. Various techniques and methods may be employed at each level to ensure lasting effectiveness within the cooperating agencies. The high rate of personnel turnover in agencies requires that these efforts be frequent and systematically scheduled.

TRAINING

Training, as developed here, is viewed as a dual responsibility of both agencies. It is required at all levels of administration and operation. Orientation in this context then begins with the first inquiry the social worker makes of the vocational rehabilitation counselor. Information exchange can take place informally during a coffee break session, but the "channelers" themselves are dependent upon and require the formal support of the agencies involved. Identification of the criteria for and what constitutes appropriate referrals becomes possible by means of conferences, seminars, case staffings and other innovative methods of staff development.

Following the state-wide joint agency conferences, a series of joint training seminars were directed toward: (1) strengthening program understanding, (2) broadening the knowledge base of the departments involved, and (3) soliciting local commitment to the Integrated Action Program. The seminars included selected professional staff from three departments: local welfare agencies, Commission for the Visually Handicapped, and Vocational Rehabilitation.

It is from the involvement of these three cooperating state agencies that a "counterpart" system of staff selection was developed and designated to carry out the resource exchange and staff development procedure between the cooperating agencies. Because it provides opportunities for professional staff to exchange ideas and information, supplies a common forum for the understanding of each agency's uniqueness, and enables staff members to develop a comprehensive view of the goals to be achieved. For many, this marked their initial introduction to any communication with their counterparts in the corresponding agencies. Because of the acceptance and effectiveness gained in the early meetings, the stage was set for future joint activities.

Interagency training sessions have confirmed the compatibility of workers from multidisciplined agencies. Although not designed as such, many training sessions resembled low-key sensitivity groups with the result that agency representatives could, some for the first time, effectively and objectively examine limitations both professionally and in terms of service application. Usually, after members had engaged in several days of problem solving, they were able to see that common problems should be approached jointly to effect appropriate solutions. Also, after recognition of mutual problems was aired, members demonstrated increased interest and enthusiasm in working toward overcoming barriers.

PROCEDURES FOR SERVICE DELIVERY

The counterpart system was implemented through the development of four expansion projects made possible by the appropriation of federal funds. These expansion projects were placed under the administrative directions of the Department of Vocational Rehabilitation. The expansion projects are presently operating in four demographically different geographic areas of the state. The basic make-up of staff consists of a project director, counselors, social workers, project aides, and job placement counselors together with needed clerical staff.

With the aid of expansion grants, innovative means of service supply are being developed, and additional training needs are being identified. Not only were additional points of emphasis identified as vital to the improvement of the rehabilitation process, but also the necessity for more diversified training material became evident in order to encompass other relevant service systems. An example of this approach occurred when persons from private and public sheltered workshops, a representative from Health, Education, and Welfare Region III, graduate students and faculty members from Virginia Commonwealth University subsequently came together to participate in joint agency training sessions.

As public welfare and vocational rehabilitation personnel have become more adept in using the techniques of counterpart relationships, the roles of other state agencies (e.g. the Virginia Employment Commission, Department of Mental Health, et al.) became increasingly significant as vital elements in a comprehensive service plan for the disabled. Nevertheless, the persistent need for continuing training as previously described, coupled with active participation by other service agencies has evolved from the very positive atmosphere of commitment which has been experienced. This creates opportunities for broadening the scope and range of interagency concern for joint service to the client.

Case Staffings

A productive technique for effective staff training has been the utilization of case staffings. The mechanics of case staffings follow: the social work supervisor initiates the staffing process by selecting several cases which may be considered for referral to vocational rehabilitation. Persons participating in such "staffings" might include a combination of (1) social workers involved with the particular case, (2) social workers not directly involved yet who might contribute to a correct assessment of the case and in the process, develop awareness of the resources available from vocational rehabilitation, (3) community resource persons who may be working with the case (e.g. the visiting health nurse), (4) the vocational rehabilitation counselor, (5) the counselor aide and (6) the vocational rehabilitation field supervisor.

Any similar combination of these resource persons can measurably contribute to a comprehensive and realistic plan for joint services. Limiting the staff number to approximately eight prevents "staffings" from becoming unduly cumbersome or from impeding individual participation.

Case staffings as an administrative tool not only represent a good use of time since they are client-oriented activities but also result in innovative approaches to service. Additionally, follow-up staffings, to include the client as a participant, is also a promising possibility provided the client has agreed to and been thoroughly prepared for the experience. Case staffings generally provide the worker with an in-depth understanding unlikely to be gained otherwise. Most important, it enhances the responsibility of role functioning with greater clarity and precision. Just as helping the client is a process, so are the worker's activities on behalf of the client a process which has to be nurtured and sustained.

Through improved methods of interagency training and closer working relationships, the efficiency of the referral method can be improved. The referral method must be an accepted, prescribed procedure which initiates and supports a continuing system of information exchange. Follow-up efforts are the responsibility of both agencies and must be coordinated to support the services provided by the agencies. The coordination of services and the positive relationship between the social worker and counselor is of paramount importance and cannot be overemphasized. In a comprehensive and supportive role the social worker and counselor must be aware of the individual's total personality in its often abortive efforts to relate to an estranged environment. Further, the integration and development of the service plan, oriented toward a vocational objective, needs to be (1) reality oriented, (2) attainable, (3) progressively implemented and (4) updated in relation to changeable needs. If this homeostatic approach is not employed, a breakdown in the service plan is apt to occur. In addition, the attitudes of the professionals involved play a significant role in the client's progress toward reaching the vocational goal, and these attitudes may only be improved by means of enlightened interagency training devices.

Attitudes Toward the Poor

Attitudes toward the poor and the disabled are significant in the enabling process. There is a strong tendency not only to offer, but also to impose upon the client middle-class ideals and standards, judging him pejoratively when he does not achieve or at least make heroic attempts to reach these ideals, many of which we have not attained ourselves. Put yet another way, we have a natural affinity for measuring ourselves by our own good intentions and ideals, and for judging the other person by his overt acts. To accept an individual as he exists is a difficult task, and, in making the effort, it is helpful to understand the life experiences which affect the individual's present ability to cope.

The non-judgmental attitude is an unattainable goal for which the provider of human services strives. The plain fact is that professionals are called upon to make judgments in both professional and personal endeavors. The salient ingredient, however, providing the crucial difference is reflected in the professional acceptance of the applicant or recipient of service, and the belief in his rights and dignity as a human being. The inculcation of these concepts in the helping professions prevents our judgments from becoming unnecessarily destructive and disruptive to the individual.

When a recipient of service is unable to benefit from rehabilitative efforts, a reexamination of methods by which services are offered and provided is needed. The point is to determine where the service delivery system has broken down as well as what services could have been supplied to maximize the recipient's potential.

In the past, the temptation has been to hide behind phrases such as "not motivated," "not feasible," "not cooperative," "inability to cope," thereby transferring from the professional the onus of responsibility for the client who does not achieve in spite of the most ingenious, professionally preferred efforts. Today, such phrases have lost their meaning and value and have become antiquated clichés of the profession. Without understanding the dynamics of the individual's needs, one may easily propel the client into a maze of services with little consideration given to wishes and needs expressed by the client. Often our abilities to assess problems outweigh our abilities to listen to the client's expressed needs. He has therefore become the object of our occupational affection but the victim of our personal misunderstanding. The pertinent question remains, "When the client fails, according to our standards, is it not really a breakdown in the system that has failed the client?"

An answer to this question is one which practitioners in the rehabilitative art continue to seek.

RESEARCH

Periodic screening of public assistance cases by the social worker for prereferral exploration is a useful tool. At the same time as the screening occurs, some contact should be initiated with the vocational rehabilitation counselor to inquire about the possibility of services. Once the appropriateness of the referral is established, the social worker's role is to work with the client and his family members in soliciting support for the client and interpreting the referral plan. Following assessment of the case for potential referral to vocational rehabilitation, it is necessary to follow-up with a written referral to the rehabilitation counselor. The information usually required on the referral form would include:

1. Client's name
2. Address
3. Social Security Number
4. Age
5. Suspected disability
6. Social Worker's name and
7. Phone number

There are rudimentary procedures which the rehabilitation counselor will reasonably expect the social worker to have performed at the onset of referral: (1) whether the avenue of referral has been explored and discussed with the client so he is aware of why he is seeing the vocational rehabilitation counselor, and (2) whether motivational and supportive casework services have been identified and initiated. These are fundamental procedures essential to the preparation of a referral, and their consumation depends both on the social worker's knowledge and understanding of vocational rehabilitation services and on the vocational rehabilitation counselor's reciprocal knowledge of services available through the local welfare agency.

ECONOMIC BENEFITS

In Virginia, the individual case service cost of rehabilitating the disabled welfare recipient averages less than five hundred dollars. There are some obvious economic benefits which operate to increase incentive for the vocational rehabilitation agency to work with the welfare recipient. For example, medical expenses subsumed by Medicaid for those eligible recipients has cut vocational rehabilitation expenditures. Also, there is provision of day care by the welfare department for children of mothers either employed or in training.

Homemakers

Another supportive service available from local departments of welfare which increases the chances of rehabilitation is the homemaker service. The homemaker program is a service available from some local departments of welfare which attempts to support and sustain the disabled client throughout the rehabilitation process. The focal point of this program is the strengthening of family life through helping the family or its individual members attain self-sufficiency. This is accomplished by working to improve or restore capacities for personal functioning. This service presents a practical plan for holding families together in times of crisis and stress. The homemaker can help families maintain household stability when, for instance, one caretaker is sick or away, thereby enabling the other caretaker to continue training or employment without excessive loss of time. The homemaker carries specific responsibility for a specialized service child and adult care, as well as for training in home management. The homemaker is responsible to the agency which is, in turn, responsible to the client and to the community for the quality of service provided. Homemaker service is an organized agency service related to client and agency program goals. As such, it is derived from the coordinated effort of the homemaker, the social work staff and other professional personnel who may be involved in the client's total plan for social and physical rehabilitation.

Some local welfare departments now have the services of case aides who can provide, on an individual basis, escort service and transportation for the client to prescribed appointments, assistance in the purchase of personal items, and help to the uninitiated in guiding them through the system.

Group Dynamics

The use of group dynamics as a method in the rehabilitation process has not been fully explored either by welfare or by vocational rehabilitation personnel. It is a technique which may provide a client an acceptable outlet for social intercourse, an advantage often otherwise absent. For many disadvantaged persons, group work has proven to be the initial step in developing meaningful relationships with others. The lack of social interaction, among other factors, has been identified as one of the impediments in the process of positive motivation toward effective personal management in social situations. Such motivation can be realized in the enabling process. For example, the push from one's peers may have a different meaning for the individual than is found in the "one to one" relationship.

If the counselor or worker wishes to develop his group work skills, he can be helped through the use of staff groups. In the staff group each member has a job responsibility and in this sense the approach is different from the client group. Similarities in the groups, however, include the following: the dynamics of group interaction, the group as an education tool, its use in the problem solving process, and the practice of social roles within the accepting atmosphere of the group. The professional interested in developing his skill with groups can develop and improve his abilities in the process through the experience of participating in a staff group. He can then be helped to relate the experience to his work with client groups.

The group process furnishes for its members an opportunity to share similar, related problems which affect their unemployability. It prevents individuals in the group from feeling that they are entirely alone and isolated in their personal anxieties and fears. The group setting reduces the potential presence of an inhibiting authority by diluting the group worker's control, and concomitantly de-emphasizing him as a figure of authority. The group worker then helps the group evolve an indigenous leadership from among its own members. Whenever possible, the group worker should take a nondirective role; as in an educational model, where the learning process occurs as the members "teach" each other. The group worker helps the group focus its corporate attention on a part of a problem to which each member should be able to relate. A group might be formed around a common set of problems such as a group of public assistance clients who need help in accepting the realities of work. The more choices the group can make, the more the feeling of "our group" evolves and enables the client to make more responsible choices. The task-oriented group will be the most successful if its members are commited to the group's purpose.

In the initial phases, direction should focus on some aspect of employment and/or the mechanics of securing employment. As the individual group members begin to feel comfortable, the dynamics of their life experiences should begin to unfold.

It should be pointed out that the authors do not view the group approach as equivalent to group therapy since the majority of social workers and counselors are not skilled in therapeutic techniques. They are, however, trained in group counseling, and in the dynamics of groups. Therapeutic benefits may be derived by the individuals in the groups, but this is ancillary to the prime purpose of group work. The group worker, therefore, should not attempt to tamper with what he perceives to be the client's psychology since this could have a damaging effect on the participant.

The incorporation of a social worker and counselor as co-workers in the group setting may serve a useful purpose in clarifying for group members the respective roles and sanctions of the two agencies. This integration of effort would aid in the process of coordinating supportive services.

Work with groups is an expeditious and effective way of dealing with the growing number of needy cases that otherwise would go without individualized services. It is one way to maximize services and at the same time, to increase the client's ability to function in a mobile society.

SUMMARY

As a result of substantial joint and multi-agency staff training and program planning, the authors make the following observations:

There are many public and private service agencies that are available to render services to disabled and non-disabled individuals. These agencies offer fragmented services primarily because of internal policy and procedural restrictions. Many persons are in need of and eligible for services from these agencies, and the staff members of these agencies are primarily "client oriented." Nevertheless, many clients are not served due to staff misunderstandings and misconceptions of other available community resources. Once these misunderstandings and misconceptions are clarified, agency staff members are most receptive to a coordinated integrated service delivery system that will meet the needs of the individual needing help. Experience and practice has demonstrated that there are more people needing joint agency services than will be served by a unitary approach. Previous training conferences and seminars confirm the need for interdisciplinary training approaches in rendering services to people.

There are, however, three ingredients which the authors suggest are vital to the success of this integrated approach to service. These ingredients are identified and rank ordered here:

1. Commitment,
2. Communication,
3. Coordination.

It is also beneficial to have an accepting and supportive atmosphere built on an "ounce" of trust to expedite the process.

CHAPTER XIV

ATTITUDES AMONG PROFESSIONALS WHICH AFFECT SERVICES

W. Alfred McCauley*

"We begin life with the world presenting itself to us as it is. Someone—our parents, teachers, analysts—hypnotize us to 'see' the world and construe it in the 'right' way. These others label the world, attach names and give voices to the beings and events in it, so that thereafter we cannot read the world in any other language or hear it saying other things to us."

Sidney Jourard[6]

Introduction

Bases for Attitudes

Summary

References

T HE DICTIONARY DEFINES "attitude" as a position or disposition with regard to a person or thing; a way of thinking, acting or feeling. So then, in dealing with attitudes of professionals as they affect their services to others, one must treat any discussion of them in cognitive, behavioral and emotional aspects, both on conscious and less than conscious levels.

*Appreciation is acknowledged for the collaborative contribution to this chapter by Samuel Finestone, Professor, Columbia University School of Social Work.

269

INTRODUCTION

The effectiveness of rehabilitative services depends upon opportunities and attitudes in society, the adequacy of service programs, and the skills and attitudes of those who deliver the service. Since the focus of this chapter is on attitudes of professionals that become barriers to rendering effective service, the origins of attitudes and their impact upon delivery of services will be the prime content.

Rehabilitation and social work professionals, especially among all professionals serving the welfare recipient who is disabled, are presumed through professional training to have acquired self-awareness and self-discipline, but they inevitably share attitudes of the larger society, transmitted through their own family experience, which reassert themselves in subtle ways. Therefore, the importance of reviewing the process of attitude formation seems justified in order to identify attitudes which may impede effective service.

Stuart Chase[4] has given to us a classification of universal needs and functions that are satisfied by thousands of different customs found in every society so far studied and which will help us understand the problem of our task better. They are:

1. Language—the most important of all.
2. Status of the individual in the group. Who outranks whom?
3. Family and other social groups.
4. Methods for dealing with food, shelter, clothing, and other vital materials.
5. Government and law. These can be informal but are always there.
6. Religion and ethics.
7. Systems for explaining natural phenomena—magic, mythology and, lately, science.
8. Rules regarding property; who owns what, and methods for barter and trade.
9. Art forms: the dance, stories, songs, poems, architecture, handicrafts and design.

Although every child will acquire a means of dealing with these needs and functions, no child knows the answers intuitively. Every detail must be taught him by the culture. It is, of course, well understood that even within the same society there are generalized cultural universals but there are also sub-cultural elements that stem from that environment closest to the individual. These are the basis for the child's *real* education in contrast with the formal education taught in our schools. Thus, one's earliest attitudinal conditioning tends to prevail through life unless one can work through reconditioning by actual experiences that provide attitudinal reconstruction and reorganization as a result of the impact of such experiences. Change comes more from involvement than intellectualization.

Although the thrust of the content of this book is to the rehabilitation of the "welfare client," such a client is the disabled person receiving welfare assistance benefits. We must understand that the poor do not constitute a homogeneous group, however. Among this group, so classified because of low economic status, there is a wide variety of subcultural styles of life, races, socioeconomic levels, intelligence groupings and religious affiliations.

Attitudes, then, can relate to any aspect of these general global characterizations of the poor or disabled poor in ways unique to the experience or lack of it with any of these subgroups. Blanket stereotyped class attitudes that most professionals have absorbed from the American culture are often the basis for their inability to establish and maintain meaningful relationships with the poor who need their help.

It is difficult for professionals to put themselves in the roles of the poor and understand and empathize with them in their needs. Although the professional is well-intentioned in his reaching out to this clientele, it is difficult to conceal his feelings of superiority. Thus, we are tempted to do a lot *for* the poor but usually not very much *with* them. And too often we do not understand the difference!

BASES FOR ATTITUDES

Attitudes derive from a number of sources: the family, group status or ethnic and social class, occupational or professional grouping, and bureaucratic or agency-specific in which a professional helper may be attached as a base for service. The context of attitudes derives from conflict of values, conflict of statuses and communication of assumptions that may be invalid.

In considering attitudes there is the temptation to treat "human nature" as the basis for them as a universal. We humans tend to universalize "human nature." For example, in Southeast Asia there is a profound sense of the limited quantity of goods. While there is a certain fatalism about the unequal access to goods which a *few* rich families and *many* poor families have, there is a sense of competition for each family's share of the total available at the expense of the others' shares. In contrast, a basic attitude of westerners is that goods are a result of work and ingenuity so that the total amount of goods can be increased and each producing unit can improve its own share by its own efforts. These two pervasive attitudes say a lot about human nature and motivations in these two cultures.

Most training for counselors and social workers, on the other hand, deals with limited conceptions of human nature, and psychology, especially, tends to do this in its clinical therapeutic focus in training for the helping professions. This lack tends to allow invalid universalization of "human nature" which plagues the service delivery process among professionals serving the disabled individual and the welfare recipient.

We can see that the cultural characteristics of any people are not haphazard, although each of us is apt to interpret them as "human nature" rather than trying to come out of our isolated life to find out more about them. We fail to recognize that from the days of our earliest childhood we have really had few connections with humanity. Our family isolates us. Our community isolates us more than we are aware. Our whole way of living inhibits that necessary intimate contact with our fellow men, which is the art of knowing human nature. Since we do not find sufficient contact with our fellow men, we may become indifferent to them or even become their enemies. Our behavior towards them is often mistaken, and our judgments frequently false, simply because we do not adequately understand human nature. Nor does our contemporary education give us a valid knowledge of human nature. Each of us is left entirely to himself to evaluate his experiences properly and to develop himself beyond his classroom work. Contact with humanity, alone, is not enough, however; there must be *experience* as well. Only the contrite sinner, or those having the gift of identification, the gift of empathy, can understand the nature of human nature, understand the good and the bad sides of life and, thus, better comprehend the problems which the barriers of attitudes pose to those who serve.

Prejudice as Basis for Attitudinal Bias

There appears to be serious prejudice against people who are poor, disabled, or otherwise less capable to compete in the "American way" and which results in damaging discrimination. Let us look briefly at prejudice in general—at its origins and application.

As children, we are not born with prejudice. We are taught that prejudices stem both from psychological sources in the individual and from the social norms which have developed over a long period in a society. Oscar Cohen[5] has summarized ideas of the late Gordon Allport[1] as they relate to attitudes toward blind persons, and has set out psychological needs which can be briefly summarized here:

1. Deprivation and frustrations, which individuals suffer, are taken out on some convenient object and may be blamed on a race, a religious group, a class, an agency or government.
2. Guilt and evasion—the projection of one's behavior upon that which one is acting against because "they" deserve it. Hitler blamed the Jews for the things he was doing!
3. Fear and anxiety—in times of stress (no matter what provokes it), when danger threatens, one or a number of groups are blamed. (*The present attack upon the Black Panthers by the organized police effort is an example.*) (Italics added.)
4. Self-enhancement—one suffering inferiority feelings may look down upon another group, thus enhancing one's own self-esteem.
5. Conformity—adherence to custom, mores, social norms, and modes of thinking shapes one's response to those who violate any such norms.
6. Tabloid thinking—people frequently simplify issues by blaming "them"—blacks, Catholics, Jews, Democrats, etc.

Traditional victims are not only rejected but even hated by prejudiced individuals. There seems to be widespread in society a dislike for differences, an impatience with people who present problems. Many agencies in which professionals are employed (and even the professionals, themselves) are often accused of perpetuating postures of helplessness and dependence among those with problems and whom they serve. Thus, both those who have problems and those who would help them to solutions suffer rejection among prejudiced minds. This prejudice has impact upon responses of both the person with problems and he who works with him, and modifies in unconscious ways the behavior of both, causing them to respond in irrational ways when examined as outlined by Allport above.

Myths as Basis For Attitudinal Bias

Unaware of the impact of their cultural heritage, professionals, like all other men, tend to evaluate those who need helping services, and the institutional systems for rendering such services, as discreet entities, as if they were unrelated, except as one can be made a "fit" for the other. This fit is perceived (and often applied or withheld) from a basis of mythical thinking about the individual needing services. Some such myths are:

1. Every individual born in American society has the opportunity and responsibility to take full advantage of the physical, social, economic and educational resources to "get ahead" in life; therefore, those who do not do so are less worthy in our concern.

2. All socioeconomic classes aspire to achieve and consume at least to the level of American middle class; therefore, those who do not manifest such drive are less deserving.

3. Given the open opportunity, all underprivileged members of the society will take advantage of the chance to get ahead by actively becoming involved within the services and resources offered to them that will fit them economically and socially; therefore, those who do not do so are less worthy and less deserving of our help.

4. Misfortune must be the result of malappropriate living; therefore, one who deviates in body or mind or station must deserve whatever has occurred to him. Thus, worth and value of the individual in society is conditional upon how misfortune is judged appropriate.

5. Anyone from another ethnic, racial or socially or disadvantaged group belongs to the "out-groups;" therefore, he is less worthy and valuable to society than those of "my" own class (generally middle-class as professionals).

6. Persons who are disabled, lacking in one essential capacity, must be limited in all other capacities, including moral and

judgmental, because they are not whole; therefore, proscription of their basic liberties, rights and pursuits is not deemed punitive or unusual.

7. The "out-group" individual does not have the characteristics or perceptions about what is meaningful to the practitioner and valued by that group; therefore, he does not deserve equal consideration nor concern or judgments about his capabilities, needs or desires.

8. Persons who take from society economically without working for it in return are not capable of contributing to it in other supportive ways; therefore, such do not deserve consideration for other valued attributes beyond mere sustenance.

9. One who deviates from social mores and gets caught deserves what he got and should pay the penalty; therefore, there seems no inconsistency that he goes on paying, even beyond the limits prescribed by the law.

10. Persons who are socially and economically disadvantaged and yet who have "things" representing attributes of affluence must have obtained them undeservedly because, in "my" economic strivings, I worked hard for what I have attained; therefore, they must have obtained "things" inappropriately and possibly have more than what visible evaluation reveals.

Such myths, too often believed by middle-class professionals, become the assumptions by which values of others are set and become the basis of attitudes prejudicial to those who need the professional's help. Such is particularly true among professionals who serve those in our welfare systems and among the general middle-class and upper-class public. The subtleties of attitudes, conditioned by service systems and their rewards, supported by the middle-class public, more often than not become barriers to the best quality of services to those who need them.

Professionalization and Attitudinal Barriers to Service

Professionals in social service are under impossible demands for performance and are generally defensive about not meeting them. Their practices are generally locked into bureaucratic structures as a basis for services. Here, where they are subjected to organizational demands, determination from legalistic and regulatory origins, and evaluations of performance by nonprofessional peers, they allow responses within these sets to condition their response to client needs. Subtle seductions by rewards from the organizational structure for response to its goals lure the professional to shortcut the response to client's needs by rationalizations that in more reflective moments he would abhor.

Both rehabilitation counselors and social welfare workers reveal rigidity and defensiveness toward change while, at the same time, revealing flexibility and receptivity to changes. This ambivalence is a consequence of their stage of professionalization. They both deal with a great deal of ambiguity about roles and functions, sharing common areas of skills while also demonstrating unique aspects of knowledge and skills complementary to total service to mutual clients. In seeking more concreteness in role, conflicts often arise from suppressed jurisdictional boundaries in practice, as each seeks to develop status and maintain it in the complex service settings where more of their practices now take place. More recently, both professional groups have seen the *non-professional* deliberately introduced into the service operation as an added manpower resource. If this individual performs aspects of role and task in both fields and takes on professional orientation without legitimation, he adds further to the ambiguity of role and threatens professional status. Psychic energies involved in response to such threats too often generate barriers to ample service for the client whom they mutually share in service.

Similarly related is the response of professionals within agencies where specific role components (such as division of labor, controlled by specific rules and regulations set down by organizational authority) come in conflict with internalized goals, definitions of practice and standards of practice as a result of training. The professional's general resistance to rules and organizational standards, his chafing under bureaucratic supervision, and his conditional loyalties to the agency in contrast to his perceived loyalties to his client, generate behavior responses that may get into the processes for service, as reflected by Allport[1] earlier in this chapter.

There appears to be developing a trend toward relieving the surplus manpower problem among the unskilled, the disabled, and the public welfare groups by giving them training as public service workers, many to be employed by the same service systems which served them. Such employment contributes to role strains with professional social welfare and rehabilitation workers. The obvious greatest strain is in response to the individual as a client who may also become an agent in the service process. The uncertainty about responsibility in such a situation is bound to generate attitudinal barriers that may affect services to such clients, particularly, in scope and focus for vocational outcomes.

Both social work and rehabilitation counseling are striving to reflect the aspects of clinical behavior and judgment as the basis for unique skill and, subsequently, status, as comparable to more established professions. Both professions are struggling to free themselves from dependence upon the agencies in which they are employed; yet, it is the agency which thrusts upon them the various forms of intervention that shape the roles and functions and gives richness in greater responsibility for solutions to complex problems. The ambiguity surrounding what is to be considered professional and nonprofessional dimensions will generate attitudes that will affect how each responds to service demands in the context of serving the whole individual or family. The sorriest aspect of such behavior is that, too often, there develops an absence of conscious subjective awareness that locks professionals into a closed system which shuts out the prime reality of man.

Social Change and Attitudinal Bias Affecting Services

Traditionally, the professional's role in human service situations has focused on specific operations without much consideration as to how that role could also contribute to agency policy formation, to help the agency more realistically respond to increasing demands for service. Professionals need to help in such situations with planned strategies rather than to respond in piecemeal fashion to episodes of crisis.

All professionals, as well as agency administrators, in social service agencies are having to be concerned with the inadequacy of old models for serving increasing numbers of clients which require more categorical services. All have to face up to the trends of increased services as our society moves to a post-industrial status economically and to a more service-oriented status. Politically, finding new ways and means to help clients more to become program participants, thus, promoting self-help and demonstrating a model for change, is a new factor in professional practice.

Policy decisions supporting such changes through application of social psychological processes and research utilization will be the prime routes for involving professionals in strategic decisions. Professionals must be trained for such participation in order to assure that clientele do not get caught in unnecessary battles as a result of spill-over of attitudes with negative psychological investments of the professionals who may be caught unknowledgeably in such changes.

It is predicted by Pearl and Reissman[7] that professionals will function more as supervisors of casework, as group work leaders, as trainers of support staff and as innovators for experimental methods rather than providing direct service to clients. Accommodating this shift in professional self-image in new contexts and methods for serving is apt to generate attitudes and behaviors that will directly or indirectly affect best service response with clients.

Professionals are being asked to explore new experimental mechanisms for enhancing service meanings to clients and drawing upon other disciplines to contribute in the service processes that have not traditionally been involved. Such therapies as music, dance, drama, recreation, encounter, meditation and other insight and self-enhancement processes to make life more meaningful and enjoyable outside the traditional contexts of serving will be much more accommodated as legitimate parts of the service program. Professionals in traditional systems will be tempted to reject such "high falutin" components in the rationale that such types of service are not needed, deserved, nor contributory to client growth. Unconsciously, such responses are reflected out of a position of looking backward out of their own experiences, or lack of them, rather than forward to that which enhances recovery, enlargement of capabilities or well-being of clientele.

More positive attitudes supportive to change can only develop from enlightened self-interest. This, in turn, can derive primarily through well-developed programs of continuing education focused to growth and personal development of the professional and those who work with him in directly serving people.

The Work Ethic and Attitudinal Barriers to Service

"The guiding principle of welfare reform is the work ethic requiring employable welfare recipients to secure income through work rather than to rely upon welfare alone."

MARTIN REIN[8]

Vocational rehabilitation programs, both federal and state based, have played up the economic advantages of rehabilitation goals and outcomes and administrators have sold their program values to governmental appropriating bodies on the basis that for every tax dollar spent in rehabilitation, various amounts ranging from $5.00 to $35.00 in tax dollars would be returned in the work life of the "rehabilitated" individual. The vocational goals and outcomes of rehabilitation programs have shaped the types of services and the primary techniques and practices in service delivery mechanisms and include a wide service range in total potential application. The federal law and regulations are supportive to almost any service a disabled person needs to help him reach vocational goals. Some limitations are imposed by state plans, particularly if states impose economic eligibility standards for certain services to be rendered.

Over many years rehabilitation agencies have served "welfare clients," but accepted only those for services who had characteristics of problems, the resolution of which would reasonably be expected to result in remunerative or gainful employment or its equivalent and, thus, remove them from welfare rolls. The professional rehabilitation worker usually made this administrative decision whether to accept such a client for service or reject him. The threshold of feasibility or eligibility for service, thus, became a function not only of the characteristics of evaluative data about the client and his problems but also a function of the rehabilitation worker's level of skills for interpreting vocational potential. In this latter issue there is a great deal of latitude for the operation of attitudinal bias that may operate negatively in the decision to accept or reject the client for services. An interesting area for research would be that in which the decisions to accept or reject such clients for service in rehabilitation programs were studied over a sample of public rehabilitation workers and matched against the attitudinal sets of those same workers!

Such rationales as: "Too old for the labor market," "Not motivated to work," "No job in client locale at his level of potential skill," and all other such statements that justify rejection of welfare clients on the basis of vocational factors are frequently heard by social welfare workers about referrals they make for rehabilitation services. Many such welfare workers are aware that the level of age is not an absolute in cut-off from the job market, that motivation is learned, and that job availability generally relates to skills acquired. Too often many such clients have been served to enable them to enter the labor market at its lowest level of accommodation, thus reducing the investment that agencies would otherwise have to make to raise clients to higher productive capacity.

Attitudes set out earlier in this chapter play in decision-making in some situations. On the other hand, limitations imposed by administrative plan may prevent the rehabilitation worker from being able to render the full scope of services needed to bring the welfare recipient to a sufficiently higher level of vocational potential which will make it worth the client's self-investment to move to an economic level higher than the level of welfare payments he received. In many cases the level of net income after rehabilitation would be little higher than the welfare payment when costs of taxes (social security and income), deductions for hospitalization, cost of transportation, work uniforms, meals, and other such factors required in employment are considered.

Bourque[3] points out: "Rehabilitation counseling has assumed, over time, a directive leading and, at times, coercive style, in the expectation that vocational adjustment is a matter of rational, goal-directed decision. Characteristics of client behavior are, therefore, of the sort that conform to the system. When conformity does not take place there has been developed a set of numerical status categories which account for the client's place in the process but which do not foster resolution of his life problems."

Attitudes which underlie counselor behaviors, as reflected by Bourque, stem from uncritical acceptance of administratively im-

posed standards which undergird the structure of vocational rehabilitation programs focused to respond to values derived from
the work ethic. Counselors may have motivation to serve clients
with nonvocational goals, but the law and regulations may not
allow it within their service structure, although not denying opportunity for them to use other complementary structures in the
community to do so as a part of the client's rehabilitation plan.
Attitudes that have impact upon limiting services to only those
emanating from their agency will, in turn, limit the perspective,
judgment, and decisions to serve or not to serve welfare clients
even though the total community has resources which, when put
together, could have potential to respond to the totality of client
needs. Thus, attitude sets from within service structures in which
professional rehabilitation and social welfare workers predominantly practice are allowed to limit unnecessarily their perceptions of a total service response capability in the larger community. Such attitudes also limit one's vision to see that rehabilitation can focus on improved competence in the client's social
roles in the family and community and is equally as worthwhile
as focus on the work role and which skill could really enhance
the latter goal.

Also, the subtle seduction of some agency goals and rewards
for their attainment will generate attitudes, as implied by Bourque
above, which will cause professional workers to forget attitudes
of underlying respect and dignity of clients who are engaged in
the service process in that system. Any subverting of professional
goals through inappropriate attitudes in serving people is a di-
minution of professional character and practice against which one
must always be on guard.

Residuals of Elitism, Racism and Sexism Affecting Services

"At birth, the rich and the poor begin with nearly equal abilities,
but with time the educational reinvestment process assures uneven
development and unequal opportunity between the two. The more
wealthy generally pass on to their children the means by which
their higher status can be maintained, while most of the children
of the poor are left with little recourse but a future on welfare."
BARRY BLUESTONE[2]

The situation set out by Bluestone above provides the frame

which in our society contributes to attitudes of elitism, racism and sexism that have negative impact on services to clients.

We are taught in our culture that certain styles, forms and manners indicate a person's worth. For example, one should be clean, one should use proper grammar, one should dress in appropriate style, one should reflect good health, and on and on *ad infinitum*. Those from "poor" subcultures cannot usually respond with such social and physical attributes. Professionals too often communicate in unconscious ways "class supremacy attitudes." Under such circumstances, there can be very little honest communication, just as there can be very little honest dialogue between blacks and whites because our society is pervaded with white supremacist attitudes. It is really very difficult for whites in this country to put themselves into the "skin" or "the shoes" of a black person and *feel* what it is like to be black. It is equally difficult for professionals to put themselves in the shoes of the poor and to understand and have empathy with them.

To reverse or change this attitudinal bias of elitism or racism in one's professional behavior requires actually living or becoming personally involved in the experience of the poor or racial group. It is no different from trying to help certain workers in certain industries without some knowledge and experience in their work setting. A personal example will illustrate.

In my early experience as a rehabilitation counselor, I served a territory in which coal mining was the basis of the economy. Many cases of industrial accident were assigned to me by Workmen's Compensation referral. I had never worked in a coal mine, although I grew up on the fringe of a coal mining area and had known some miners casually.

When I called at the home of an injured miner for an initial interview, I often found the man confined to his bed a wheelchair, or in some similar immobilized position, usually amid squallor and filth because of the generally low expectations for health, sanitation and comfort in most coal company controlled communities. I, in my white shirt, suit and tie, would try to establish rapport with my client, in his soiled and sometimes ragged clothes, with children's elbows propped on his knee listening to our efforts at conversation. This man and his whole family knew that I knew nothing about mining, its dangers, its trade vocabulary, its life style, the fatalistic attitudes about its dangers and other such aspects that reflected my ignorance. They usually gave me "yes" and "no" answers and the minimal information when questions were put in an interview style for soliciting information, even though they knew I was there to offer help.

After some months of this kind of experience, I persuaded my supervisor, after substantial argument, to allow me to actually live for a time in a mining community and share their community life, their work situation and their culture in general. I lived in a clapboard YMCA, ate from wooden benches around a family style table seating twenty, slept with my door unlocked, played pinochle by a wood-burning stove and an oil lamp. Having grown up in a rural area, I was not unfamiliar with many of the accommodations in this setting. However, it was in the work setting that I really began to appreciate the life style of the miner. He was paid in scrip which had full value at the company store, but was discounted when converted into cash at the company bank. His selection of food and clothing was whatever the store manager had available. The children went to a company-built school, painted dingy barn red like all other buildings, and played on a grassless plot of ground. The company doctor and managerial personnel lived usually away and higher on the hill in homes of a different style and quality from those of the miner in the valley, along the yellowed stream.

I learned, however, that "rib" meant a wall of coal left between areas of diggings to help hold up the ceiling of rock or slate. "Machine" meant the cutting machine which worked in the high coal veins. A "trip" meant a train of underground cars loaded with coal and pulled by a motor car, driven by a motorman and ridden on the rear by a brakeman. And I could go on.

Later in my interviews when a miner would tell me that he got his pelvis "busted between the rib and the machine," I would interrupt to say, "Yeah, the jack slipped, eh?" Immediately, the man's face would light up and he would ask, "Hey, have you worked in a mine?" and would continue his dialogue in a relaxed manner. I learned also to leave my tie in the car (I often wore a colored shirt) and sometimes even wore a non-matching jacket when making contacts in some mining communities. My tie was put on and my suit matched when, on the same trip, I called upon company officials and the style of relationship was shifted.

This experience represents only superficially the many other apects of my involvement in a subculture set. Of course, now in those same hills, the miners live in better housing or in nearby towns, are paid in cash, and bank at the regular bank, drive automobiles to the work site, send their children to high school and college and share a middle-class culture. The techniques of mining are automated with the miner as a skilled mechanic, a machine operator from a remote control panel or inside the mine.

Such progress is not yet available to the ghetto dweller, the Indian, the Mexican-American, the migrant worker and others who make up the large welfare groups in our society, but we professionals need to know them by living a "little bit" with them to better understand them if we are to avoid continuing attitudes that can be barriers to our service to them.

Parenthetically, it might be said that the experience set out above was necessary as a technique in overcoming inappropriate attitudes. It also reflects the need among professionals working as helpers of the welfare recipient to develop a real understanding of the world of work and the subculture of the client. It is my impression that social workers and rehabilitation counselors simply do not know about the world of work: its technical requirements, life styles, interpersonal patterns, physical and emotional strains, etc. Sheer ignorance, as well as elitism, is an obstacle to empathy, understanding and service.

Sexism is becoming less of a problem in attitudinal response with clients. However, there is still evidence of discrimination in many places in serving housewives in the context of vocational rehabilitation goals where one must rationalize that the contribution of a disabled housewife can be measured in "kind" if not in cash in remunerative employment. So also, can the focus of vocational counseling for career choice with a female client reflect attitudes of sexism when she comes from a poor family and professional attitudes cast an expectation that her aspirations and potential attainment in the work world would be proper for a charwoman or a laundry worker, even though her capabilities in all spheres reflect potential for a higher vocational order.

Even though women in the lower economic levels make up a heavier proportion of working females in our society, their general level of income is much lower than that of men. The gains from manpower programs, focused to help the poor to raise their skills, have been small.

According to the U. S. Department of Labor,[10] "For those who completed training under the Manpower Development and Training Act (MDTA) during the middle 1960's, only three out of five advanced in pay and the increased earnings were negligible.

According to the latest study of MDTA, involving over 100,000 institutional training graduates, the average wage for males after training was only $2.06 per hour, 27 percent higher than the average pretraining wage. For females, the post-training wage was boosted to $1.53 per hour, less than 20 percent above the pretraining average earnings." We find that in government policies to reverse uneven development economically and in service areas, women still suffer much discrimination.

Social service workers, including rehabilitation counselors, largely come from groups that like to think of themselves as middle class but who really come from upward striving working class family backgrounds. They have a common affliction as first level white collar workers—they need to feel themselves as better off than those whom they serve.

Henrietta Tolson[8] has indicated that "we in the helping professions rationalize our strivings to seem superior by insisting that maintaining authority is essential to providing services. Whether we communicate our attitudes directly through scorn or paternalism, or indirectly through fawning or overcompensation, our behavior delivers the same condescending message to the client. . . . We can detect a counselor's embarrassment that labels us inferior even when he is not aware that his feelings exist, for racial and elitist reactions often stem from unconscious attitudes in the counselor."

Rehabilitation and social service personnel make moral judgments about how clientele spend the little money they may have. A new car, a color TV, fancy shoes or hot pants dismay us when we detect material yearnings in the welfare recipient. Yet, again, we would respond more positively when we see a "good" book or a literary magazine instead of *True Story* on a client's table or chair.

Equally so, we become particularly concerned about moral aspects of our client's behavior. If we find the evidence of a weekend party still around on Monday morning when we visit in a client's home we are upset. The evidence in our own home, including the cans and bottles, will have been cleared up only earlier, perhaps on Sunday morning or afternoon.

In the area of sexual behavior, our judgments about our clients are always in relation to *our* standards of judgment about what our client *does* rather than *who* he is or *why* he does it. Thus, we are always challenged in our helping roles to be honest, being able to question our own motives, examine our reactions, and analyze our methods in making decisions and judgments in relation to our clients and their backgrounds and subcultural status. Perhaps if we could understand that most of our welfare clientele are only responding from motivations to have a larger share of the power and wealth around us and equal treatment in our social systems, our attitudes would be different.

Our clients are becoming more and more impatient with much of our traditional behaviors in responding to help maintain the *status quo,* rather than to help them improve their status instead. Could it be possible that our client's feelings of not being understood is the central cause of the declining credibility of our professions?

Individual Psychological Factors That Relate to Attitudes

Up to this point the material focuses mainly upon societal, subcultural, familiar and "professional" sources of attitudes. It is suspected that there are idiosyncratic elements which also may interfere with service.

Increasingly, the disabled individual is, himself, now entering into training and practicing as the helping professional. He has "made it." On occasion, some clients report that they have been exhorted by their disabled counselor to assume that "because he has 'overcome' his handicap, certainly I should have more confidence in being able to achieve my goals." At times, such counselors unrealistically, if subconsciously, find it difficult to accept any lesser degree of motivation among their clients than that equal to their own. Similarly, such attitudes sometimes are manifested by professionals of racial or ethnic background different from the predominant groups in social service programs when they exhort their clients to emulate their own example.

On the other hand, there is the case of the "able bodied" professional who is unconsciously threatened by disability. There is much evidence that attitudes emanating from this basis contribute to compromising behaviors and underdemanding expectations about what the disabled person can accomplish. This idiosyncracy among rehabilitation workers allows for the stereotyping of classes of disablement and for vocational counseling that leads disabled individuals to vocational choices that have now become stereotyped as for the disabled (i.e. watch repair for those confined to wheel chairs). This behavior continues to be prevalent among all professionals who deal with disabled persons in spite of continuous examples manifested every day that many disabled persons chafe under such compromising attitudes and behaviors, suspecting that they threaten many "able bodied" professionals.

Occasionally, one hears a professional reflect that a particular client does not deserve the "break" that rehabilitation service is giving him. This may be the client whose background reflects antisocial behaviors, arrests, drunkenness, divorce, prostitution, or abuse of others. Again, this attitude is a function of the worker's own personal needs and self-image which interferes with an objectively empathic approach to the individuals with whom he is working. It is not so much that the professional's relations to him require unusual sympathy or detachment, but rather, the necessary combination of objectivity and empathy which permits real respect for the dignity of the disabled individual who now needs the professional's services.

SUMMARY

Our whole attitude development toward our fellow man is dependent upon our understanding of him; an implicit necessity for understanding him, therefore, is a fundamental of the social relationship. Human beings would live together more easily if their knowledge of human nature were more satisfying. Disturbing social relationships could then be obviated, for we know that unfortunate adjustments are possible only when we do not understand one another. In ordinary life and helping relationships, an error in judgment of another human being need not be followed by dramatic consequences because these occur long after the error is made and the connection may not be obvious. We still can see the great misfortunes that follow decades after a misinterpretation of a fellow man. Such misfortunes should teach us something of the duty of each of us, professional or not, to acquire a better knowledge of those for whom our professional lives can give better meaning in service.

The uniqueness and individuality of a human being consists in *what* he perceives and *how* he perceives. And perception is more than a simple physical phenomenon. It is a psychic function from which we may draw the most foregoing conclusions concerning the inner life—be it our own or someone else's. How can we perceive if we wear the blinders of prejudicial attitudes? How can we serve adequately if we cannot correctly perceive?

REFERENCES

1. Allport, Gordon: *The Nature of Prejudice.* Reading, Mass., Addison-Wesley, 1954.
2. Bluestone, Barry: The welfare crisis: No exit, *Urban and Social Change Review,* 5, No. 2, Spring, 1972.
3. Bourque, Ellsworth J.: The university student as an agent of change in rehabilitation, *Special Report, Research Utilization, Conference on Rehabilitation in Poverty Settings,* Boston, Northeastern University, Monograph #7, May, 1969.
4. Chase, Stuart: *The Proper Study of Mankind.* New York, Harper and Row, 1948, 1956.
5. Cohen, Oscar: Prejudice and the blind, *Attitudes Toward Blind Persons,* American Foundation for the Blind, New York, 1972.
6. Jourard, Sidney M.: *Disclosing Man to Himself.* Princeton, Van Nostrand Co., Inc., 1968.
7. Pearl, Arthur, and Reissman, Frank: *New Careers for the Poor.* New York Free Press, 1965.
8. Rein, Martin: Work Incentives and Welfare Reform. *The Urban and Social Change Review,* 5, No. 2, Spring, 1972.
9. Tolson, Henrietta: Counseling the "Disadvantaged." *Personnel and Guidance Journal,* 50, No. 9, May, 1972.
10. U. S. Department of Labor, Manpower Administration: The Influence of MDTA Training on Earnings. *Manpower Evaluation Report,* No. 8, December, 1968.

PART V

Research Findings in the Rehabilitation of the Public Welfare Recipient

The Economy and Rehabilitation

Innovations Needed in Public Welfare and Rehabilitation for Effective Rehabilitation Services

CHAPTER XV

RESEARCH FINDINGS IN THE REHABILITATION OF THE PUBLIC WELFARE RECIPIENT[1]

CARL E. HANSEN

CONSUMER NEED

W ITH THE LAST DECADE, a growing body of research in the area of rehabilitation and public welfare may be noted. Undoubtedly, the surge of research in this specific area is due to urgency assigned to the "welfare problem" by society in general, and more specifically, by Congress. The awareness of current research and what it means to the rehabilitation counselor should be given top priority.

[1]Assistance is gratefully acknowledged to Mr. Stephen Moore, Graduate Assistant, Department of Special Education, University of Texas, for his work in the preparation of this chapter.

In some instances, the rehabilitation counselor may be directing a research project, but more often he is a consumer of research. To become a consumer of research, one must first have the research available to review, digest, and reflect upon. It is only after the research is made available that change can be brought about in programming based upon the research findings. It seems important that this chapter serve not only as a review of current research in rehabilitation of the public welfare recipient, but also point out resources that are available to the rehabilitation counselor that will keep him abreast of current research.

One major source of information is the "Research and Demonstration Brief" which is a one sheet, two page summary of completed research projects, and is published monthly. The "Briefs" are published by the Research Utilization Branch; Division of Research, Demonstration, and Training; Social and Rehabilitation Service; Department of Health, Education and Welfare; Washington, D.C. 20201.

Engstrom describes the "Briefs" as:

> . . . being created to meet the need of all practitioners—rehabilitation and social service—to keep abreast of research despite little time for reading. The summaries are kept brief because the Branch realizes that 'final reports' from research studies are generally too long and too technical for easy reading and yet contain information vital to administrators, social workers, counselors, and the like in their efforts to more effectively serve recipients. Each issue summarizes the final report of a particular project or group of projects, paying special attention to the research findings and their implications for the field worker. Since 1967, the series has dealt with such diversified subjects as aging, architectural barriers, corrections, counseling, deafness, dependency, heart disease, juvenile delinquency, mental illness, mental retardation, public assistance, and workshop administration (1970, p. 3).

The Research Utilization Branch also publishes *Research,* an annotated list of all projects supported by the Division of Research and Demonstration and the Division of Research and Training Centers. For example, the 1970 edition of *Research* listed 3,500 projects dealing with all aspects of health and welfare and representing an expenditure of over $200 million (Engstrom, 1970).

RESEARCH UTILIZATION SPECIALIST

At the local level of dissemination of information, the rehabilitation worker may turn to the Research Utilization program found within his region. Engstrom (1970) notes that in the spring of 1969, SRS made a grant for a 5-year demonstration project in one state of each HEW region to demonstrate the advantage of placing a Research Utilization Specialist (RUS) in the state vocational rehabilitation agency to work toward the effective use of research findings. The RUS serves as a link between research and state program needs. The RUS is often in a position to supply the rehabilitation counselor with ready information about a particular subject. The RUS is often a change agent helping to disseminate research information. Appendix A lists the Research Utilization Specialists by name, address, and region.

KEY WORD INDEX AND ABSTRACTS

The RUS is also one of the best resources from which to obtain copies of SRS sponsored research abstracts.

From 1954 to 1971, those agencies now comprising the Social and Rehabilitation Service have sponsored about 2,500 research and demonstration projects. These projects have ranged over the entire field of rehabilitation, social welfare, aging and child welfare. Since many of the resulting reports are out of print or inaccessible to the administrator or practitioner who might find the material of value, the Research Utilization Branch of SRS has contracted with the Computer Management Corporation of Gainesville, Florida, to produce a set of abstracts for the first 1,700 project reports submitted to SRS. The Computer Management Corporation has been more recently contracted by SRS to engage in the preparation of additional abstracts beyond the original contract calling for 1,700 abstracts. If SRS funding continues at an adequate level, the Computer Management Corporation, in time, could produce an abstract on each piece of SRS sponsored research.

Because of government printing and contractual regulations, the SRS Research Utilization Branch was only able to contract for 25 copies of the abstracts and associated indexes. The University of

Florida Regional Rehabilitation Research Institute staff has reproduced additional copies of the indexes so that those agencies and programs which want to make a wider use of the abstracts can identify the materials which have value for them. However, the person who has identified the abstract or report in the index must then turn to one of a small group of organizations to secure a copy of the abstract. The groups having a complete file of the abstracts resulting from the Computer Management Corporation Project are the Research Utilization Specialists and the six Regional Rehabilitation Research Institutes (Computer Management Corporation, 1971). The requester of an abstract will usually need to pay a nominal fee for any duplicated report that he wants.

The research in rehabilitation and welfare is available to interested individuals. The "Research and Demonstration Briefs," *Research,* The Research Utilization Program and the *Key Word Index* for Social and Rehabilitation Service Abstracts are all valuable resources to which one may turn when he is interested in the results of research. The important aspect of SRS research materials is that the resources are not only available, but that their information is continually up-dated. A chapter such as this, which deals with the research findings in the rehabilitation of the public welfare recipient, quickly becomes out-dated and is significant from only a historical viewpoint. The aforementioned resources will afford the rehabilitation worker the opportunity to continually up-date his knowledge of current research in the area of the rehabilitation of the welfare recipient.

STATE AGENCY CONDUCTED RESEARCH

Development of Sponsored Research

A major contribution to the fund of welfare-rehabilitation information has been the research conducted by the state rehabilitation agencies. These research efforts have been either partially or wholly sponsored by research and demonstration grants from SRS. The research typically orients itself toward the rehabilitation of the *disabled* recipient of public assistance. It should be remembered that the emphasis has been on the disability of the public welfare recipient, not upon the welfare recipient's low income status. The clients included within these research projects, for the most part, had to meet the three basic criteria established for rehabilitation eligibility: (1) Must have a disability, (2) must be a vocational handicap, and (3) there must be a chance for remunerative employment.

In 1962, the state rehabilitation agencies hoped for substantial increases in service to welfare clients. The previous cooperation was based on a history of rehabilitation and welfare agencies working together for nineteen years. Although the mechanism for cooperative efforts was set up at all governmental levels—federal, state, and county—the actual utilization of this mechanism varied. Many of the cooperative efforts were producing gratifying results while others had been sporadic in nature and differed widely in their achievements.

The number of public welfare recipients rehabilitated by state rehabilitation agencies had been about 16 percent of all persons rehabilitated during 1960 and 1961. In fiscal year 1960, the proportion of rehabilitants receiving public assistance during their rehabilitation program was 31 to 35 percent in four general state agencies, 20 to 29 percent in eight agencies, and 19 percent or less in the remaining forty-two agencies. In states with separate agencies for the blind, the proportion of blind rehabilitants receiving public assistance was 30 percent or more in twenty-two agencies, 20 to 29 percent in seven agencies, and 19 percent or less in the remaining seven agencies. The fact that some agencies had rehabilitated twice the national average while some state agencies were well below the national average of clients reflected the wide range of effort exerted. Although it was not possible to determine the total number of public welfare recipients who could be returned to work, there was no doubt that concentrated effort could yield substantially more than the approximately 16,700 public assistance cases rehabilitated in 1962 (Howard, 1963).

Following the passage of the Public Welfare Amendments of 1962 (Public Law 87-543), vocational rehabilitation intensified its efforts in collaboration with the Bureau of Family Services of the Welfare Administration. A special Committee on Public Welfare was appointed within the Council of State Directors of Vocational Rehabilitation to review joint plans and recruit the full cooperation of state vocational rehabilitation agencies.

As a result of the 1962 amendments, national action was focused on three areas designed to strengthen and expand the teamwork between State Vocational Rehabilitation Agencies and State Public Welfare Agencies. One area concerned itself with research and demonstration projects.

Additional impetus was given through a series of selected demonstration projects based on successful programs developed several years earlier in Fulton County, Georgia, and Hillsborough County (Tampa), Florida, to rehabilitate welfare clients. These two projects involved experiments in which special staff members were designated by both agencies to conduct a closely coordinated effort in selection, referral, and service to clients. The development of projects based on these successful prototypes was given priority by the Office of Vocational Rehabilitation (now known as Rehabilitation Services Administration).

The series of selected research and demonstration projects provided for the establishment of joint working arrangements, social workers, rehabilitation counselors, and necessary specialists who would work together as a team (Zinni, 1969).

Sufficient research and demonstration grant funds under the Office of Vocational Rehabilitation were made available to start nine projects during fiscal year 1963. In fiscal year 1965, a total of twenty-six research and demonstration projects were in operation across the nation (Rehabilitation Record, 1967).

The twenty-six projects, plus other less well-funded projects, focused heavily on inter-agency cooperation, the development of early referral techniques, improving methods and techniques in the welfare-rehabilitation caseload and the development of programs for comprehensive services.

Agency Cooperation

Terwilliger (1967) reported that the New Mexico Division of Vocational Rehabilitation and Bernalillo County Department of Public Welfare effected a three-year cooperative agreement to increase rehabilitation services to disabled welfare recipients. A caseworker and a counselor were assigned to the project and worked jointly with the clients. The caseload for the team was limited to sixty clients and averaged between forty-five and fifty-five clients. The upper age limit was established at sixty years of age.

The major result of the New Mexico three-year project was the referral of 329 individuals of which 175 were rejected for various reasons. Eighty-one of the 146 accepted cases were rehabilitated, sixteen cases were closed not rehabilitated, eight cases were transferred to other districts, and forty-three clients remained on the caseload at the end of the project. The savings to the Department of Public Welfare was estimated at $40,000 per year.

Of the 146 cases accepted, most clients were receiving Aid to Dependent Children. Most clients were males between the ages of 20 and 34, who were married, and had orthopedic disabilities. Most clients located their own jobs after rehabilitation services were provided and received $50 to $90 per week at the time of closure. They were rehabilitated in an average of three to nine months at a case cost of $200 to $500. Prior to closure, they had received $150 to $190 per month in public assistance payments.

Selling (1967) reported a tandem approach developed in New Jersey. A rehabilitation counselor and a caseworker from a welfare agency worked as a team in the provision of respective agency services to mutual clients. In this research study, the welfare-rehabilitation cases served as the experimental group. One hundred thirty cases referred by the county welfare boards to the rehabilitation commission as regular referrals and independent of the project were selected as the control group. The criterion for inclusion was the same for the experimental group.

The 200 cases served by the tandem approach resulted in twice as many rehabilitation closures as the control group. The experimental group had fifty rehabilitation closures (26%) as compared to thirteen closures of the comparison group (10%).

Mullins (1967) reports that in a three-county area of Kentucky a project was conducted with the rehabilitation counselor and the public assistance caseworker coordinating services with each case. Of the 738 disabled public assistance applicants or recipients who were referred for rehabilitation services, 376 people were accepted for services. The largest single category of disability among the accepted cases was that of orthopedic handicaps.

From the pool of referrals accepted for rehabilitation services, 220 clients were closed as rehabilitated, forty cases were closed as not rehabilitated, and 116 cases were transferred to a general caseload when the research project was completed. The average cost for rehabilitation of each client was $600.

Information is lacking in the Kentucky research report in terms of comparisons between rehabilitants and non-rehabilitants. The factor of cooperation between rehabilitation and public welfare stands as the major emphasis of this study.

The three selected pieces of research from New Mexico, New Jersey, and Kentucky, as well as research completed by Miller (1968), Novak (1966), Jarrell (1966), Mosmeyer (1966), Singer (1968), and Baldwin (1968), all demonstrated the effectivenes of the team approach in the rehabilitation of disabled public assistance recipients. Taylor (1971) points out that the implementation or further integration of this type of approach in new or ongoing programs would seem to merit consideration.

Early Referral

Merrill (1967) demonstrated in a California study the importance of early referral in the rehabilitation of the welfare recipient. Nine vocational rehabilitation counselors were assigned full-time to work in seven different county welfare departments. The offices which were selected represented a cross section of the state's welfare cases. The cooperative relationships were established in communities where a vocational rehabilitation district office existed in order to provide supportive services to the counselor. The selected counselors had substantial experience with the agency and welfare clients. In several instances, the counselors had worked for county welfare departments.

After an exploratory study, the following procedures for early identification and orderly referral of potential clients were established:

1. All applicants for Aid to Needy Children (ANC) would be screened by the Welfare intake caseworker and disabilities which would interefere with employment would be identified at that time.

2. When welfare assistance was granted, the County Welfare De-

partment would refer all such cases to the rehabilitation counselor.

3. Prior to interviewing the recipient, the counselor would discuss the referral with the welfare caseworker and a coordinated plan for referral preparation by the caseworker and follow-up by the counselor would be developed.

Of the 2,939 cases evaluated during the first year of the project, 14 percent of the cases were accepted for service. Rates of acceptance in the eight project locations varied from 8 percent to 29 percent in the ANC category. Overall rates of acceptance from Aid to Disabled and General Relief recipients were 3.8 percent and 6.9 percent respectively with substantial variation from office to office. Nearly 45 percent of referrals were not accepted for services because of either a lack of interest in rehabilitation or an unresolved child care problem. From the experience and information the project supplied, it is estimated that about 34 percent of the applicants for ANC were disabled and of this group approximately 3,400 clients (29%) would be eligible for rehabilitation services. The flood of referrals (5,900) to the nine counselors required the counselors to retreat from their casefinding activities and to temporarily discourage referrals.

O'Neil (1968) demonstrated in a Washington D.C. study that early referral for rehabilitation services diminishes the crystalization of dependency patterns of public assistance recipients. The major results of the O'Neil study demonstrated that specialized units of social workers and rehabilitation counselor teams could work effectively in the provision of services. The teams were able to provide their most effective services after intake procedures were established to interview and refer prospective clients to the project at the time of their application for public assistance. During the three-year project, 119 welfare recipients were closed as rehabilitated, representing 46.87 percent of the cases accepted into active statistics. The average case cost to both agencies per rehabilitation was $868. The monthly income of the average rehabilitation client increased from a public assistance grant of $115 to $297 from remunerative employment.

It would appear that as greater rehabilitation success can be realized in the early referral of the traumatically injured client, greater rehabilitation success can be realized with the early referral of the welfare client. The research seems clear that early referral of the disabled welfare client and a closely coordinated program between welfare and rehabilitation can result in a higher number of successfully closed areas.

Comprehensive services as reported by Burkhart (1967) and Holdship (1965) play an important corollary role with early referral. Early referral without closely supervised, comprehensive services to the welfare-rehabilitation client may be relatively meaningless. The Wood County Project, to be discussed later in this chapter, will amply demonstrate the importance of early referral in combination with comprehensive services as a viable approach to the rehabilitation of the welfare-rehabilitation client.

Project Summary

In one of the more comprehensive research reports, Grigg (1969A) discusses the evidence from fourteen Research and Demonstration sponsored projects involving 7,694 clients. The following points summarize Grigg's findings.

1. Of 7,694 applicants in the fourteen projects, 2,786 (36%) were accepted for services, and complete data was available on 2,614 of the applicants.
2. 1,146 (44%) of the 2,614 cases were closed as rehabilitated and another 879 clients (34%), some of whom would become rehabilitated, were still being served.
3. Only 6 percent of the 1,146 clients who were closed as rehabilitated indicated they were unemployed after their case was closed; compared with 78 percent before services. Of those clients rehabilitated, 68 percent were working in the competitive labor market, and 78 percent were working fulltime (some in sheltered settings), compared with only 5% when referred.
4. With all other factors constant, the cost-benefit ratio for Negroes was lower than for Whites and Latin Americans, due largely to the higher expected cost of services. In this regard, the difference between Negroes and Latin Americans was especially noteworthy, and prevailed also with respect to the percentage still being served in the projects: 58 percent of Latin Americans vs. 20 percent of Negroes.
5. Of the 2,614 clients for whom data was analyzed, 56 percent were men, 44 percent women; 62 percent were White, 26 percent Negro, and 11 percent Latin American. Their ages ranged from under 20 to over sixty, with 90 percent of the clients' ages spread

rather evenly between twenty and sixty.

Forty-two percent of the clients had less than eight years of schooling; only 17 percent of the clients had twelve years of school or more.

Prior work experience of the clients had been mostly in service, semiskilled, and housewife areas, 46 percent having such work backgrounds.

Seventy-seven percent of the clients were on AFDC. In all, about 72 percent were receiving some form of public assistance, but 28 percent were getting no aid when referred.

Seventy-nine percent of the clients had not been referred for services to the State Divisions of Vocational Rehabilitation during the four years prior to acceptance into these projects.

6. All of the clients accepted were disabled in addition to being economically dependent. The most frequent primary impairments were amputation and orthopedic or bodily deformities (28%), psychiatric and behavioral disorders (14%), and cardiac problems (6%). A full range of impairments was present in the total group, and at least one half of the clients suffered also from secondary disabilities.

7. In brief, the majority of those clients served were functioning only marginally in our society, as shown by their low educational attainment, skimpy work histories, and economic dependency.

8. Major reasons for nonacceptance into projects were little or no functional work capacity, "declined services," no substantial disability, and combination of disability, illiteracy, and lack of skill.

9. Of eleven social services rendered to project clients, health care was used most often, followed by vocational and financial and self-support help.

10. The AFDC group, which received more public welfare services under matching funds than other public assistance categories, had a better rehabilitation rate than any other public assistance group. The study data does not, however, tell us whether or in what manner welfare services affect rehabilitation outcome.

11. The most frequently used of ten rehabilitation services were diagnosis, maintenance and transportation, surgery and related treatment, training and training materials, prosthetic appliances, and hospitalization. Those clients who were rehabilitated received more of these services than those clients who were not rehabilitated.

12. Needs and types of service varied by race and ethnic group. Whites needed more major medical attention and Negroes needed more job training or retraining. Negroes received relatively more maintenance and transportation, but their urgent training needs were not met.

13. Those clients who were rehabilitated had an average treatment cost of $561, compared to $502 for those not rehabilitated.
14. The average increase in weekly earnings after successful rehabilitation was $46, with men and those with higher educational attainment gaining the most.
15. Expenditures were greater for men than for women, and greater for those clients with higher levels of education.

This section has been examining research primarily completed by the state agency supported by R & D. These research reports could be criticized for their lack of sophistication. Many were conducted by individuals without any training or background in research. Although some projects filled this lack of research sophistication with expert consultation, many did not.

On the more positive side, the projects were funded with R & D money which meant it was not only a research project, but also a demonstration project. Many of these projects helped demonstrate to the participating state agency that a stronger, more unified approach to working with the welfare agency and public assistance clients could be achieved. In many instances, the R & D project was really "seed" money to get a project started so that an idea or concept could be woven into the fabric of the agency, as opposed to any real degree of research interest.

TWO MAJOR PROJECTS

Impact of Research

It is doubtful that total agreement within the field of rehabilitation can ever be reached regarding the question of which research effort has had, or will have, the most significant impact upon the rehabilitation of the public welfare recipient. Numerous projects have contributed data rich in information, insight, and program direction. To single out two projects for discussion in a chapter such as this becomes most difficult for the writer and can become misleading to the reader: misleading because the reader may feel that the reported research in this chapter is "all" that exists, when indeed the reader is only being exposed to what the author of the chapter feels is important. Because of chapter size limitations, only a limited number of research studies can be reviewed in depth. The Wood County Project and the San Antonio Project have been selected for inclusion because of their comprehensive nature, as well as, for their probable impact upon our thinking in the rehabilitation of the welfare-rehabilitation client.

The Wood County Project

The Wood County Project, as reported by Wright, Reagles and Butler (1969), was designed to demonstrate the potential benefits of extending rehabilitation services to *all* handicapped persons within a prescribed geographical area. The concepts of vertical and horizontal program expansion were introduced in this study. The project established an experimental agency which was expanded vertically to include a larger number of medically-handicapped clients and horizontally to include culturally (non-medically) handicapped clients. The project successfully demonstrated that the techniques of state rehabilitation agencies can be effectively applied to a much broader range of unemployed and underemployed individuals. Wright, Reagles and Butler (1969) report that the five year Wood County Project was the first major longitudinal study of vocational rehabilitation clients, although there have been many follow-up studies of rehabilitants. They further report that the project was one of relatively few field rehabilitation R & D projects to follow an experimental design which allowed the assessment of the treatment effect (i.e. the expanded program). The Wood County Project has been the only such project to examine the multifaceted impact of rehabilitation services on clients, intra-agency processes and the community. Since the project required extensive and detailed analyses of data obtained under conditions emphasizing maximum delivery of service and minimum effects of the monitoring process, instrumentation and procedures should have wide applicability to similar research in field settings. Instrumentation was developed in a number of areas, e.g. in measurement of client feasibility, of client satisfaction, of rehabilitation gain and of intra-agency processes. In addition, techniques devised in related fields were applied, as in the analysis of cost-benefits. This R & D project was one of a small number in which independent, unbiased research observers were responsible for evaluating the treatment effects. The Wisconsin DVR provided client services, whereas the University of Wisconsin conducted the research.

Wood County, Wisconsin (population 59,000 in 1960) was selected for expansion of the vocational rehabilitation program because of its diversified economy, geographic location, and good educational, vocational and medical resources. It is rural-urban in composition and primarily Caucasian in population. The county had been served by a counselor from the Eau Claire district office who devoted 20 percent of his time to Wood County. The professional staff of the Wood County agency was enlarged tenfold and there was a proportionate increase in caseloads and funding for purchased services. Eau Claire County was chosen as the principal control area because of its similarity to Wood County. Six other Wisconsin counties were also used for comparisons.

The major highlights and conclusion of this research may be summarized in the following points:

1. Culturally-handicapped clients are as feasible for rehabilitation services as are the medically handicapped.

2. There was a 65 percent overall reduction in public assistance payments to the Wood County clients.

3. Eighty-five percent of the culturally disadvantaged cases had competitive employment at closure, comparable to 80 percent for the medically handicapped.

4. A client satisfaction scale indicated that rehabilitation services can be expanded to a broader range of the handicapped (the culturally as well as the medically) without reducing the level of satisfaction expressed by the client.

5. The total mean cost per rehabilitant was significantly lower for culturally-handicapped clients than for the medically handicapped within the Wood County Agency.

The single most important feature of this research points to the fact that rehabilitation services should be expanded vertically to serve more medically disabled and expanded horizontally to serve the disadvantaged welfare client. An argument against serving the public assistance client based on expense is short-sighted.

A study of the roles of Wood County welfare recipients showed that 62 percent of all clients had received public assistance prior to referral while only 5 percent received any public assistance following services. The Wood County public welfare budget was reduced in all categories of assistance and totaled over 50 percent, i.e. from approximately $1,200,000 to $600,000 annually.

The San Antonio Project

The San Antonio Research and Demonstration Project was implemented in recognition of the need to provide better rehabilitation services to AFDC recipients (Beck et al., 1967). Essentially, the project goal was to investigate and demonstrate ways to eliminate or reduce vocational handicaps and dependency characteristics of AFDC recipients to the extent that they would become gainfully employed and participate more effectively in the community.

Initially, a staff composed of two Public Welfare caseworkers, a Public Welfare Supervisor, two vocational rehabilitation counselors (with one doubling as Project Director), and clerical workers was assigned to the project office housed in a Federal Housing Project near the downtown area. The full spectrum of vocational rehabilitation and public welfare services was offered with three significant supplementary features (Zinni, 1969). These features consisted of:

1. in-house counselor-caseworker team approach
2. intensive case work
3. special prevocational evaluation-adjustment facility.

The in-house counselor-caseworker team, and the provision of intensive case work is similar in respect to numerous other welfare-rehabilitation research projects discussed in an earlier section of this chapter. The significant feature of this study lies with its special prevocational evaluation-adjustment facility. Prevocational evaluation refers to the assessment of work attitudes and behaviors associated with employment, rather than with the skills or behavior associated with a specific job. The goal of the prevocational adjustment program is to assess and shape the development of work attitudes and behaviors associated with employment.

The San Antonio Project designed a highly specific sixty day prevocational adjustment program for all welfare-rehabilitation clients involved with this study. The prevocational adjustment, or enrichment program, focused on the following seven points:

1. Understanding the world, utilizing current events on a base beyond the client's narrow scope of information.
2. Utilizing information sources such as newspapers, radios,

telephones, magazines, etc. to secure employment.

3. Civic participation geared at greater understanding of the local, state and federal government; voting, police, community service agencies and social security.

4. Budgeting for home and money management.

5. Development of an adequate self-concept.

6. Tutoring in basic English, spelling, reading and arithmetic skills.

7. Completing job applications and preparing for job interviews.

Besides implementing and studying the value of a prevocational enrichment program, the San Antonio Project also tried to develop a set of success predictors; the aim being to determine what changes of measured attitudes and abilities are associated with rehabilitation success. The best predictors of success, time and efforts considered, were the Revised Army Beta test of intelligence, the Graham-Kendall test of perception, the Purdue Pegboard test of dexterity and the total score on the Work Attitude Scale. Additional studies concerning the prediction of rehabilitation success with welfare-rehabilitation clients are available. Kunce (1969) described a "Rehabilitation Difficulty" index. The index consists of ten client characteristics which affect successful outcomes. Grigg (1969B) also describes factors in the decision to accept disabled public assistance clients for rehabilitation in combination with successfully rehabilitated clients.

The results of the San Antonio Project demonstrated that of the accepted cases (based on their test considered predictors), 70 percent of the cases were successfully rehabilitated. Considering all cases referred to the Project, 38 percent were successfully rehabilitated. The cost per successfully rehabilitated client was $560. Two factors seem important in this study: (1) rehabilitation success can be reasonably estimated through the use of select instruments, and (2) a prevocational enrichment program can significantly contribute to the successful rehabilitation of the welfare-rehabilitation client. The results of this research have been implemented throughout the state of Texas with its cooperative welfare-rehabilitation projects. The aspect of a prevocational enrichment program holds immense promise in the implementation of future welfare-rehabilitation programs. The most logical step of this research is to move the prevocational enrichment program into close coordination with sheltered workshops, since they are best suited to offer programs dealing with the development of "work personality" and to conduct programs of behavior modification.

Both the Wood County Project and the San Antonio Project point toward effective ways of working with welfare-rehabilitation clients. Both projects demonstrate that high rehabilitation potential can be realized for the welfare rehabilitation client at a case service cost per client lower than for many other disability groups.

RELATED RESEARCH

Public Housing Research

Low-cost public housing is often a necessity for many welfare-rehabilitation clients. During the late 1960's, the Rehabilitation Services Administration funded four major projects to demonstrate the feasibility of rehabilitating disabled clients within low-income public housing projects. The major goal of rehabilitation was to utilize its skill and resources in seeking to help low-income housing project residents break out of a prolonged cycle of dependency (Spencer, 1967).

The four demonstration projects were:

1. Pruitt-Igoe Housing Project, St. Louis, Missouri
2. Elm Haven Housing Project, New Haven, Connecticut
3. El Pueblo and Columbia Park Housing Project, Pittsburg, California
4. Carver Park and Outhwaite Homes, Cleveland, Ohio

The Pittsburg Project was classified as "rural, nonfarm," while the rest were located in major urban ghettos. The demographic characteristics of the projects were similar in that all were predominantly populated by blacks with low incomes; high unemployment rates were common, and at least half the residents received welfare benefits (Spencer, 1967).

Discussion of these four projects will be limited to the St. Louis and Cleveland projects. Although all four projects have serious implications for the rehabilitation of the welfare recipient, the St. Louis and Cleveland projects tend to typify the significant rehabilitation outcomes found in all four projects.

Cleveland Project

The Friendly Inn Settlement Project of Cleveland, Ohio was designed to demonstrate the effectiveness of a vocational rehabilitation program in a low income, densely populated, predominantly black housing project. The plan was to combine social work and rehabilitation ideas while implementing the program through the techniques and facilities of a settlement home. The three-year project was completed in cooperation with the Friendly Inn Settlement for the residents of Carver Park and Outhwaite Homes—two low income housing areas.

The purpose of the project was to eliminate the inability of the residents of the low income area to "establish useful and appropriate relationships within the family and within the community" and to provide better health and education services (Minton, 1968). Efforts were directed at changing personal attitudes and creating self-esteem by strengthening interpersonal relationships with a goal of employment.

In November of 1965, an inter-disciplinary team of a rehabilitation counselor and welfare caseworker was assembled under the director of the Friendly Inn. The majority of clients suffered from the long-time effects of racial discrimination, family problems, poor education and low income rather than physical disabilities. Most clients were women of approximately thirty-eight years of age. Varying techniques of rehabilitation were used and modified throughout the project. Although the services were intensive and various, the actual monetary cost was relatively low at $132 per case closure (Minton, 1968).

The vocational rehabilitation counselor assumed a client case load of sixty-six persons. Referrals came from the neighborhood case workers. The workers gave supportive services to clients with severe problems, organized neighborhood clubs, and urged general public participation. New lighting for streets, police protection, and revised traffic patterns were a result of the neighborhood club actions. Project TEACH, an inter-faith youth group, sought to end racial differences and cultural differences between the children. Of the sixty-six clients referred, a total of thirty-eight persons or 57 percent of the referrals were rehabilitated successfully. New involvement and concern for people as well as utilization of community resources were a direct result of Project Friendly Inn Settlement. It was also concluded in the research that families who received services had a strengthening of their family unit because of their new sense of community awareness.

The most promising aspect of the Friendly Inn Settlement Project is that rehabilitation can be achieved among persons suffering from cultural deprivation and family breakdown. The team approach was comprehensive and effective, although a large amount of resources, energy, and agency cooperation is needed. The study also shows that flexibility of the staff and program must be maintained if true progress is to be made in the family and community. In September of 1968, the Project was terminated and the Friendly Inn resumed its original community role.

Pruitt-Igoe Project

In the early 1950's, the Pruitt-Igoe Public Housing Project was conceived. The project was originally designed as two separate, racially segregated housing projects for the disadvantaged people of St. Louis, Missouri (Kunce et al., 1969). However, court action concerning the separation of races caused such an uproar that many whites did not participate, making the project participants primarily black. Applicants were expected to be working people with varying incomes, and rent was scaled according to ability to pay. The St. Louis Housing Authority was prepared to admit 10 percent welfare recipients, but a larger percentage was admitted until the majority of cases was of welfare status.

The project was built at a cost of $36 million and contained thirty-three modern buildings. Utilities and landscaping were modern in design but actual costs required many deletions. Accompanying the sparse plumbing and heating fixtures was an overcrowding problem. A total of 12,000 people forced their existence into the fifty-seven acres of land taken from the worst slum area of St. Louis.

Crime was the major problem outside of economics at Pruitt-Igoe. People could not leave their rooms because of fear of rape, robbery or theft. Criminals outside of the project would daily attack the eleven story high-rise and attack victims in the darkened stairways. The residents of the project became the victims of their economic distress, both criminally and psychologically.

The Missouri Vocational Rehabilitation Department staffed the project with a director and eventually three counselors. A viable program of rehabilitation did develop after a period of rough adjustment. The Rehabilitation Department received 60 percent of its referrals from the Welfare Department and 14 percent were self-referred. Approximately 40 percent of all referrals declined or were denied acceptance. Of the people who were accepted as clients, 75 percent were rehabilitated successfully and the percentage of clients on welfare dropped from 60 percent to 46 percent. The Missouri DVR found that the bulk of culturally disadvantaged clients needed a job commensurate with their present functioning and many clients needed further help after employment.

Presently, the Pruitt-Igoe project buildings are being demolished because of the many slum conditions. Although the housing project has ended on a dismal note, the research information is significant to rehabilitation counseling. The ability of a culturally-disadvantaged person to be rehabilitated was clearly demonstrated and was one of the brightest points of the project. Clients who are culturally disadvantaged have identifiable characteristics which pose as much a barrier to employment as do physical handicaps. The counselors learned that immediate help is essential in disadvantaged cases and the assistance must be tangible to be of any value. Also, counselors learned that short-term goals are most effective but must be followed by later counseling or prevocational training. Most importantly, research demonstrated that society has increased poverty problems by its well-intended projects which were emotionally based and not thoroughly researched. Solutions must be investigated not on their current popularity or simple nature, but on the values they will lend to the quality of life.

Sheltered Workshop Research

The contributions made by sheltered workshops have long been recognized in the rehabilitation of disabled clients. It has only been in recent times that we have begun to see sheltered workshops explore more and varied programs for the disadvantaged welfare client. Sheltered workshops offering the services of vocational evaluation and work adjustment services will undoubtedly play a significant role in the future of the rehabilitation of the welfare recipient. In a study reported by Button (1968), over 1,200 workshops were estimated to be in existence throughout the United States. More importantly, Button stated:

These findings further emphasize that sheltered workshops are urban institutions located at the pressure points of contemporary social problems where the incidences of high unemployment, poverty, chronic disease, disability, and welfare recipients are highest.

Evidence points to the fact that workshops are at least strategically located to contribute to programs aimed at disadvantaged urban population (p. 14).

Vocational evaluation and work adjustment projects are going on for economically dependent groups (Atlanta, 1969), welfare recipients (Arkansas, 1970) model city areas (Illinois, 1970) and the rural poor (Mississippi, 1970). Hoffman (1970) noted a study by Hillman and Martin of Florida State University involving fourteen SRS sponsored research and demonstration projects. The selection of welfare clients for these projects was based primarily on practical situations and job samples common to sheltered workshops. Of 2,614 cases for which complete data was available, 44 percent of the clients were closed as rehabilitated and 34 percent were still being served. Only 6 percent of 1,147 recipients were closed as rehabilitated and were unable to get employment after their case was closed, compared to 78 percent before rehabilitation services. The Department of Labor, in cooperation with the Association of Rehabilitation Centers, showed that rehabilitation facilities could be effective in serving the hard-core unemployed.

The research available at this time concerning the value of the sheltered workshop in serving the public welfare recipient is limited. Scattered reports are available, as noted in this discussion. The results of the research relating to welfare client success and rehabilitation still must be considered speculative. The early studies do show promise and point to a bright potential to the rehabilitation of the welfare client through the use of sheltered workshop services.

The 1968 Amendments to the Vocational Rehabilitation Act authorized the state rehabilitation agencies to carry out a program of vocational evaluation and work adjustment services for disadvantaged people, regardless of whether they were physically or mentally disabled. This section of the Rehabilitation Act has as yet received no funds. If and when funds become available, the services of vocational evaluation and work adjustment will play a vital role in the rehabilitation of the disadvantaged welfare client. The stimulus for research is certainly present, both from the possible funding for evaluative services which would stimulate even greater workshop growth and development, as well as early research reports favorably describing the outcome of workshop programs dealing with the disadvantaged.

REFERENCES

Arkansas Rehabilitation Research and Training Center: *Behavior Modification of Hard-core Welfare Clients for Sustained Competitive Employment.* Hot Springs, Arkansas, 1970.

Atlanta Employment Evaluation and Service Center: *Demonstration of Effects of Comprehensive Community Services to the Culturally and Socially Deprived and Including the Traditional Rehabilitation Client.* Atlanta, Georgia, 1970.

Baldwin, W.H.: *Rehabilitation of Disabled Recipients of Public Assistance or Those Whose Children are Recipients.* Final Report, RD-1333, Arkansas Rehabilitation Service, U.S. Department of HEW, SRS, 1968.

Beck, R.B., Pierce-Jones, J., Lamonte, A., and McWhorter, C.C.: *The San Antonio Rehabilitation-Welfare Report.* Final Report, RD-1513, Texas Rehabilitation Commission, U.S. Department of HEW, SRS, 1967.

Burkhart, J.M.: *Vocational Rehabilitation of Disabled Public Assistance Clients.* Final Report, RD-1533, Kentucky Bureau of Rehabilitation Services, U.S. Department of HEW, SRS, 1967.

Button, W.H.: "Sheltered Workshops in the United States: An Institutional Overview." In Button, W.H. (Ed.): *Rehabilitation, Sheltered Workshops, and the Disadvantaged.* Cornell University Regional Rehabilitation Research Institute, Ithaca, New York, 1970.

Computer Management Corporation: *Key Word Index.* Gainesville, Florida, 1971.

Engstrom, G.A. "Research Utilization." *Welfare in Review,* Sept.-Oct., 1970.

Grigg, C.M.: *Vocational Rehabilitation of Disabled Public Assistance Clients: An Evaluation of Fourteen Research and Demonstration Projects.* Final Report, RD-1323-G, Florida Division of Vocational Rehabilitation, U.S. Department of HEW, SRS, 1969A.

Grigg, C.M.: "Selective Factors in the Decision to Accept Disabled Public Assistance Clients for Vocational Rehabilitation." In Margolin, R.J., and Goldin, G.J. (Eds.): *Research Utilization Conference on Rehabilitation in Poverty Settings.* New England Rehabilitation Research Institute, Northeastern University, Boston, Massachusetts, 1969B.

Hoffman, P.R.:"Where Do We Go From Here?" In Pacinelli, R.N.: *Vocational Evaluation and Work Adjustment Services in Manpower, Social Welfare and Rehabilitation Programs.* University of Pittsburgh Research and Training Center and International Association of Rehabilitation Facilities, 1970.

Holdship, M.W.: *Vocational Rehabilitation of Disabled Public Assistance Clients.* Final Report, RD-1338, Arizona Division of Vocational Rehabilitation, U.S. Department of HEW, SRS, 1965.

Howard, P.: Rehabilitation Instead of Relief. *Rehabilitation Record, 4,* 1963.

Illinois Division of Vocational Rehabilitation. *Intensive Services for Socially Disabled.* Progress Report, Springfield, Illinois, 1970.

Jarrell, J.P.: *Vocational Rehabilitation of Disabled Public Assistance Clients.* Final Report, RD-1417, Georgia Division of Vocational Rehabilitation U.S. Department of HEW, SRS, 1966.

Kunce, J.T., Mahoney, R.J., Campbell, R.R., and Finley, J.: *Rehabilitation in the Concrete Jungle.* RD-2326-G, University of Missouri Regional Rehabilitation Research Institute Research Series No. 3, U.S. Department of HEW, SRS, 1969.

Merrill, S.M.: *Early Referral: A Demonstration of Early Evaluation of Rehabilitation Potential of Public Assistance Recipients.* Final Report, RD-1119, California Department of Rehabilitation, U.S. Department of HEW, SRS, 1967.

Miller, W.J.: *Vocational Rehabilitation of Disabled Public Assistance Clients: An Evaluation of Fourteen Research and Demonstration Projects.* Final Report, RD-1323A, Florida Division of Vocational Rehabilitation, U.S. Department of HEW, SRS, 1968.

Minton, E.B.: *Vocational Rehabilitation Service in a Program to Help Low-Income Public Housing Families Improve the Quality of Family Living.* Final Report, RD-1851-G, Friendly Inn Settlement of Greater Cleveland Neighborhood Centers Association, Cleveland, Ohio, U.S. Department of HEW, SRS, 1968.

Mississippi Division of Vocational Rehabilitation, State Department of Education: *Emergency Concentrated Services in a Rural Area.* Jackson, Mississippi, 1970.

Mosmeyer, H.: *Vocational Rehabilitation of Disabled Public Assistance Clients.* Final Report, RD-1648, Texas Rehabilitation Commission, U.S. Department of HEW, SRS, 1966.

Mullins, B.T.: *Vocational Rehabilitation of Disabled Public Assistance Clients.* Final Report, RD-1534, Kentucky Bureau of Rehabilitation Services, U.S. Department of HEW, SRS, 1967.

Novak, F.A.: *An Intensive Program of Vocational Rehabilitation Services to Disabled Public Assistance Applicants and Recipients.* Final Report, RD-1329, Nebraska Division of Rehabilitation Services, Department of HEW, SRS, 1966.

314   *The Big Welfare Mess*

O'Neil, R.: *Vocational Rehabilitation of Disabled Persons Receiving Public Assistance Grants.* Final Report, RD-1639, Washington, D.C.: Department of Vocational Rehabilitation, U.S. Department of HEW, SRS, 1968.

Rehabilitation Record. Highlights of the Reorganization. 1967, *8.*

Selling, L. *Vocational Rehabilitation of Disabled Public Assistance Clients.* Final Report, RD-1206, New Jersey Rehabilitation Commission, U.S. Department of HEW, SRS, 1967.

Singer, D.M.: *The Vocational Rehabilitation of Disabled Public Assistance Clients.* Final Report, RD-1494, Massachusetts Rehabilitation Commission, U.S. Department of HEW, SRS, 1968.

Spencer, G.: *A Comparative Study of the Reduction of Dependency in Four Low-Income Housing Projects.* New England Rehabilitation Research Institute, Northeastern University, Boston, Massachusetts, 1967.

Taylor, R.D.: *Social and Rehabilitation Service Abstracts.* Abstract of Project RD-1332, Computer Management Corporation, Gainesville, Florida, 1971.

Terwilliger, A.R.: *Vocational Rehabilitation of Disabled Public Assistance Clients.* Final Report, RD-1737, New Mexico Division of Vocational Rehabilitation, U.S. Department of HEW, SRS, 1967.

Wright, G.N., Reagles, K.W., Butler, A.J.: *The Wood County Project.* Final Report, RD-1629, The University of Wisconsin, Regional Rehabilitation Research Institute, U.S. Department of HEW, SRS, 1969.

Zinni, M. *Teamwork in the Vocational Rehabilitation of Public Assistance Recipients,* Unpublished Master's Thesis, The University of Texas at Austin, 1969.

Research Utilization Specialists

Region I

Mr. Edward Tully
Massachusetts Rehabilitation
Commission
296 Boylson Street
Boston, Massachusetts 02116

Region II

Mr. Adriano J. Marinelli
New Jersey Rehabilitation Commission
Labor and Industry Building
John Fitch Plaza—Room 1005
Trenton, New Jersey 08625

Region III

Mr. Paul Basset
Staff Development Research
P.O. Box 11045
Richmond, Virginia 23230

Region IV

Mr. Homer L. Jacobs
Alabama State Department
of Education
2129 East South Boulevard
Montgomery, Alabama 36111

Region V

Dr. William Sather
Wisconsin State Division of
Vocational Rehabilitation
1 West Wilson Street—Room 720
Madison, Wisconsin 53720

Region VI

Mrs. Anne T. Kohler
Texas Rehabilitation Commission
Medical Park Tower
1301 West 38th Street
Austin, Texas 78705

Region VII

Mr. Edwin J. Buchanan
Vocational Rehabilitation Section
State Department of Education
Farm Bureau Building
1448 W. Dunklin
Jefferson City, Missouri 65101

Region VIII

Mr. Charles LeBaron
136 East South Temple
1200 University Club Building
Salt Lake City, Utah 84111

Region IX

Dr. George H. Allen
3557 Imperial Way
Sacramento, California 95826

CHAPTER XVI

THE ECONOMY AND REHABILITATION

MONROE BERKOWITZ

INTRODUCTION

H ISTORICALLY, REHABILITATION'S MAIN function has been to prepare disabled persons for work. The assumption has been that if those who are disabled are restored physically and given necessary training, they would find useful and productive work at the end of the road.

Rehabilitation counselors find themselves frustrated from time to time with the whole process. The client may be highly motivated, the physical restoration surpass expectation, the retraining or training successful, but still, at the end of the road, may lie nothing. When the client is unable to find a job, all of the restoration and all of the rehabilitation would seem to be for naught. Who can blame the rehabilitation counselor for believing it is not the client who may need repair and restoration, but the economy. It is not the retraining of the client which is necessary, but perhaps the restructuring of society and the economy. Perhaps our priorities are awry, and perhaps our values are not those conducive to the maximum employment of all well persons, let alone the handicapped.

THE GOALS OF REHABILITATION AND THE ECONOMY

Our first task will be to examine the overall performance of the economic system. But before we do let us recognize that no matter how the economy functions, this is the world for which rehabilitation is preparing people. There may well be other goals for rehabilitation; persons can be rehabilitated for life in a commune, or life in a society where not a great deal of value is placed upon work. But if we look first at the traditional program of rehabilitation, it is obviously both the preferred goal and the legislative intent that persons be given jobs in the open market.

In this day of women's liberation it is obvious that this goal should apply to women as well as to men. If we restore persons to jobs as housewives, we ought to recognize this as a job of measurable economic value, even though the contribution of housewives to economic well-being is often overlooked. The rationale for including housewives as productive members is at least twofold. One is that they work in every sense of the word although their contribution is not included in overall economic calculations simply because it does not pass through the market. But secondly we recognize more and more that necessary work within the home must be performed by one person or another so that rehabilitating a housewife to a useful position in a family will, perhaps, enable someone in the family to participate in the labor force. Modern economic theory recognizes that labor force participation decisions are based upon family considerations rather than individual ones.

THE GROWTH OF THE ECONOMY

One method of examining the performance of the economy is

to look at its overall product or what is officially called its Gross National Product. GNP is a measure of the goods and services produced by the economy during a particular year. Since it includes diverse types of goods and services, it has to be measured in terms of some common denominator and this is dollars. The clear implication of this measure is that the more goods and services produced, as valued in terms of dollars, the better off we are. Hence, we associate a higher GNP with an increase in welfare.

An immediate protest can be made that this is not a very good measure of anything approaching welfare and that we may need less growth rather than more growth. Growth brings with it pollution, overcrowding, ghettos, urban problems, and so forth. We will look at some of these problems associated with growth and higher levels of GNP, but first, let us examine the record. Whatever the problems associated with growth, we cannot ignore the fact that what we are talking about is more food, more clothing, and more housing. The problem of poverty is that there is not sufficient food, clothing, and housing for a proportion of the population. One way to get more food, clothing, and housing is to produce more, and this means higher levels of GNP. It is often pointed out that complaints about growth stem not from the poor in the ghetto, but from the fairly well-off urban middle-class who can afford to be concerned about problems of growth, having themselves attained a sufficient amount of this world's goods and services.

Postponing these considerations for a moment, we note that GNP measures include first all goods and services consumed during the period in question. The object of economic activity is to produce these consumer goods which satisfy human wants. In addition the economy requires investment goods. These goods are not to be consumed during the period in question, but lathes, factories, and all other capital equipment will enable us to be more productive in the years to come.

One large difference between a developed country and a less-developed country is the amount of physical capital available to it. Countries like Bolivia, Nigeria, and Pakistan are poor because they do not produce sufficient goods and services. One reason they do not is their lack of capital equipment, and one reason they do not have sufficient capital equipment is that they must use all of their productive capacity to satisfy their immediate wants. Thus, they are caught up in a circle which, like all good circles, turns out to be a fairly vicious one. We are able to use about 15 percent of our Gross National Product each year for investment purposes without strain. This enables us, of course, to do much better in the years to come.

About three-quarters of GNP is in the form of personal consumption expenditures and investment; the balance is net exports and the government purchases of goods and services, an increasingly important sector of the economy.

GNP was more than $100 billion in 1929, it dropped thereafter until the low point of the depression in 1933 when it was $55 billion, and it climbed reaching the 1929 level only after 1940. GNP has been climbing since then, surpassing the $500 billion mark in 1960, climbing to $977 billion in 1970, and today it is over a trillion dollars. But revealing as these figures are about past economic history, they are unsatisfactory for at least two reasons. Prices have changed during these years and population has increased. It is more meaningful to talk about "real" GNP, that is, GNP in constant dollars. We can pick any one year but it's convenient to look at 1958 dollars and also to divide GNP by the varying number of people in the economy so that we can get a per capita figure.

In terms of this measure, real per capita GNP in 1909 before the first world war was $1,300. This increased but then fell again. In 1935 it was approximately at the same level, but from that point on it shot up rapidly and in 1970 was over $3,500 for each man, woman, and child in the United States.

There is no question but that the economy is growing and that it has reached an amazingly high level of per capita GNP. If we compare present levels with that of other countries of the world, about forty-eight countries with more than half of the world's population in 1965 had per capita GNP's of less than $150. About 85 percent of the countries have per capita GNP's of less than $1,500, so the United States finds itself in an elite group among the nations of the world.

The growth rate of the United States obviously has been a rapid one but we are by no means the fastest growing country. As we get higher and higher GNP's, it becomes more and more difficult to register dramatic percentage rates of growth. Thus in the period 1960 to 1964 when our annual growth rate was less than 3 percent per year, Japan's was over 10 percent, Germany's was 3.5 percent, France's was 3.9 percent, and Italy's was 5 percent. We cannot be complacent about our present performance if we want to maintain a pre-eminent position.

What are the sources of the U. S. economic growth? Edward Denison[1] estimates that about one-quarter of the total growth of the United States between 1929 and 1957 came about because of an increase in the quantity of labor and about 15 percent due to the increase in the quantity of capital. This leaves still about a quarter of the growth rate to be explained by improved education and training and about 20 percent by improved technology.

REHABILITATION AND GROWTH

Rehabilitation activities thus have a direct role to play in the growth rates of the economy. The physically or mentally disabled person or the culturally and socially disadvantaged person who is not a participant in the labor force is not contributing to GNP. Rehabilitation, plays a direct role in improving the quantity of people in the labor force. But rehabilitation does much more. It is an investment in human capital and we recognize, as Denison does, that it is not only the *quantity* of labor, but the *quality* of labor that counts. Labor is not a homogenous unit of undifferentiated automatons, but a differentiated group of persons, each of whom comes to the work place with differing amounts of human capital. Rehabilitation is an investment in human beings, and like any other investment, one which requires resources now in terms of future productivity later.

COSTS OF GROWTH

Let us be clear, however, about the costs of growth. Growth requires investments whether they be investments in terms of human capital or physical capital. These investments do not yield immediate return, the economy must give up some goods and services

---

[1]Edward Denison: *The Sources of Economic Growth in the United States.* New York, Committee for Economic Development, 1962.

in order to provide these investments.

There are countless examples. Obviously, the metal that we put in a lathe today will not be available for use in pots and pans. We hope, however, that through the building of the lathe and the using of that piece of capital equipment, the economy becomes more productive in the future. Possibly one-fifth of the improvement in growth comes about because of improved technology.

In just the same way, if a man spends time in a rehabilitation process he is investing in his own human capital, and this requires the use of resources that are not available for other production. Specifically, this includes the time of the rehabilitation counselor, his supervisors and administrators.

Another real cost of growth is that it brings with it change, and change is disturbing in the lives of people as well as in the economy as a whole. In an economy that is growing, machines become obsolete and unfortunately so do people. Persons who are trained as skilled engineers in one endeavor, find that their skills become obsolescent with changes in technology or consumer's tastes or as new products appear on the horizon. This poses terribly difficult problems for the rehabilitation counselor. He may train a whole group of people as computer programmers and after they learn esoteric program languages, they may find that changes in technology enable machines to be programmed by the use of the English language.

The economist is content to note that there can be no ideal solutions to a problem of this kind. If growth is to continue, then it must be accompanied by change. Change brings with it uncertainty and inability to forecast accurately what the demand will be in years to come for particular types of jobs. Just as importantly, it means that individuals may face the prospect of not one, but two or three jobs during their lifetime.

Growth also brings with it problems mentioned earlier. GNP is hardly a perfect measure. It is undiscriminating, counting the products of war together with the products of peace in impartial fashion. It values only as does the market, without attention to someone else's scale of values, or the comparative worth of the artist versus the truck driver, and so on.

Also, growth brings goods and services which, far from adding to man's satisfaction, may detract from it. Industrialization causes deterioration of the environment. Landscapes become spoiled, highways cut through pristine forests and factories bring with them smoke which may cause air pollution. Airplanes increase our ability to travel rapidly from place to place but bring with them noise pollution and noxious exhausts which clog our nostrils. People who look with despair at our crowded cities tend to recall romantically a simpler era when persons lived a less complicated type of life on farms. Higher GNP brings more available health services, and at the same time vast increases in accident rates, ulcers, and suicides. At the same time we cannot ignore the fact that it is growth that brings increases in social mobility and the ability to move from one place to another, from one job to another, and the ability to sample much more of the goods that the world has to offer. As in all economic matters, we come down to choices. It is not a question of one or the other, but how much of growth do we want accompanied by how much of the identifiable ills. There are ways of approaching this problem even if there are no ideal solutions.

Our conclusion must be, however, that on the score of size of the GNP, comparisons with other countries of the world, growth rate and such other macromeasures, the United States' economy performs well.

THE PROBLEM OF POVERTY

An argument can be made that the United States' economy as a whole is doing well, and surely it is doing better than the less-developed countries since it has had more time, population, and natural resources to work with. However, the accusing finger is pointed at the fact that so many of the people in the United States are not faring well and are not sharing in economy's fruits of progress. Let us examine this question.

If we want to look at the problem of poverty, we have to have some definitions, some lines to divide the poor from the non-poor. There are at least three different ways of doing this. The first is the Social Security Administration's method of setting some poverty line or threshold, and then rather arbitrarily saying that anyone who is below this line or threshold is poor and those above it are the non-poor. Such an attempt was made in 1964 when the Social

Security Administration constructed a budget based on the Department of Agriculture's emergency food budget, the cost of food for a "nutritionally adequate" family diet (the least expensive food items necessary to maintain a family in relatively decent health). Once this minimum diet was determined and priced, the judgment was made that families would spend three times this amount as their total budget, taking into account all other expenditures for clothing, shelter and any other of the necessities of life.

Based upon this rather arbitrary calculation we have the rather familiar figure of $3,000 for a non-farm family of four as being the poverty threshold. Periodically, one can change the cost of the fixed budget in accordance with the changes in the price level, and today it is over $4,000.

Using a similar philosophical outlook but with no precise definition, President Roosevelt could say in 1933 that we live in a nation that is one-third ill-clothed, ill-housed and ill-fed. You can test your colleagues by asking a simple question. Since the heyday of the Johnson administration have the number of poor people in this country increased, decreased or stayed the same? My guess is that most rehabilitation counselors will respond that the number has increased, especially if they have had contact with the urban ghettos and some of its terrible social problems. Yet the facts are that if we define poverty by some fixed standard, adjusting it only for the price level, the numbers have decreased. This is simply because our economy has grown, GNP has become larger and has brought up more and more of the people at the bottom of the income scale.

If this is not accepted then one must look to some other definition of poverty. One such is to adopt not a budget approach, but an income share approach, and define as poor some proportion of the population at the bottom of the income scale.[2] Poverty thus is defined not as a lack of absolute command over goods and services but the relative lack, and that type of poverty line would automatically change with the growth of the economy. Thus, when we use the fixed standard defining poverty as an income of less than a particular fixed real dollar amount a year, the percentage of

2See The President's Commission on Income Maintenance Programs, Background Papers. Washington, D. C., Government Printing Office, 1970, p. 11.

families in poverty decreases almost half between 1959 and 1965. But defining poverty as an income of less than one-half the national median income, the percentage of families in poverty during this period has increased a little. The percentage of total money income, going to the bottom 25 percent of families and unrelated individuals has hovered around 5 percent since 1947.

INEQUALITIES

It is possible to have a third definition of poverty. And as our society does become more affluent, poverty can be defined not only as the lack of components of a subsistence level of living, but "also the lack of opportunity for persons with limited resources to achieve the quality of life enjoyed by persons with an average amount of resources."[3] This is not an absolute definition but a relative one. The trouble is we are no longer necessarily talking about poverty. Persons at the bottom of the economic pile do not have what the persons with an average amount of resources have. At the same time, they may by somebody's definition be rather comfortably well-off. Consequently, what we are really talking about is not poverty *per se,* but the distribution of income or inequalities of income. The dissatisfaction of many persons with our present-day economy is that it does not distribute income or wealth in anything approaching an equal fashion.

If we compare the percentage of people in the economy and the percent of income they received, if absolute equality prevailed, 20 percent of the people would receive 20 percent of the income, 60 percent of the people would receive 60 percent of the income, and so forth. That is hardly the case. The lowest 20 percent of the people in 1967 received 5 percent of the income. The lowest 40 percent received only 17 percent. To put it in another way the families with earnings of $15,000 and up were only 10 percent of all families and individuals, but together they received 29 percent of the income. If we look at the income of persons earning $10,000 or more we have 29 percent of families and individuals, but together they earn 55 percent of the income. What is happening over time is fairly difficult to find out and it depends a great deal

---

3President's Commission on Income Maintenance, Background Papers, *op. cit.,* p. 8.

upon how the matter is calculated. It is clear that inequality is definitely less than it was back in 1929, but not very much different today than it was in the period immediately following World War II.

GOVERNMENT INTERVENTION

Government, of course, is not indifferent to the distribution of income. Through the income tax and transfer payments, it clearly influences the distribution of income. We do not each pay the same income tax rates. Some pay a higher percentage than others and this results in redistribution. Also there are those of us who receive transfer payments by reason of past contributions to the economic system (Social Security), or by reason of being recipients in a particular program, whether it be Unemployment Insurance, or Public Assistance Programs. The President's Commission on Income Maintenance estimated that as much as 29 billion dollars were redistributed through federal taxes including the Social Security taxes in 1966.[4]

At least two other aspects of this poverty-income-inequality thesis should be discussed. One thesis which has gained some currency among rehabilitation counselors, social workers and others in the helping professions is that basic changes have taken place in the economy. Theobald[5] argues that basic changes in the whole economy have altered the relationship between work and money. The thesis is that if we are to remain a viable country, somehow the work-income nexus has to be broken. We have to have some new way to legitimatize claims on income in the United States lest too many people find themselves unable to participate in the normal work processes and without any legitimate claims on income. The thesis is carried further to note that growth in the United States' economy is going to leave in its "backwash" a number of persons who are unable to take advantage of the increases in prosperity.

Why should this come about? Apparently it is because of increasing automation in the economy which improves our ability to produce without adding to the capacity to consume. But as

---

4President's Commission on Income Maintenance, Background Papers, *op. cit.*, p. 22.
5Robert Theobald: *Free Man and Free Markets.* New York, Clarkson and Potter, Inc., 1963.

Gallaway[6] points out this thesis is similar to the underconsumptionist arguments that have appeared in economic literature over the years, going all the way back to Malthus and Hobson. The empirical evidence in support of this thesis is slim. It consists first of all of the concern about aggregate unemployment rates which we will discuss below, and possibly unhappiness with the rate at which people leave poverty levels.

We have stressed the fact that persons in poverty are increasingly a smaller proportion of the total population. Between 1947 and 1956 the poverty rate in the United States declined from 31.7 to 22.2 percent or a 9.5 percentage points decrease. The calculation pertains to the percent of families with less than $3,000 in annual income at 1963 prices. However, as Gallaway points out, between 1956 and 1961, the decline was only another 1.3 percentage points, from 22.2 percent to 20.9 percent. And of course, it was just at this period that the concern with poverty began. Michael Harrington's *Other America*[7] was published in 1962. Yet for whatever the reason, whether it is the whole complex of programs that have been introduced or whether it is simply normal economic growth taking place, the dismal predictions made at the beginning of the 1960's just have not been carried out. The number of families with incomes below $3,000 has been a much smaller proportion of the population than could ever have been expected in the 1960's. As mentioned above, percentage was about 12.8 percent in 1968, a percentage which the Council of Economic Advisors in 1964 predicted would not be reached until 1980. But although insufficient evidence exists to support the dramatic world of Theobald where income would be available without work, nonetheless, there is little room for complacency. As we do push the percentage of persons in poverty down to say 10 percent or less, it is obvious that we are down to hard-core cases and that economic growth may not be sufficient to continue to do the job. Once we are down to this relatively small number, it is obvious that poverty concentrates in particular groups. These may be the non-whites,

---

[6]Lowell E. Gallaway: *Manpower Economics.* Homewood, Illinois, Richard D. Irwin, Inc., 1971.

[7]Michael Harrington: *The Other America: Poverty in the United States.* Baltimore, Penguin Books, 1964.

the aged, women, and of course the disabled with whom the rehabilitation counselors are particularly concerned.

Another aspect of the backwash thesis is the idea of structural unemployment in the economy, the notion that as automation progresses there are those people who find themselves unable to compete in the labor market. An unemployed person is one who decides that he wants to participate in the labor force but, for one reason or another, finds himself without a job. It is clear that persons who do not participate, either because they are housewives, students, retired or not yet ready or of an age to begin work, are not counted as unemployed. During the depths of the depression years possibly as many as 25 percent of the labor force were counted as unemployed. This number declined during the war years when the economy was running at forced draft and under strict controls to something less than 2 percent. Probably 2 percent is an unescapable minimum level since there will always be people between jobs. Unemployment increased after the war years and in the early 60's reached over the 5 percent mark. Nineteen hundred and sixty nine unemployment declined to 3.5 percent, but in 1970 rose again to 4.9 percent and it has hovered in that area ever since.

In this short discussion a number of things ought to be noted about this unemployment rate. First, it is one thing to talk about an overall unemployment rate, and another to talk about particular groups in the economy. In 1969 the overall unemployment rate was less than 4 percent, but for whites it was 3.1 percent and for non-Whites 6.4 percent. Women, teenagers and the disabled likewise show much higher rates than the overall average. The second factor to note is the immeasurable amount of hidden unemployment in these data. As unemployment rates increase, people become discouraged from looking for jobs and consequently drop out of the labor market.

We also cannot ignore a relationship between the unemployment rate and the level of price inflation in the United States. As noted throughout this chapter, economists are fairly unpopular creatures. They point to no easy solutions but rather to choices that have to be made. And apparently it is not easy to escape the choice between a low unemployment rate and a high rate of change in the price level. This so-called "Phillips curve" relationship postulates a trade-off between inflation and full employment. When the Viet Nam war heated up and caused a rise in spending, and when we lacked the courage to tax or to tighten our money supply sufficiently, prices began to rise. The trick began to be one of trying to bring down a 6 percent rate of inflation to 3 percent or less without retarding the growth in the economy as a whole, and thus cutting off employment opportunities, especially for the marginal groups. We tread a very fine line in trying to "fine tune" the economy in this fashion, but these dilemmas are posed constantly. Although the phenomena of rising prices was shared by other countries of the world, it is hardly any solace for us.

It is clear, however, that both inflation and unemployment affect those on pensions and other fixed incomes, whereas unemployment, hits hardest those with the least marketable skills. Again, we speak here of the non-Whites, the aged, women, the teenagers who have not yet had time to acquire a great deal of marketable labor skills, and above all the disabled groups.

THE RELEVANCE TO REHABILITATION

The rehabilitation program deals of course with all of the groups in the problem areas. The demographic subgroups particularly hard hit by current trends; the female-headed households, the aged, the disabled, the blacks, the inmates of institutions, are all persons who find themselves disproportionally represented on the unemployment rolls, and of course in the poverty population.

The traditional area of concern for vocational rehabilitation has been the disabled. This term, as the rehabilitation counselor knows, is a fairly elastic one. But if we define it as those who have some physical impairment which interferes with their full participation in the labor force, possibly nearly one-sixth the civilian noninstitutional population age eighteen to sixty-four was disabled for a period longer than six months according to survey conducted in 1966.[8] About half of these disabled workers did not work at all, and of those that did work, 36 percent were employed full time, 12 percent part-time and 3.9 percent were unemployed.

---

[8]Social Security Survey of the Disabled Adults 1966. This survey has been reported in a series of papers and the basic data can be found in Lawrence D. Haber, "The Effect of Age and Disability on Access to Public Income Maintenance Programs," Report No. 3, July 1968.

The disabled can be divided into three categories. Those who are severely disabled, those who are occupationally disabled, and lastly those with just some secondary work limitations. These last are people who are able to work full-time at their job but subject to some limitations on the kind or amount of work that can be done. Eighty percent of the severely disabled did not work as compared with 35 percent of the occupationally disabled and 27 percent of those with secondary work limitations.

The chances of a non-working disabled family head keeping his family out of poverty were six in ten. About half of the families with the disabled head under age fifty-five were in poverty. Most of the persons who were disabled received no public income maintenance support at all, either because they were not seriously disabled enough to qualify for the Social Security payments, or because they were not eligible for them.

Vocational rehabilitation has expanded its sights beyond the physically and mentally disabled to include those who are handicapped for other reasons, including cultural and social reasons. As the case loads increase, harder and harder cases come in for consideration.

Vocational rehabilitation has been criticized for clearing people over the eligibility hurdles only if it is sure that they can get a job, and also for training persons for jobs which are not very much in demand. (Note the conflict in the twin criticisms.) Sixty percent of the people completing training were in occupations such as service, homemakers, and unpaid family workers. It is not clear, however, that this is because of any lack of knowledge on the part of the vocational rehabilitation counselors about where jobs are, but rather because of the increased difficulty of training a person with great limitations, perhaps in motivation, skill and background for sophisticated jobs which are increasingly becoming available in the economy as a whole. We cannot overlook the fact that the employer may also discriminate against the welfare recipient.

ECONOMIC RATIONALE FOR REHABILITATION

There is no reason in the world why vocational rehabilitation counselors or administrators should think like economists, but if they did, and it is an interesting game to play, they would pose these kinds of questions about the program. Why is it that governmental or public funds should be used for the program? Why is it that individuals themselves cannot provide or buy vocational rehabilitation services? They would then purchase the mix of goods and services which would yield them the greatest satisfaction. All of the answers to this question are by no means in. However, it ought to be noted that vocational rehabilitation has the virtue, from the economist's point of view at least, of not providing a *fixed* set of services applicable to all who apply to the program. It is true that services are provided at less than cost to individuals who qualify, but at least a wide range of services that can be tailored to the individual's need are offered, thus preserving a wide degree of freedom of choice.

Nonetheless, some rationale is needed for expenditure of public funds and possibly two can be advanced. One is that this is one method of redistributing income, and society has deemed it wise to engage in these income redistribution activities in order to have a more equal distribution of income. A second rationale might be that there are certain "external benefits" to be gained. Society, as a whole, may gain from the individual who participates in the program. If individuals complete the program successfully, there is a reduction in disability *per se*, which might have utility for the nondisabled. In addition the disabled may now participate in the production process and now help finance public goods by paying taxes in a manner that will reduce the burden on the non-disabled. There is a good bit of evidence to support this in the cost-benefit studies that have been conducted.

The second general question that the economist would raise is whether or not this is a rationale program from the allocation point of view. If we are going to allocate resources to the program, how should they be allocated and to whom? Are the costs of the program greater than or less than the benefits to be derived, either by the individuals or by society as a whole? Such benefit and cost criteria might serve to allocate resources among the subgroups in the population waiting to be served and among the state agencies.

Let us consider first the costs involved. One cost not counted but one that ought to be counted, is the foregone earnings of the persons going through the rehabilitation program. In many cases such costs will be positive. An individual undergoing rehabilitation may be foreclosed from participating in economic activity, and the amount of money sacrificed is a cost from the point of view of society as a whole.

In addition, of course, there is the whole cost of the administrative apparatus that is involved in the joint federal state program. In addition to case service expenditures, possibly 5 percent of the program's expenditures are for general administration, 25 percent or more for vocational guidance, and another 8 or 10 percent for the establishment of facilities and workshops. Of course there are also expenditures involved in research, demonstration and expansion projects.

In addition, there is the usual notion of costs valued in case service expenditures, whether for diagnostic procedures, surgery and treatment, prosthetic appliances, hospitalization, training, maintenance, tools, equipment, licenses, time spent in rehabilitation or adjustment centers and workshops.

If these are the costs, what are the benefits to be derived? Their measurement poses a great deal of difficulties. Obviously, if a person who is living in a state of dependency can find himself transformed to a life of independent living without the necessity of constant attendance, he has gained a great deal in satisfaction. Such psychic satisfactions are a very real benefit that ought not to be discounted. Although it is not usually measured, it ought to be recognized as a plus factor, and used to inflate the benefits that are measurable.

In general, however, the method used is to assess the earnings of the worker at the time of acceptance and contrast these with his earnings or the value of work at closure. This is not an ideal method of measurement and is subject to at least the following difficulties. There is a tendency to assume that if the worker was not earning at the time of his acceptance he would not have been earning for the rest of his life. We cannot say that simply because the client came to the agency at a moment of zero earning status he would continue that way. Time alone may have brought about an increase in his earnings, even without any vocational rehabilitation services. Future benefit estimates require some better estimates of what the earnings over a lifetime would be for those workers who did not take advantage of the rehabilitation facilities.

Whatever this post-rehabilitation figure is, it contrasts with the clients' earnings at closure. The difficulty is that the records indicate his earnings for a period of thirty days, a quarter, or in some studies for six months. Again, what we want to know is what the earnings would be over the rest of his useful working life, after appropriate adjustments are made for mortality, unemployment and other factors. There is also the technical problem of the rate of discount to be used, but this need not detain us here.

The attempts that have been made at cost-benefit analysis turn out favorably for vocational rehabilitation. Studies show that there is an increase in earnings and value of work over the working lives of about $11.00 for every dollar spent.[9] In Conley's estimation, taxes regained from increased earnings were two to four times the cost of the program. The highest earnings at closure tended to be from white male, well-educated married clients with orthopedic difficulties. These, however, were also the most expensive to serve.

CONCLUSIONS

What is important in these results are not the particular figures. These are subject to change. Hopefully, more sophisticated detailed studies are being made all of the time. What is important is the approach. It can be disregarded entirely and one can look at vocational rehabilitation as a social service program which stands on its own rights. If one advocates the idea of no connection between work and income, one might seek an entirely different basis for vocational rehabilitation. Certainly if one feels that the structural changes in employment and the economy are gross and that we are moving on to an economy where work and income are separated, then the whole traditional basis of vocational rehabilitation is eliminated.

However, as far as the evidence available indicates, this is just not the case. The traditional economic problems are very much with us. We live in an economy which is growing. We live in an economy where the numbers of people in poverty are being

---

9Ronald W. Conley: *The Economics of Vocational Rehabilitation*. Baltimore, Johns Hopkins Press, 1965; Conley: A benefit-cost analysis of the vocational rehabilitation program. *Journal of Human Resources, IV*: 226-252, Spring, 1969; Charles M. Grigg; Alphonse G. Holtmann, and Patricia Y. Martin: *Vocational Rehabilitation of Disabled Public Assistance Clients: An Evaluation of Fourteen Research and Demonstration Projects*, Institute for Social Research, Florida State University, 1969; and Department of Health, Education, and Welfare: *An Exploratory Cost-Benefit Analysis of Vocational Rehabilitation*. A Report for Rehabilitation Services Agency, 1967.

diminished, perhaps not as rapidly as we would like, but going down nonetheless. But we also live in an economy where the labor market demands persons with skills which fit the jobs available. As we become more productive in an economy, the low-skill non-productive jobs necessarily fall by the wayside. It is the persons with training, education, and skills that are able to compete. Consequently, particular groups in the economy necessarily suffer as the economy as a whole advances.

The solutions to this problem lie in a whole gamut of programs, including attempts being made to eliminate discrimination by reason of age, sex or disability; training programs, relocation programs, stimulation of industry in particular sectors, etc. Vocational rehabilitation fits neatly into the whole scheme of things. It is a program which can aid growth in the United States, not retard it. It is a program which can help people come out of poverty, not push them further into it. It is a program that is designed to aid the particular groups that may be left out in the general progress. By making people's skills more marketable, by increasing their training, by hardening them to the rigors of the work place, it helps add productive members to the labor force, increases productivity and keeps down rates of inflation.

At least such are the objectives of the program. The degree to which it carries them out is subject to economic analysis, but alas the data are not always present. The rehabilitation counselors tend to shy away from economic criteria feeling that they will perhaps do better by appeal to the human condition of man.

I would argue that these two objectives are not incompatible and that what is desperately needed is better information about what goes on in the vocational rehabilitation process. This system, which fits so neatly into the overall economic scheme and which is so necessary as our economy becomes more complex and its pressures increase, deserves better information. We should know more about the clients that enter into the programs, and we must know more about the clients who leave. As the pressures on the economy increase, it will be necessary to make intelligent choices among those who seek services and to rationalize in some intelligent economic way both the methodology and the outcomes for those who pass through the program.

CHAPTER XVII

INNOVATIONS NEEDED IN PUBLIC WELFARE AND REHABILITATION FOR EFFECTIVE REHABILITATION SERVICES

RUSSELL A. NIXON

Research and Demonstration Utilization

A Dynamic On-Going "Incapacity" Determination Process

A New Service Mix—From Assistance to Work

Rehabilitation for Sure Employment:

The Biggest Innovation—Coordination of Welfare, Rehabilitation and Employment Services at Federal, State and Local Levels

Finally—An Innovation to Avoid: A Shift of Rehabilitation From a Voluntary Opportunity Program to a Forced Work Program

References

A SIGNIFICANT COALESCENCE OF MANPOWER, welfare, and rehabilitation concerns and programs is developing. This coalition is being forced by the pressure of ineluctable conditions: the stubborn persistence of the incapacity of millions of people to find realistic and satisfying work roles in our society; the explosive growth of a population dependent on public assistance which includes a large portion of actual or potential employable adults; the inescapable fact that there continues to be several millions living in the country so disadvantaged by physical, mental, and/or social handicaps as to be excluded from the opportunities shared by others. These are interrelated and overlapping conditions which feed upon themselves and demand coordinated and comprehensive remedial public action.

For whatever the reasons, beyond discussion here, the largely uncoordinated programs of the 1960's . . . the varied manpower, anti-poverty, expanded and revised educational, vocational, and rehabilitation programs . . . failed to break the cycle of social and economic exclusion and dependency that afflicts so many people. Now new policy efforts are being aimed at a part of this problem. Comprehensive manpower legislation, welfare reform, and large-scale public service employment programs are all on the national agenda. These are strongly complementary programs, and their success probably depends on the degree to which they are coordinated. These proposals reflect the experiences and lessons of the last decade and require extensive adjustments, changes, and innovations in our basic human service delivery programs.

The manpower experience of the last ten years proved two things: *First,* all the remedial and training efforts on the labor supply side come to very little unless there is a meaningful job available. Moreover, the employment setting is by far the best location for remedying employability defects, for job preparation, and occupational capacity development. *Second,* those who are disadvantaged in the regular labor market are adversely affected by a multitude of difficulties which include physical, mental, and cultural factors. To treat these wounds, which lie at the base of particular individuals' limited employment capacities and potentialities, requires a multi-faceted approach to the whole person in the whole situation. Thus it is essentially the rehabilitation process which has by necessity turned out to be required as the larger human resources development programs have evolved. Rehabilitation services can accept this trend with satisfaction, but it means also that both quantitative and qualitative expansion of rehabilitation is required. To the gratification of confirmed experience must be added the problems of an extremely complicated added target population and new service needs.

In the midst of the Congressional legislative process no one can be certain as to the content of the legislative package that brings together the manpower, anti-poverty, welfare and rehabilitative areas. It is clear, however, that more than problems have coalesced. Program remedies and processes in these areas have tended to come together too, and the legislative and bureaucratic lines have been forced into a closer and more integrated relationship. Whatever the legislative delays and diversions may be, it seems clear that the necessary effort to reduce welfare dependency must essentially involve a far reaching program to render employable and employed as many of the adult welfare clients as possible.

Rehabilitation services are found in the center of the evolving human resources development system. The target population that is the welfare population moves to the rehabilitation screening and care process, and from there either quickly or slowly as each case demands moves on to the more usual manpower sequence of job preparation and placement. The essence is that this is a *process,* with its parts not only overlapping but intimately and continuously interconnected.[1] For the rehabilitation system to fit into this picture to the full extent of its constructive potential and to play its crucial role, will require program adjustments and changes. While gimmicks are not called for, innovations are needed and the following suggests what some of them might be.

RESEARCH AND DEMONSTRATION UTILIZATION

It may seem odd and even superfluous to suggest that as a new program evolves the knowledge and experience gained in the past should be applied. But this cannot be taken for granted, and in the case of rehabilitation services is of special importance because of the extensive research and demonstration effects that have been carried on.

The rehabilitation service has long been giving increased attention to the poverty population and has been studying ways to make the services more relevant to the poor. Particular groups have been given special attention as HEW priorities have been aimed at ghetto areas, neighborhood services, family planning, model cities, aging, and motivation to work. Ex-offenders, alcoholic and narcotic victims, foreign language groups, youth, have all been given special emphasis. Legislative amendments to the Vocational Rehabilitation Act in 1965 and especially in 1968, have increased the focus on the poor, on the welfare area target population.[2] Demonstration projects, program evaluations, problem oriented institutes, and research of widely varied content has been carried on to clarify the ways and means of successful vocational rehabilitation. To a very large, and perhaps unrecognized extent, this research and development has been unique, not duplicated in other human resource related areas. It now has a particular timeliness and applicability and should be reviewed for its usefulness in building the new welfare—rehabilitation—employment sequence. It should also be reviewed for maximum feasible exposure to the public assistance and manpower agencies and personnel involved.

In a larger sense, the rehabilitation process and experience needs to be shared with all components of the new sequential system. It is necessary to put aside the possible bureaucratic jealousies and "turf" considerations and recognize that expanded and adapted, the method of seeking rehabilitation through careful diagnosis, total person consideration, and an individually-designed program is uniquely the method required to deal with the dependency creating wounds of our welfare population. This approach, central to rehabilitation, has not been central to our welfare and manpower systems. Now the emphasis in pending "welfare" legislation on an individual "employability plan" for as many as three million persons would provide massive application of the basic rehabilitation approach. It is possible that rehabilitation personnel themselves fail to see the special relevance of their process in the new setting. Enriched, improved, and expanded the lessons, experiences, and model of vocational rehabilitation should be carefully shared.

A DYNAMIC ON-GOING "INCAPACITY" DETERMINATION PROCESS

It is inevitable that there must be a channelling of welfare clients into categories of "ready to go" employables, potential employables after rehabilitation, and unemployables. The relevant legislation, as well as administrative realities, will require this differentiation which turns on a definition and a determination of what is meant by "incapacity."

The definition agreed upon by the National Task Force on Welfare Reform and Rehabilitation Planning states:

"Incapacity means a medically determinable physical or mental impairment which by itself or in conjunction with age, education, vocational experience, and similar barriers to employment, prevents an individual from engaging in suitable work."[3] This is a thoroughly sensible and defensible definition. But it is necessary to caution at once that this concept is a very complex compound, dependent upon a wide and varying set of factors. It possesses all the uncertainties and vagueness that applies to the term "employable."

Facing the practical requirements of screening and referral of clients, the Social and Rehabilitation Service has given much attention to the development of standard guides and models for this purpose. Specific referral guides have been developed and widely adapted by states in administering Disability Insurance under Title II of the Social Security Act.[4] A special project of the American Rehabilitation Foundation titled "An Evaluation of the Processes of Referral of AFDC Recipients For Vocational Rehabilitation and Other Employment—Related Programs" has developed a model screening guide based on tested experience in several welfare—employment settings. Other approaches to guidelines are being explored, but all tend to develop a mechanical model applicable in a rigid and standard fashion to varied people under varying conditions and situations.

There is both a virtue and a danger in this process. Given the large population involved and the limits in personnel and agency resources, some very practical methods of screening and referral are required. Much of the "screening in" and "screening out" will be almost automatic and self-evident. But it is in the marginal cases . . . and these may be a very large part of the total . . . that critical problems are faced and bad effects will result unless carefully avoided. The mechanical screening process could well threaten to eliminate for many clients the very essence of the rehabilitation process which evaluates a person in all the existing complexity, makes an individual assessment in which the "art" of evaluation rather than an "enumeration" process is essential.

There is a danger here in the understandable inclination to extrapolate already tested and applied methods that have been used for the disabled and the traditional physically and mentally handicapped. The danger is that this "logical" extension may be very wrong for the new complexities and subtleties involved in the poverty population. As is well recognized there are important cultural and social variations which can directly affect the access to "suitable work." Enormous problems of motivation, and suspicion versus trust in the system, have decisive impact on the contemplated process of rehabilitation. Furthermore, the state of the demand for labor, the availability of jobs in the private sector, the possibility of a new category of "sheltered" jobs or work half-way houses, and the availability of a large scale public service employment program adaptable to those whose employability has been limited in the competitive labor market, all could have widespread effect on "capacity to engage in suitable work."

The innovation required here is to combine the essential mechanical screening and referral system with a dynamic, flexible, case by case process which imaginatively judges the potentialities of each individual. Especially for those "screened out," the case should never be closed except for obvious situations, and the review should be on-going. To achieve these potentialities suggests that the application of incapacity tests especially needs to be a team effort, with neighborhood and indiginous participation.

A NEW SERVICE MIX—FROM ASSISTANCE TO WORK

For the public welfare system the work and rehabilitation objective means a new service emphasis for familiar clients, for the rehabilitation system this means familiar services for relatively new clients. For both systems adjustments are required. Particularly, the professional case worker and rehabilitation counselor need to change by addition to their knowledge and capacities. For the public assistance case worker there is a whole new need of awareness and competency relating realistically to the world of work, to the labor market, to the methods and possibilities of employment and employability rehabilitation. The vocational rehabilitation counselor will be required sensitively and intelligently to relate to a new population whose essential characteristics are dependency, poverty and deprivation.

Although the contemplated new welfare to work via rehabilitation sequence is enormous both in number of people involved and in the complexity of programs and services, very little has been done to upgrade and add to the capacity of existing personnel or to create new sources of new personnel. The basic outline of the Work-Fare Program or the Family Assistance Plan was presented by President Nixon in August, 1969, and the Work Incentives Plan was added to Title II, Aid to Families with Dependent Children, Social Security Act in 1967. Almost five years have passed without serious attention to personnel for new social service tasks. It has been estimated that "enactment of a reasonable approximation of the administration's Family Assistance Plan is expected to double the size of the employment service staff involved in job placement, training referrals, and counseling in the 1968 to 1975 period."[6] The authors of this estimate conclude by asking "Can programs such as the Family Assistance Plan be implemented without far-reaching changes in the public employment services of the United States." A similar estimate and question is appropriate for the welfare and rehabilitation services.

Two suggestions seem warranted. *First,* an adequate plan for preparation of professional manpower to perform new tasks should be implemented in every state. This should involve "in service" training for those already in the welfare or rehabilitation system. In addition, new curriculum and emphasis should be built into all schools preparing persons for jobs as social workers in public assistance and a vocational counselors, trainers, and administrators. Perhaps a new breed of workers in these areas is now required.

Second, if this welfare to work process is to succeed it must combat the suspicion and distrust that most public assistance clients have for the welfare, rehabilitation, and public employment Establishment. Besides the issue of credibility, the subtle factor of familiarity and "neighborliness" is probably decisive. This program, to be successful, has to proceed on a cooperative rather than a conflict basis. To achieve this involves many difficult considerations which may prove to be very difficult. But one essential is to devise a new and effective method of "maximum participation" of the community and the client in all levels of the program. This means purposeful use of New Careers personnel, of "self-help," and of teams for screening, referral and rehabilitation services. The examples of the Neighborhood Health Centers, Model Cities,

Community Mental Health projects, and Community Action Agencies suggest a kind of "peoples' involvement" which has not yet been applied to the coordinated welfare—rehabilitation—employment model. This could jointly assist in meeting the need for effective program personnel and provide an essential element of democratic participation by clients and community.

REHABILITATION FOR SURE EMPLOYMENT:

On the basis of the work training programs of the past ten years, the Work Incentive Program and the vocational rehabilitation program, the absolute core for success is assurance of a decent job at the end of the rehabilitation—work preparation process. Lacking that, all the best laid plans come to nothing, or worse, to deep frustration and resentment. This means that every effort and advocacy must be directed to the integration of welfare rehabilitation with actual employment. It would be hard to overstate this requirement, as everything depends on it. Its absence has bedeviled all the anti-poverty manpower efforts, and frantic job development that is not job creation is of little help.

The alternative is not to engage in the employability development effort, and not to design programs for that purpose except as the linkage to work is established as a prerequisite. This is necessary not only to avoid the obvious negative effects of "no job at the end of the line," but also because effective job preparation and training require a real and not a spurious occupational outcome. The advantages of on-the-job training are very great. It avoids irrelevant training, unrealistic educational requirements, and spurious entry credentials. But most important, it reflects the most essential need of the rehabilitative process, which is the realistic prospect of meaningful work in the social company of others similarly gainfully employed.

THE BIGGEST INNOVATION—COORDINATION OF WELFARE, REHABILITATION AND EMPLOYMENT SERVICES AT FEDERAL, STATE AND LOCAL LEVELS

By the very nature of the problems and the programs, the plans to reduce the relief rolls by a combination of rehabilitation and employment services cries out for comprehensive integration of the services involved. Real progress in genuine coordination of the public assistance, rehabilitation, and manpower agencies would be the major innovation. It is easy for an "outsider" to pontificate about the need for a unified system, and it is necessary to recognize the very real difficulties in bringing together governmental units with long-separate traditions and experience. It is especially difficult when this is attempted in a grant-in-aid system which essentially consists of fifty distinct state, political and bureaucratic systems.

The fact remains that a degree of cooperation and coordination within the various involved agencies of HEW, and between HEW and the Department of Labor, far beyond anything so far achieved is essential. Token "joint" declarations unmatched by functional integration will not be sufficient. The "active manpower programs" which have had relative success in many western industrial societies have been planned and nationally coordinated programs. An "active human resources development program," and that is what the welfare-rehabilitation-employment sequence involves, needs similar unification.

Such coordination does not imply a diminished role at the state and local levels. Quite the contrary, such non-Federal leadership in planning and implementation is essential. Some very encouraging examples of local coordination have developed which suggest it is "at the point of production" that bureaucratic barriers to unification are mostly easily overcome.*

The real art, and the real need, in designing the new system is found in the search for a new method and success in evolving a smooth, coordinated and comprehensive manpower development plan which preserves the qualities of overall Federal standards, with the effective relevancy of localized application.

FINALLY—AN INNOVATION TO AVOID: A SHIFT OF REHABILITATION FROM A VOLUNTARY OPPORTUNITY PROGRAM TO A FORCED WORK PROGRAM

There is a danger for rehabilitation in the present context of welfare reform consideration. A majority of the Senate Finance Committee recently proposed a welfare-work formula which elicited

---

*See Bourgea, Ron: Briefs in public assistance activities. *Rehabilitation Record,* May-June, 1971, pp. 27-30.

the sharp condemnation of the Secretaries of Labor and HEW, because of its rigorous compulsory and punitive character. From the English Poor Laws to the present, there have been pressures for treating work in relationship to welfare as an exacting test of laziness, and as punishment for dependency. That such an approach is held by powerful influences affecting public policy today, is very clear.

The Rehabilitation Service has always been part of a voluntary and opportunity creating system. Its fine reputation and its real accomplishments have been based on this foundation. The participation of rehabilitation clients has reflected motivation based upon free choice and pursued opportunities. The same motivation has moved all the professionals, administrators, planners and service personnel in the rehabilitation system. As has been well said "Rehabilitation is a social movement with a prophetic mission . . . a consequence of . . . society's inadequate expression of the humanitarian impulses and equalitarian ethos, which support action to overcome the social deficits of members of our culture."

In developing legislative and administrative moves to relate work and welfare, it is of crucial importance that the vocational rehabilitation system, avoid any compromising of its traditional and basic voluntary and opportunity premises. In the *first* place, compulsion and punishment will not work for rehabilitation. Without positive voluntarism and the magnet of attractive and newly created opportunities, the process of rehabilitation cannot work. *Secondly,* the philosophical and social-moral precepts of forced work and dependency punishment are contrary to the deepest impulses of the people who have built and maintained the social service called rehabilitation. To subvert this foundation would threaten the entire structure.[8]

The welfare and the rehabilitation systems can work together, so long as rehabilitation can apply its skills, methods and experience for curing vocational wounds in a voluntary and opportunity framework that builds on the best instincts and motivations of people to participate in and contribute to society.

REFERENCES

1. Department of Health, Education and Welfare Social Rehabilitation Service, Rehabilitation Services Administration: *Disability, Incapacity, and Rehabilitation Referral Under Welfare Reform,* Report: Issue No. 3, January, 1972, by National Task Force on Welfare Reform and Rehabilitation Planning. DHEW Publication No. (SRS) 72-25011.
2. Criswell, Joan H.: Research Utilization in Poverty Settings. *Special Report Research Utilization Conference on Rehabilitation in Poverty Settings,* Northeastern University, Monograph No. 7, May, 1969, pp. 9 and 16.
3. Department of Health, Education and Welfare Social Rehabilitation Service: *Disability, Incapacity, and Rehabilitation Referral Under Welfare Reform. op. cit.,* p. 26.
4. Newman, Edwards: Commissioners Letter Number 70-20, December 30, 1969.
5. Thoreson, Richard W., and Haugen, John L.: Counseling Practices: The Challenge of Change to the Rehabilitation Counselor. In *Rehabilitation and the Culturally Disadvantaged,* University of Missouri, Research Series No. 1, 1969, pp. 85-110.
6. Lecht, Leonard A., and Cobern, Morris: The Family Assistance Plan: Its Staffing Impact upon the State Employment Services. In Niland, John R. (Ed.): *The Production of Manpower Specialists,* Cornell University, Ithaca, N.Y., 1971, pp. 171-180.
7. Sussman, Marvin B.: The prophetic mission of rehabilitation: Preface. *Journal of Rehabilitation,* January-February, 1968, pp. 26-32.
8. Meyers, Jerome K.: The prophetic mission of rehabilitation—curse or blessing? *Journal of Rehabilitation,* January-February, 1968, pp. 26-32.

INDEX